ft Fitness Trainers

Swimming for Fitness

ft Fitness Trainers

Swimming for Fitness

Kelvin Juba

A & C Black • London

Dedication

To Edward and Charlotte, for all the enjoyment of our shared times.

Thanks

To David Fychte, Nick Juba and Dr. David Hunt.

Published in 2001 by A & C Black (Publishers) Ltd
37 Soho Square, London W1D 3QZ

Copyright © 2001 by Kelvin Juba

ISBN 0 7136 5825 8

A CIP catalogue record for this book is available from the British Library.

Note: Whilst every effort has been made to ensure that the content of this book is as technically accurate and as sound as possible, neither the authors nor the publishers can accept responsibility for any injury or loss sustained as a result of the use of this material.

Acknowledgements
Cover photograph courtesy of David T. Hewitson.
All line illustrations by Dave Saunders.

Typeset in 10/12pt Minion Display

Printed and bound in Great Britain by Biddles Ltd, Guildford and Kings Lynn.

Contents

I Introduction

II Swimming for fitness

III Planning your swimming year

IV Training for competition

Part I
Introduction

Come on in, the water's fun

Swimming as an activity has probably been around as long as man. Examples of man swimming can be found in a number of ancient documents and hieroglyphs emphasising the enjoyment the sport has brought to people over hundreds of years. The key difference between swimming as a sport now and swimming all those years ago lies in the reasons for taking part. Whereas years ago man swum for enjoyment, to fight wars and hunt for food, now we have very different objectives. Over the last 100 years, swimming has moved from being a sport associated with pleasure, competition or safety to one with a fourth and equally important objective – health and fitness.

Until the beginning of this century, swimming was always referred to in books as being an art. Again, it is only over the last 100 years that it has been increasingly talked of as a science. In the ensuing pages, it will be considered as both.

In 1999, there were 3353 leisure centres and swimming pools in the UK, 816 of which had a pool only.[1] There were a further 2500 health and fitness clubs, around 62% with swimming pools. Mintel found in their research that the swimming pool is by far the most popular facility at leisure centres, with 61% of visitors using an ordinary swimming pool, 22% a fun pool and 19% a children's pool. Given that in the same year, leisure centre and swimming pools admissions amounted to 340 million people,[2] the number of people swimming in the UK – a country surrounded by water – each year is enormous. If the number of people who swim in the sea or inland waterways is taken into consideration, the overall total is even greater. Swimming can proudly boast that it is among the top leisure pastimes in the UK, and much of this is due to the explosion in the number of people swimming for fitness. In adult competitive swimming alone, the level of interest is increasing. Some 7000 people from 53 countries took part in the 7th World Masters Swimming Championships in Munich in 2000.

More and more people are beginning to recognise the benefits of being fit in order to lead longer lives. A sensible diet, less stress and plenty of exercise are just a few ways of counteracting the pressures of modern life. Swimming very much fits within this. It is one of the few sports that can build stamina, flexibility and strength, while placing less strain on the heart due to the fact that a person can exercise without the additional burden of body weight. Swimming is also one of the few sporting activities that you can take part in throughout life.

---

[1] Mintel Leisure Centres and Swimming Pools, *Leisure Intelligence*, February 1998 and Mintel 2001
[2] The Audit Commission and Mintel Leisure Centres and Swimming Pools, *Leisure Intelligence*, February 1998 and Mintel 2001

There are very few secrets in swimming. There are, however, many important ideas and handy hints to pass on that may help the general swimmer who wants to get fit or who is looking to maintain fitness. This book is directed towards those people who belong to this group. It assumes a certain level of swimming competence, in that the reader can already swim all four of the key strokes – backstroke, breaststroke, butterfly and freestyle – but that some updating may be necessary. Many of you who read this book will not have swum for many years. Remember, swimming can be great fun. Where else could one obtain such a high level of pleasure while truly benefiting in health terms? Let this book lead you down to the water! Come on in, the water's fun!

The basic properties of water

Water has many unique properties. It is 1000 times more dense than air, so it offers great resistance to a swimmer's forward movement and therefore, compared with land-based forms of exercise like running and cycling, makes swimming an inefficient form of movement. Here are a few basic factors that effect the body and make water a unique medium in which to develop fitness.

Hydrostatic pressure

Water exerts a pressure on your body, which contributes to a lower heart rate during exercise (*see* also p. 19) and provides a massaging effect which can help reduce muscle tension and leave your body feeling less stressed.

Buoyancy

If you jump into the deep end of a swimming pool, your body displaces the water, causing it to rise and push you upwards towards the surface, reducing the effect of gravity and giving you a feeling of weightlessness and floatation. This can help to promote a greater range of movement in the joints (*see* also pp. 65–75), but also increases the intensity of any movements in which you are pushing down against the water – e.g. the downwards kick in freestyle and backstroke – so that it can help improve muscular strength and endurance (*see* pp. 76–84). (*See* also the factors that affect a swimmer's buoyancy, p. 16.)

Resistance

The forces acting against you as you swim from one point to another are known collectively as water resistance, or drag, of which there are three types:

· form or frontal drag – water exerts a multidirectional resistance to every move you make, so that every movement potentially demands a greater muscular exertion and greater energy expenditure than on dry land. In general, the larger the area presented to the water, as well as the faster the speed, the greater its effect will be – hence the importance of achieving a streamlined swimming position

· viscous or frictional drag – water molecules cause friction when coming into contact with your body, so some competitive swimmers shave their bodies in the belief that this will reduce its effect, as well as creating a feeling of speed through water

- wave drag – this turbulence at the surface is created by your swimming action, which often creates bow waves that press back against your body and can slow your forward progress. Good stroke technique can help overcome this – or lessen its impact.

> ### Action–reaction
>
> Newton's third law states that for every action there is an equal and opposite reaction. In other words, when you push water backwards – or cause it to accelerate backwards – you will move forwards with an equal amount of force.

A lifetime activity

Apart from the fact water is such a unique medium in which to exercise, swimming is much more than just another sport. It is a life skill, something that can be learnt early, retained and enjoyed throughout an individual's life. Here are a few examples of people who have swum virtually throughout their lives. Roy Romain of Otter, one of the best known Masters swimming clubs, was European Champion in 1947 in the 200 m breaststroke. Swimming butterfly at a time when you could choose either stroke in a breaststroke race, he won the event in 2 minutes 40.1 seconds. Roy was still swimming butterfly well into his 80s and holds the British record for the 80 to 84-year age group of 52.17 seconds for 50 m.

But Roy is far from being the only one. Consider John Harrison of the Royal Navy, who set British Masters' records in the 85 to 89-year age group of 35 minutes 15.45 seconds for 1500 m and 2 minutes 2.85 seconds for 100 m. There have been even older record setters than John Harrison. In the USA, Tom Lane set world records of 2 minutes 5.49 seconds for 50 m in 1994, and 4 minutes 25.98 seconds for 100 m freestyle in 1995, in the 100 to 104-year age group. In Australia, Mary Maina set a world record of 5 minutes 10.84 seconds for 50 m freestyle in 1994 in the 100 to 104-year age group. Swimming is a lifetime activity. You can start by visiting the water when you are only a few months old and still be swimming for fitness when you are well over 100.

The oldest known British Masters partnership is that of husband and wife Yvonne (79) and Roy (88) Hodges. Their daughter Jayne, a 46-year-old mother from Edmonton, also competes in Masters events and holds European and British Masters records. Roy started swimming in the early 1920s.

Scheduling swimming into your life

The first great problem is overcoming inertia. Modern life is comfortable and you may not want to break out of your routine. Be positive at the start. Once you have decided to commit yourself to getting fitter, plan one or two hours of regular swimming into your working week.

Try to plan the time of your sessions a month ahead and stick to it. Recognise that a level of fitness will not be achieved without a certain amount of effort. The aim of this book is to guide you through the various stages necessary to reach a reasonable level of fitness, and to help you overcome any discomfort in steady steps.

In scheduling your swimming, try to avoid days when you already have other physical activities, family distractions and time pressures. For example, if you are going to swim for an hour then you need to swim for an hour – not 45 minutes because you find you have to spend time drying your hair, putting on a suit and getting back to an important meeting at the office.

Contact the pool you plan to swim at and find out when 'lane' swimming normally takes place. Pools have a variety of names they use for adult swimming, from 'jogging' to 'aqua fitness' to 'swimfit': try to find out when the pool is reasonably quiet and whether there is a resident group of adult swimmers who meet on a regular basis. The answers to your questions will also probably tell you whether the pool management is reasonably sympathetic to adult fitness swimming. You will then be able to plan your month's swimming timetable. In doing so, look to the long term. Remember that the true benefits of your swimming programme will not be felt for a number of months. For more information on planning your swimming sessions, *see* Chapter 9.

Where to go for advice

Let us now consider some of the initial problems your might encounter, and where you can go to find out more in order to tackle them. (Contact details for all the bodies mentioned below can be found in the Further information section on p. 151.)

If you are having difficulty finding a suitable swimming pool, the leisure department of your council should be able to make suggestions. If, however, this proves fruitless, you might like to contact the Institute of Sport and Recreation Management or the Institute of Leisure and Amenity Management who may be able give you further ideas.

If your difficulties are related to the future content of your swimming sessions, it is probably best to contact the Institute of Swimming Teachers and Coaches at Loughborough. Alternatively, the Amateur Swimming Association has a Masters Swimming Committee directed towards adults.

Any medical problems or queries should be addressed in the first instance to your own GP, but if help cannot be obtained the ASA should be able to guide you through the good offices of one of their medical advisors.

You may be in the process of moving to work abroad, and thinking about taking up a swimming programme once there. If so, you may need to find out if there is a suitable swimming pool in the area in which you will be living. The details of each country's national swimming body is held by the Féderation de Natation Internationale. These national bodies should be able to guide you in the right direction.

What type of swimming facilities to look for

Increasingly, swimming pool authorities have recognised the need for adult fitness swimming. Now whole lanes are set aside at certain times of the day or whole pools given over to fitness swimming. Unfortunately, in some pools this tends to only be carried out when requested by the public.

A 25 m pool is ideal, offering the opportunity to break your swim on a regular basis. Any longer, and this can be initially quite tiring for someone trying to regain fitness. Avoid pools that have poor shower, footbath and toiletry facilities – this lack of attention may well be replicated in the way they look after pool water. Also, avoid pools where there is either a lack of discipline shown by the swimmers using the lanes, or where the etiquette of lane swimming is not recognised.

Most pools keep the outside, poolside temperature slightly higher than that of the water itself. Pools where the water is kept at a very high temperature are best avoided as they can make lengths swimming very uncomfortable.

Wearing the right equipment

As with any sport, wearing the right equipment is important. The main considerations are comfort and efficiency, and all equipment should add something of both to your overall personal performance. Most of the items below can be purchased from a leisure centre, swimming pool, website or by direct mail. It may take trial and error for you to find the equipment that is right for you, but here are some handy hints that may prevent you wasting time and money in the first place.

Swimsuit

Enthusiastic swimmers never go anywhere without a swimming costume in their briefcase or handbag, just in case they have the time and opportunity for a quick swim. The swimsuit is obviously your most important piece of equipment, and you should aim to choose one that suits you with comfort and convenience in mind. Go for a swimming costume that doesn't trap air or water, and avoid a suit that rubs under the arms.

Nowadays, most swimming costumes are made of lycra to reduce the effect of drag (*see* p. 5). The range of available swimwear has increased with fashion, meaning that the traditional suits have been supplemented with knee-length or full body suits. Manufacturers claim that the design of such suits has been achieved through biomimetics – in other words, they mimic various amphibians such as sharks. All of these suits are practical for the fitness swimmer and will dry quickly.

The life of a swimsuit can be increased by washing out pool chemicals. Sand, salt and suntan oils can also damage swimsuits. At the end of your day, soak your costume in ordinary tap water to preserve its condition.

Goggles

Lightweight goggles are common; some are better than others. Anti-fog goggles prevent misting. If you do find that your goggles mist up, licking the plastic eyepieces prior to putting them on may help. Those swimmers who are returning to swimming and are not used to goggles should take care in putting them on, to avoid eye injuries. Place the eyepieces over the eyes first. Then, while holding the eyepieces firmly over the eye sockets, pull the elastic band circuitously over the forehead and top of the head until the elastic band fits comfortably on the back of the head.

Swim cap

Most serious swimmers wear a latex hat to keep long hair out of their eyes, rather than to keep their hair dry. A swim cap can be particularly useful if you have to work after your swim. You may not get the time to wash your hair, and a latex hat will help to keep pool chemicals out of it so that you don't smell like a swimming pool while at work!

Nose clips

A nose clip is an optional piece of equipment used by some swimmers because they have difficulty in balancing the pressure of the air inside their nose with that of the water outside it. The clip normally consists of a 'U' shape that fits over the nose, with an elastic band holding it in place from the back of the head.

Earplugs

If you experience discomfort as a result of water getting into your ears, there are various types of self-moulding earplugs that can be obtained from a local chemist.

Useful swimming pool equipment

In addition to the various items of personal equipment listed above, many pools make available the following training aids. Alternatively, you can always take these to the pool with you. A precautionary word, though – build up the use of such equipment very slowly. Too much too quickly, particularly with the arm-related equipment, can lead to aches and pains and sometimes tendonitis (*see* p. 99).

Swim fins/flippers

This training aid has been around for as long as one cares to remember, and yet fins are as relevant today as they have ever been. Fins are recommended for legs-only activities, since they tend to dislocate the natural rhythm of the stroke when the arms and legs are used together. They are, however, useful for building ankle flexibility and increasing the workload on the leg and ankle muscles. Be careful when you remove the fins: your legs drop lower in the water and the levers shorten, meaning that slightly different muscles are being used.

Pull buoys

The advantage of the pull buoy is that it enables a swimmer to remain high in the water while preventing the legs from kicking. Essentially, a pull buoy consists of two cylindrical pieces of polystyrene of approximately 25 cm in length, joined by two parallel lengths of rope. The pull buoy supports the ankles or the knees and keeps the legs high in the water while preventing movement. The swimmer can then work on arm technique.

Hand paddles

Hand paddles are sometimes used with pull buoys. In general, they overload the muscles of the chest, back and arms (*see* p. 79), leading to higher resistance and requirements for work. Effectively, they strengthen the arm strokes by presenting larger surface areas to the water. Try to use paddles that are slightly larger than your hand. Paddles that follow the shape of the hand, and therefore replicate normal water movements past the hand, are of most value.

Kick boards

Don't forget to keep the ubiquitous kickboard in the back of the car in case you end up going to the swimming pool at short notice. It is a must for every keen swimmer. A kickboard or float can isolate the legs so that the swimmer can concentrate on legs-only swimming. Placed between the upper thighs, it can also be used as an aid for practising the arm strokes. Useful in building the leg muscles, the kickboard makes the legs work harder. In doing so it also exercises the heart, which has to work much harder to pump blood to the legs.

Swim pacers

Swim pacers – such as the one shown in fig. 1.1 – are a useful training aid. Originally designed for groups of swimmers, they can now be used by individuals and adjusted at the end of a length. If you are fortunate enough to swim in a group, these portable units can be pre-programmed to include different variables such as time per stroke or, number of rest intervals. You can also key in target times for your intervals. The pacers are accurate to one hundredth of a second.

The information you need is relayed via a small pacer unit under a swimmer's cap or fixed to the goggle strap. The bleeps that it emits can be used to inform you about your stroke rate and pace. The pacer can also be used to even out the stroke and build better stroke balance.

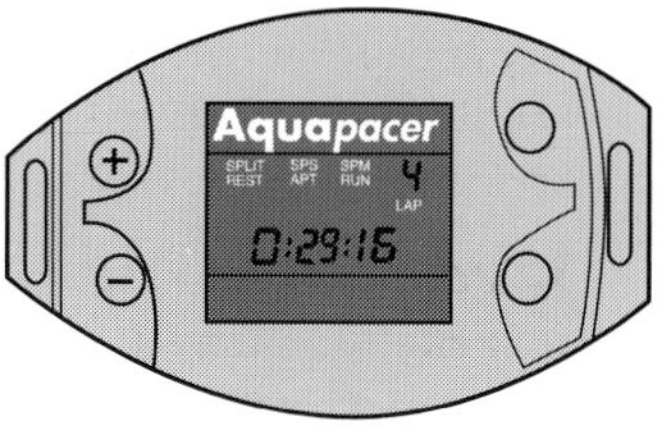

Figure 1.1 Swim pacer

Heart rate monitors

Heart rate monitors normally take the form of wrist watches, into which you can manually enter your heart rate data (*see* fig. 1.2). The monitors can be set for different heart rate ranges or a specific number of beats per minute, and they indicate the percentage of your maximum heart rate at which you are working (*see* also pp. 54–7).

The more advanced versions will also indicate the number of calories you are burning, based on the intensity of your exercise. They will show you two versions – one based on the calories you are currently burning, and a second version based on the accumulated number of calories you have burnt since the start of your swimming session. You can then take the heart rate monitor home with you and plug it into your PC in order to re-programme it ready for future sessions.

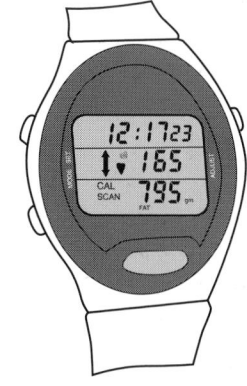

Figure 1.2 Heart rate monitor

Inner tubes

The inner tube of a car tyre can be used to isolate the arms, the advantage being that it helps to keep the swimmer's legs high in the water. By placing the tube round the ankles, drag can be increased so that both arms and heart have to work much harder.

Drag devices

These can take the form of divers' weight belts or belts made with pockets. They are used to increase the effect of water resistance.

Chamois leathers

Traditional cleaning leathers were first used by divers, but are now increasingly being used by swimmers – particularly in outdoor pool environments – since they are more adaptable than towels for drying down on a regular basis. They dry out quickly after being rung out, and are lighter and less bulky to carry.

Suit solutions

It is now possible to buy special cleaning solutions for your swimsuit. These can be used on a regular basis, preventing the rapid deterioration of your costume due to pool chemicals and sunlight.

Ear wraps

Neoprene ear wraps can be used round the head to cover ears that are susceptible to invasion by foreign bodies.

Table 1.1 *Where to obtain swimming equipment*

	Swimming pool/leisure centre	Website	Direct mail	Home-made	ASA	Normal sports shop
Goggles	✓	✓	✓		✓	✓
Swim cap	✓	✓	✓		✓	✓
Swimsuit	✓	✓	✓			✓
Nose clips	✓	✓	✓		✓	
Ear plugs	✓	✓	✓		✓	
Swim fins	✓	✓	✓			✓
Pull buoys		✓	✓		✓	
Hand paddles		✓	✓		✓	
Kickboards	✓	✓	✓		✓	✓
Inner tubes				✓		
Swim pacers	✓	✓	✓			
Heart rate monitors		✓	✓			
Drag devices				✓		
Logbook					✓	
Chamois leather	✓	✓	✓			✓
Suit solutions		✓	✓			
Ear wraps		✓	✓			

Logbooks

These will become a vital part of your overall planning (*see* also Chapter 9, *Planning principles*). A logbook allows you to plan your schedules, keep a record of your training, and compare results over a period of time. It is, therefore your swimming past, present and future!

Swimming with a partner

When swimming, you will spend a lot of time with your head under the water – often not knowing if you are making mistakes. If you are returning to the swimming pool after a number of years, try to swim with a partner or a group of friends. It has the following benefits:

- you can get a partner to look at your strokes and help you to correct any obvious technical errors you are making, both over and under the water

- a partner to swim with and compete against while getting fit can make life much more interesting

- you get a sense of teamwork, which makes the swimming mentally easier and more purposeful: there is a shared feeling that you are all 'in it together' and taking part in something worthwhile.

- you can use slipstream swimming: lane swimming often means chain swimming – in other words, following one another up on one side of the lane and returning on the other side of the lane. Swimming behind someone else in this way can give you distinct psychological encouragement.

- having someone to talk to when you get to the end of a swim is a good chance to be sociable, as well as to create points of comparison and reference while training.

If you are going to either join or form a group, try to team up with someone who prefers the same stroke and is about the same speed. If possible, look for someone who shares the same goals as you. For example, if you want to get really fit and intend to swim four or five times a week, there is little point in starting out working together with someone who won't be able to spare the time to train six months down the road.

Before you start

Before you embark on a training programme, it is a good idea to have a check-up with your general practitioner. Ask your doctor for a 'well person check-up' – these are free and will include a check on your heart and lung function. Your doctor will take your blood pressure, and if you are young and healthy, a reading of about 120 mm of mercury (HG) for systolic pressure, and 80 mm for diastolic pressure will be the target. (Systolic measures blood that is pumped away by the ventricles of the heart, while diastolic measures the troughs in between.) As you age a higher level may be acceptable so do not be alarmed if it is slightly higher and the doctor is satisfied. During training, your cardiac system will be called on to work and your blood pressure is a good indication of its condition.

It is also a good idea to get your doctor to test the efficiency of your lungs, since oxygen consumption will be important to you when you get into training. The doctor is most likely to measure your peak expiratory flow rate (PEFR). You will be requested to breath as deeply as possible and blow into the mouthpiece of a PEF monitor, three times in succession. The doctor will record your highest flow rate. The amount of oxygen consumed by the muscles during exercise is also measurable but it is very unlikely that your GP will test this as it is not a standard test. The maximum oxygen uptake is called VO_2 maximum, or more commonly VO_2max. For men, this is normally about three litres per minute (two litres per minute for women). Hereditary factors do to some extent determine lung capacity, but this can be increased considerably with training. Ensure that your lifestyle begins to take account of a new training programme. Smoking harms the lungs' capacity to work efficiently while training and should therefore be reduced or given up. Alcohol should be limited to about 20 units per week. Heart and lung fitness will become important elements in your swimming programme.

In general, common sense is the order of the day. If you are not overweight and you are under 50 years of age, you can build gradually into a training programme. If you are over 50, you should progress with extreme caution, avoiding over-extending yourself in the early stages. If in any doubt, always consult your doctor. The most important thing to bear in mind is that whatever your sex, ethnicity, age or state of health, you can take part in swimming for fitness. Swimming remains accessible to almost everyone. You can start at any time and take part at little cost without looking a fool. Let's go for it!

2 Why train?

What is the difference between just swimming up and down a pool and training? If there is little difference between the two, why not just swim?

Swimming has a number of functions – pleasure, health and fitness and personal safety – and each of these is linked. If you swim for pleasure, you will almost inevitably develop some measure of fitness, however small. If you swim for health purposes, it is highly likely you will become fitter. If you swim for fitness, you will derive pleasure and are likely to be healthier. If you swim to become more confident in water, a degree of all three will rub off.

One major benefit of training, however, is that it provides a structure to your swimming. This structure can promote variety and help you to plan your swimming in such a way that you get the most out of every one of your sessions throughout the year. Moreover, a well thought-out programme of training can help to ensure that you are doing the most beneficial things both at the right times of the year and within the same training session so that you achieve your objectives and get results.

What then should be the objectives behind your training programme? Different swimmers may have very different fitness and training goals. You may be looking to enhance your general health and appearance, in which case your swimming programme will be quite different from someone who is training for the Olympics. The following chapter outlines the basic physiological and technical elements of swimming fitness that you may wish to improve by following a training programme.

Swimming as a means of improving fitness

Swimming is the perfect medium for improving fitness. It offers a warm and friendly environment not seen in most other adult sports. Because your body is beneath the water's surface, inhibitions about shape and size are removed, so even those people who are overweight need have no fears when taking part. On top of this, the extra support that water lends whilst you are exercising makes swimming a particularly beneficial approach to fitness training for many groups of people for whom land-based activities are less appealing or indeed impossible. In short, the barriers to entry are low.

Swimming and health

Swimming can be both therapeutic and prophylactic, helping people overcome and even prevent all sorts of illnesses and disabilities. Part of the reason for this is that water buoyancy (*see* p. 16) makes it a non-impact form of exercise, removing the stress placed on the joints and therefore opening it up to people with a wide range of conditions for whom land-based activities are problematic. It is also a sport that exercises a wide range of muscle groups (*see* pp. 76–9), builds muscular strength and endurance and develops self-confidence – the following story being a good example.

Duncan Newby, the national swimming coach to Bermuda and an active swimmer himself, was diagnosed as having oesophageal cancer while still young. He was losing weight and could not swallow. Originally, he put his problems down to the fact that he was training hard for his first Master's competition. Following an endoscopy in January 1998, he was told he had cancer and had to be operated on immediately. He was given a 2% chance of survival but with the help of friends and family, he went to the most expensive cancer clinic in the world, the Memorial Sloane Kettering, New York.

The clinic told Duncan that the fact he had swimmer's lungs might give him a slim chance of survival. Throughout large courses of chemotherapy and radiation, Duncan continued to swim. Just three weeks after the operation, he swam in a 1300 m open water race! And a few weeks later, he swam in a 4 km open water race. This was despite the fact that Duncan had lost his stomach, oesophagus and part of his diaphragm.

Duncan's cancer is now in remission and he feels he owes his life to his swimming. In the summer of 2000, he swam a 10 km race in 2 hours and 55 minutes. He now plans to give talks in the UK about the wonders of swimming as a source of life extension and quality of life. This remarkable case of one man's determination to survive against the odds epitomises how swimming can help improve health even in the most serious cases.

Starting with the right mental approach

Pushing yourself can be very difficult, but that's what any fitness programme requires. As discussed in Chapter 4, your initial sessions will be all about acquainting yourself with the water, and your lengths can be swum at a very easy pace. Eventually, though, you will need to move out of this comfort zone and this is when your fitness programme will become harder – both physically and psychologically.

At this point, you will have the inevitable self-doubts: 'Why do I do this? Perhaps this isn't such a good idea after all. I think I prefer music or reading as a hobby – they are much less demanding at my time of life. Can I really keep this up?' Faced with this, try to start in the way you mean to go on. Set yourself realistic and achievable goals before you go to the pool and stick to them. If you have set yourself half an hour for your session, make sure you swim for half an hour, not 20 minutes! The right way to break out of your comfort zone is to attempt this in short stages. Build up your workload slowly; in time, your efforts will become easier as you get fitter and your body adapts to the increased level of exercise.

Components of swimming fitness

People tend to think of 'fitness' as being the ability to carry out a given activity at a fairly high intensity for a long period of time – i.e. aerobic fitness. In fact, fitness is made up of many different components, the activity you wish to take part in dictating their relative importance.

Aerobic fitness

This is the ability of the heart, lungs and circulatory system to transport oxygen efficiently around the body, and sustain low–moderate levels of activity.

- In swimming this is crucial because prolonged, low-level activity will make up the majority of your training. As a fitness swimmer you are unlikely to be training at very high intensities and therefore developing anaerobic fitness (the energy system which does not utilise oxygen – *see* p. 53). This would be utilised at the more intense competitive training levels when your heart rate reaches the 80–90% range (*see* p. 54).

Endurance

Endurance is associated with aerobic fitness and is commonly called 'staying power'. It refers to the maximum amount of time the body (cardiorespiratory system), an individual muscle or a group of muscles can maintain a specific activity.

- By making long swims, or a series of longer swims with short rest periods (repetitions), endurance becomes the main focus (*see* p. 55).

Speed

This is the rate at which a swimmer can swim a set distance.

- Speed in swimming is often developed through a mixture of swims performed at just less than maximal intensity (*see* p. 57), combined with a number of swims designed to sharpen up the swimmer's reactions, power and explosive capacities. Unlike endurance swimming, high-intensity swimming develops your anaerobic capacity.

Flexibility

Flexibility refers to the range of movement in muscles and joints. Like aerobic fitness, this is an important factor in our everyday health.

- In swimming, the body's ability to carry out the full range of movement at every joint is essential. Water is the perfect environment for improving flexibility because buoyancy supports the body and helps to mitigate the effects of gravity (*see* p. 4) – thereby allowing the joints to lift and separate, decreasing the compression experienced on land and hence improving mobility. However, land-based stretches can also contribute to improved flexibility once a well-structured programme is implemented (*see* Chapter 6, pp. 65–76).

Strength

This is the ability of a muscle or group of muscles to exert a force in order to overcome a resistance.

- In swimming, working against water resistance (*see* p. 4) will assist with the improvement of muscular strength and endurance, particularly in the large muscles of the shoulder region that pull the body through the water. Other strength benefits will come about as a result of associated land conditioning work (*see* Chapter 6, pp. 76–84).

Technically-related components of swimming

Many swimmers wishing to keep fit also want to swim technically well. A training programme helps you to propel yourself through the water more efficiently, often naturally correcting faults and generating the correct neuro-muscular patterns in your strokes.

Whether you are swimming for fitness and wish to make the most out of your time in the pool, or are more serious about your swimming and wish to train towards a specific race or competition, you will need to consider the following technical elements in addition to the general fitness elements outlined above. Please refer to p. 155 for books which discuss these in more detail.

Buoyancy

Three factors affect your buoyancy: the amount of air in your lungs, your body composition and the distribution of your body fat – which contributes to your form as you swim through the water.

Body composition

Body composition refers to the ratio of fat to lean body tissue – muscles, organs, blood and bones (*see* Chapter 7, p. 88).

- In swimming, your body composition helps determine your buoyancy, which in turn influences your capacity to float and overcome the forces of water resistance – i.e. it affects your ability to swim. Swimmers generally have a smaller percentage of body fat and a higher percentage of lean tissue than less physically active people. However, as men and women have different amounts of fat on their bodies, this also influences buoyancy.

Body form

Body form is the overall shape and distribution of fat and lean tissue in any one individual.

- As the body shape changes throughout each stroke, it presents a different form to the water at any one point in a stroke cycle. With this in mind, the general shape of the body therefore impacts on the efficiency with which it can move through the water.

Balance

This relates to the swimmer's ability to position his centre of gravity in the water effectively and to minimise unwanted movements. The primary importance of balance is that it aids stability during swimming and makes each stroke and turning movement more efficient.

Propulsion

This is the swimmer's ability to overcome and manipulate the resistant properties of water to propel himself along (*see* p. 4).

Timing

Timing determines a swimmer's ability to ensure that his stroke is continuously propulsive. If all the movements in a stroke are timed correctly in relation to one another, propulsion through the water will be more effective.

Streamlining

Streamlining is the swimmer's ability to co-ordinate a set of actions in order to bring about a body position that reduces drag and maximises propulsion. Generally this amounts to a series of flexing, extending and angular movements utilising the arms and legs in order to account for the direction and velocity of water flow.

Reactions

This is the swimmer's ability to respond to an external stimulus. Examples include the speed of entry into the water upon hearing the start signal, or a requirement to accelerate rapidly during a race to face competitive demands.

Feel

People have tried for years to define 'feel' without success. It refers to all the intangible factors that an individual brings into play in the course of swimming a distance. Some of these may be innate, while others may be acquired. The efficiency with which they are brought together has a direct bearing on speed and the ability to overcome resistance. An integral part of this 'feel' is the swimmer's ability to 'paddle' efficiently to the next propulsive phase in a stroke, but the ability to generate lift is also important.

Basic training concepts

Whatever your fitness goal, you will need to train to achieve it. The process of training involves a number of basic concepts defined briefly here.

In simple terms, training involves subjecting your body to 'stress' and then allowing it to adapt so that it will be able to cope better with similar and increased stresses in the future. Swimming is just one of many ways in which the body can be positively stressed, resulting in the development of more efficient physiological systems.

Overload

This is a fundamental training principle dictating that fitness improves only when the demands placed on the body during training are greater than those normally encountered. For example, if you have been swimming regularly for the past few years but doing exactly the same thing each time you go to the pool you will need to introduce some additional overload if you want to actually begin training.

The greatest fitness improvements are likely to come about when you begin to overload your energy processing systems (e.g. heart, lungs, circulatory system). The demands you place on your body under these conditions stimulate your body to *adapt* and, over time, to *progress*. You will know you are progressing when you can swim at maximum with a feeling of decreased effort. Normally this comes after several days of hard training followed by slightly easier training. Once you have progressed you can up your training to an increased level of intensity and the adaptation and progression process will start again, but this time at a higher level than before.

It is worth noting, however, that after initial overload the body will experience fatigue so that you won't necessarily experience positive feelings immediately. This is why rest is also a key aspect of training (*see* p. 100).

Overload can be achieved by manipulating the following three training variables:

- *frequency* – this simply refers to how often you are training. Research shows that for aerobic conditioning to occur you should be swimming three times per week

- *duration* – this is defined as the length of time you are swimming at a particular intensity, either for the total time of the entire swimming session or via a series of repeated efforts (repetitions) with periods of rest between

- *intensity* – this is basically how hard you are working and can be measured in terms of speed (*see* above), heart rate and subjective feelings ('I feel better than I did when I finished training last week').

Monitoring your heart rate

Your heart rate is a useful indicator both of your general fitness and the overall progress you are making in your swimming programme, as well as providing a useful marker of the intensity you are training at when in the pool. Your pulse shows how fast your heart is working rather than how efficiently it is working. When you begin your swimming programme, your heart will work faster during any given swim than it will later, when you are fitter.

You can measure your pulse manually in three ways:

- by pressing gently with your middle finger on the carotid artery on one side of your neck; it is situated at the side of your head and approximately 3 cm from the bottom of your earlobe

- by pressing your fingers on your heart

- by pressing the middle finger of one hand on the inside of the other wrist.

Count the number of beats that your heart makes in 15 seconds, and then multiply this by four to obtain the number of beats per minute (bpm). This can be carried out at any time during your session to monitor whether you are training at the right intensity (*see* below and pp. 54), but it's also useful to measure it at the start of your whole programme, to give you a baseline for future measurement.

The heart rate monitor (HRM)

HRMs generally consist of a sensor or transmitter that is strapped around the chest and/or a waterproof wrist monitor (*see* fig. 1.2, p. 9). They are now widely available and, if used correctly, are considerably more accurate than using manual methods for monitoring the intensity of your swim.

Working out your training intensity

A useful guide to your training intensity involves working out both your resting heart rate (RHR) and your maximum heart rate (MHR).

- Resting heart rates vary greatly from one individual to another. On average, women's are higher than men's by 5–7 bpm, but in general terms, the fitter you are, the lower it will be. To find out your RHR, take your pulse before you get up every morning for a few days and then calculate the average.

- Your MHR is basically your heart rate when you are working flat out, and this is normally achieved in swimming during interval training. For example, after a thorough warm-up you would take your pulse within 15 seconds of completing a high quality series of swims – e.g. 4 × 100 m with 3 minutes rest. However, it is not advisable for some people to push themselves to this level, so Table 2.1 gives some general guidelines for MHR according to age, though again this will vary considerably from individual to individual. As a rough guide, take the following figure – 226 bpm for women, and 220 bpm for men – and subtract your age.

Table 2.1 Average MHRs for different age groups

Age group (years)	MHR (bpm)	Swimming MHR (bpm)
20–30	200	190
31–40	190	180
41–50	180	170
51–60	170	160

- As you can see, however, this table includes MHRs for swimming. This is because, once you have reached a reasonable level of swimming fitness, your MHR in water will generally be lower by about 10 bpm than your MHR if you were training on dry land.

How water affects your heart rate

Research has shown that your heart can work both harder and for longer when you are immersed in water. This is because:

- buoyancy acts to support your body (*see* p. 4)

- you are training in a horizontal position, so that your blood is distributed more evenly around your body

- you tend to use the muscles in your upper body more than those in your lower body, so that your heart does not need to pump the blood as far as in land-based aerobic activities

- your heart becomes enlarged in water, meaning that between 10% and 20% more blood can be expelled with each contraction when swimming than when running

- the cooling effect of water on a swimmer's skin means that blood used for this purpose when training on land can be diverted to the central systems around the heart.

- When you have worked out your RHR and swimming MHR, you need to decide on the training intensity required. For aerobic conditioning, this will usually be in the 55–80% range – and at the low end of that during the early stages of your training programme – although for more intense training, this will be in more like the 80–90% range, and for anaerobic training 90% plus. (*See* also p. 54.)

- Then, using these figures apply the following formula:

(MHR – RHR) × % training range intensity + RHR.

So, if you are 40 years old, have a RHR of 70 bpm and are starting out on a swimming programme, you should be aiming at swimming at a pace where your heart rate is about 136 bpm

(180 – 70) x 60% + 70 = 136 bpm

Do check your RHR on a regular basis once your have started your training programme. It will gradually get slower as your fitness improves, so you will need to recalculate your training ranges to compensate. As a general rule, an average person needs to exercise to a level whereby their heart rate sustains 150 bpm in order to really benefit – in other words, our 40-year-old should aim to improve his swimming fitness so that he can work at about 70%.

That being said, it is important to note that your heart rate measurements relate only to *you* and to *your* performance; comparisons with other swimmers' results are not really relevant. Bear in mind, too, that an unusually high heart rate early in the session might indicate overtraining (see below), or possibly the onset of an illness. In such a case, be careful to rest or adapt your training accordingly.

You should also take your pulse five minutes after exercise. If it is still around 120 bpm or noticeably elevated, your training has been too hard. Ten minutes after exercise your pulse should be below 100 bpm and heading towards the average resting pulse rate of 70 bpm. Your body's ability to adapt needs to be developed gradually; this guideline will help to indicate when you are trying to achieve too much too quickly.

Overtraining

Overtraining is when you train too much and your body does not have time to recover adequately between sessions – failing to adapt to the demands being made of it. This can be for a variety of reasons:

- the volume of swimming is too great or intense
- there is not enough rest between sessions, sets or swims
- the swimmer has unrealistically high personal goals
- there is too high an expectancy amongst family, friends or training partners.[1]

If this happens, it is very easy to ease back before any damage is done. Often, though, you do not realise that your body has failed to adapt until is it actually happening. You therefore need to be aware of the symptoms, which include:

- an elevated RHR (*see* p. 19) – by as much as 5 bpm
- listlessness and recurrent infections due to less efficient immune system
- poor training performance – e.g. your timed swims are slower
- difficulty in concentrating at work.

Be aware of your body, ensure that you have adequate amounts of carbohydrates and fluids in your diet (*see* Chapter 7), and plan your fitness programme carefully so that it is progressive and cyclical. Please refer to Chaper 8, p. 100 for more information on overtraining.

Training cycles

The idea behind cyclical training is to provide periods where you can rest and regenerate – at certain times you will be swimming hard, but these are counterbalanced by substantial periods where you are not asking so much of your body. These periods of regeneration take place after intensive periods of hard training and they are considered necessary in order to guarantee continuous improvement. The periods employed vary from swimmer to swimmer but can include anything from 6 to 12 week cycles, with 3 weeks hard training followed by 6 weeks rest.

Longer cycles are known as *macrocycles* and are normally designed to fit in with the short-course and long-course swimming season described later in the book. They allow the swimmer to reach three or four peaks during the year. *Microcycles* refer to shorter periods lasting from a few days to one or two weeks. A *mesocycle* is a string of microcycles generally lasting for between two and seven weeks. The mesocycle always contains a period of hard work as well as an easier regenerative period.

[1] Cross, N. (1997), 'Overtraining in British swimming: a research summary', *Swimming Times*, p. 26.

By splitting your annual plan into identifiable phases and organising these into cycles, all elements of your training plan will knit together. If organised correctly, they will allow you to be at your peak at a pre-determined time – something known as *periodisation*, which is an approach used by most serious or competitive swimmers. *See* also Chapter 9, Planning principles.

Detraining and retraining

Training suggests systematisation, structure and orderliness. But what happens when a regular swimmer stops training? Quite simply, the swimmer will go into a phase known as 'detraining'. This detraining effectively means the loss of fitness gains, reversing the training process towards untrained levels. In order to move back towards the fully trained state, the swimmer will need to go through a process commonly known as 'retraining'.

The warm-up

It is common knowledge now that you should warm up the body before undertaking any form of exercise. This has the effect of preparing the heart, muscles and joints for the main part of the training session, and has several physiological benefits. Essentially, the warm-up:

- increases the temperature of the muscles, which allows them to contract more rapidly and more forcefully, and to relax more quickly

- causes a rise in general body temperature and a gradual lifting of the heart rate, opening up the capillaries and ensuring that sufficient blood is transported to the muscles to be exercised

- stretches the muscles and loosens connective tissue

- replicates the neuro-muscular patterns required in the training session

- encourages the release of synovial fluid – the fluid that allows smooth movement of bone over bone – into the joint capsules, and warms the tendons and ligaments as well as the muscles that surround each joint. The joints are therefore well lubricated prior to use.

It also has psychological benefits, preparing the swimmer mentally for the training session ahead.

The warm-up should always be gradual. If done too vigorously, muscle glycogen is depleted, and lactic acid may be present at the start of a session (*see* also pp. 69–70). Build into your training programme without over-extending yourself at first.

A simple warm-up routine on land

If possible, make the time to perform a simple warm-up on the poolside before you start your training session. Don't expect too much of yourself at first, a few light exercises are sufficient. You should set aside about five minutes before each swimming session for stretching, particularly the shoulders and the ankles (*see* pp. 23–7).

Here are a few suggestions each of which should least 15–30 seconds:

- Start by standing upright with your feet shoulder-width apart. Circle each arm through 360 degrees, or as near as possible (*see* fig. 3.1). Take the right arm and circle it forwards several times; then, with the same arm, backwards. Repeat on the other side. In order to ensure that your body is vertical throughout, look immediately in front of you while circling. Carry out these movements quite slowly so that you can feel the complete range of movement at the shoulder joint. Keep your shoulders down and your back straight throughout.

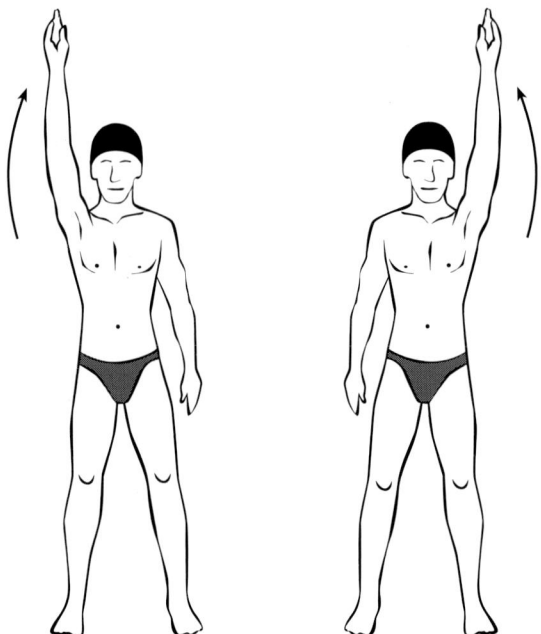

Figure 3.1 Shoulders – arm rotation

- Now you can get the feel of swimming by draping your body forwards at the hips and mimicking the freestyle action (*see* fig. 3.2). By now your shoulders should be getting used to the rotational movements, so you can make your freestyle arm movements that much quicker. Follow this by switching to butterfly arm movements. Keep your back straight and your head in alignment.

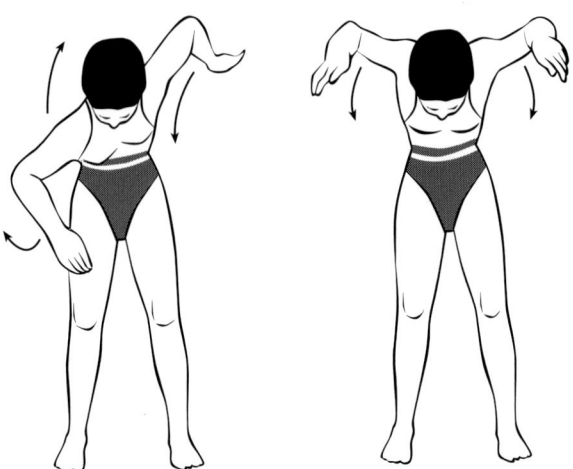

Figure 3.2 Freestyle and butterfly – arm rotation

- The next stage is to stand upright again and circle the arms together backwards (*see* fig. 3.3). The movement should be fairly slow, and when the hands reach the vertical above the head, the shoulder blades should feel as though they are going to scrape together. Again, ensure that your shoulders do not lift up during the exercise.

- Now raise your left arm and hold the elbow with your right hand. Press gently backwards to stretch the triceps at the back of the upper arm (*see* fig. 3.4). Your head and body should remain vertical and you should face forwards throughout. Hold the stretch for 15–30 seconds and then repeat on the other side. A partner, if you have one, can help you keep the whole movement steady and controlled.

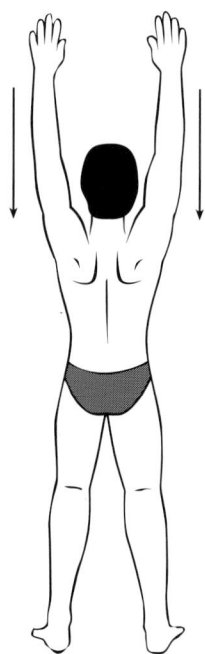

Figure 3.3 Backwards – arm rotation

Figure 3.4 Triceps stretch

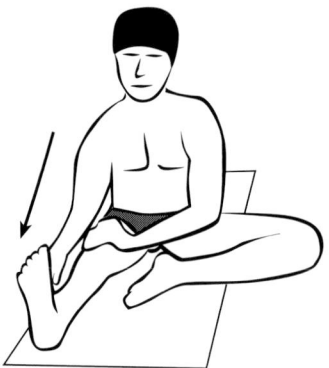

Figure 3.5 Sitting hamstring stretch

• You are now ready to move on to another simple exercise, this time stretching the hamstring muscles at the backs of the legs. Place your towel on the ground and sit upright, with one leg straight and the other comfortably bent out to the side. Bend forwards from the hips, reaching towards your toes until you feel a stretch at the back of your thigh (*see* fig. 3.5). Keep your back straight and your head in alignment. Hold for 15–30 seconds and relax. Repeat on the other side.

• Finally, bend your left leg and place your left ankle on your right thigh, above the knee (*see* fig. 3.6). Holding your ankle with your left hand, rotate your foot with your right hand through 360 degrees. When you have repeated this a few times, rotate in the opposite direction. Repeat on the other ankle.

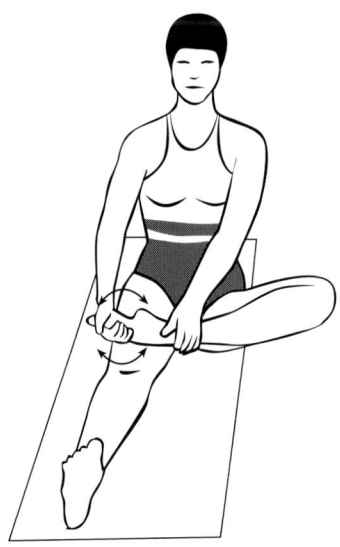

Figure 3.6 Ankle rotation

Chapter 6 covers land conditioning – strength and flexibility work – in greater detail, but these few simple exercises are all that is required to help you prepare both mentally and physically for the training session ahead. When you have got used to your quick routine, you may want to utilise two or three exercises only and to change these from session to session.

Stretching in the water

Sometimes, easy stretching in the water is preferable to stretching on land (*see* figs. 3.7–3.13). You may find, for instance, that there is little room on the pool deck – and during busy public swimming sessions, land-based exercise routines do not go down all that well with the bathing fraternity. In addition, some stretching in the water tends to get you used to the feel of steady resistance that you will encounter when actually swimming.

• Start by facing the side of the pool. Holding on to the pool deck or rail, place your feet flat on the wall and straighten your legs at the knees as shown in fig. 3.7 (incidentally, this is also a useful way of relieving cramp if you get it while training).

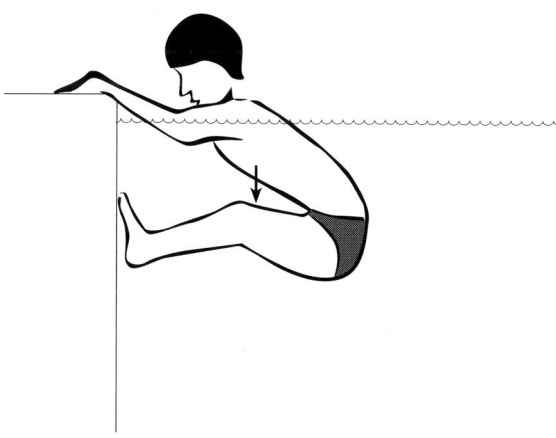

Figure 3.7 Hamstring stretch

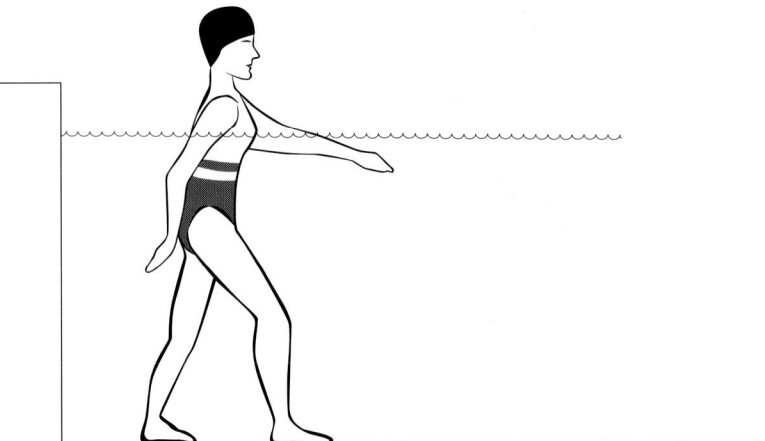

Figure 3.8 Walking stretch

- Next, stand on the bottom of the pool and walk away from the shallow end towards deeper water. Push off the bottom of the pool by pressing down through your toes (*see* fig. 3.8). Try this several times.

- Now, standing on the bottom of the pool, lift your knees one at a time. Try to get the knees as high as possible, preferably above the waist (*see* fig. 3.9). As you change legs, try to bounce gently on your feet to add rhythm to the movement. The forearms rest on the surface of the water throughout.

- Then stand on the bottom of the pool with your legs apart. Choose an appropriate depth so that your shoulders are level with the surface. Extend one arm to the side in line with your shoulder. Move the hand of the other arm in an anticlockwise direction under the water surface, in one big arc in front of the body – extending

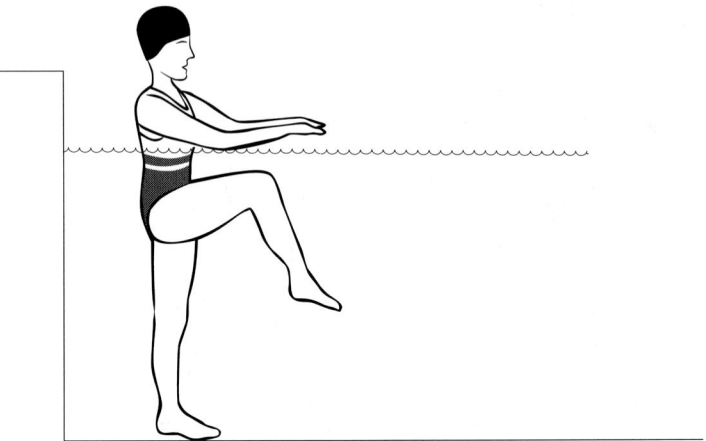

Figure 3.9 Knee raises

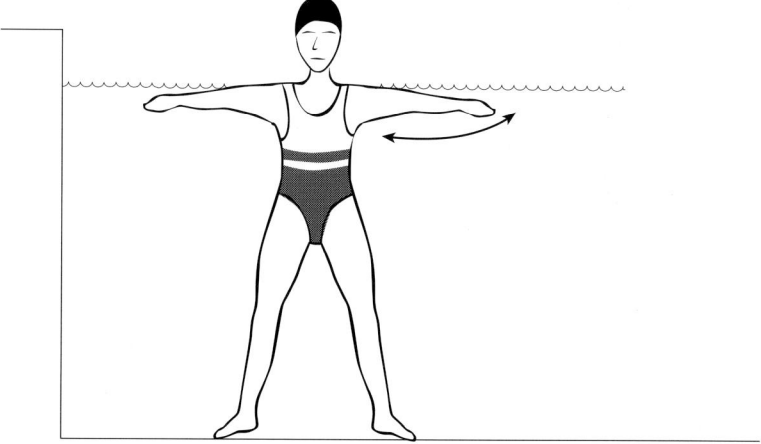

Figure 3.10 Arm rotation

the arm to its maximum (*see* fig. 3.10). The hand stays about 5 cm under the surface throughout. The arm is then returned to the start position, and the exercise repeated on the other side. Try to accelerate the hand movement through the water so that the resistance of the water increases.

- Follow this by working on some side bends. Stand upright so that the water surface is beneath shoulder level. Keeping your arms by your sides, tilt your body to the right and slide the fingers of your right hand as far down the side of your right leg as possible (*see* fig. 3.11). Repeat on the other side, making sure that you keep your hips in alignment throughout the exercise.

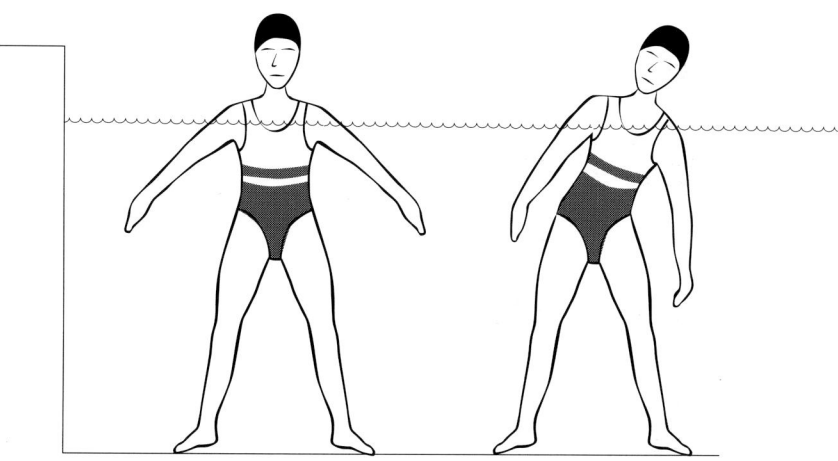

Figure 3.11 Side bends

Figure 3.12 Water squats

- Now try water squats. Stand in chest-deep water with your feet turned out and slightly further than hip-width apart. With your hands on your hips, bend your knees in line with your feet, keeping your back straight and your head facing forwards (*see* fig. 3.12). When your chin sits on the surface, straighten your legs at the knees. Repeat several times.

- The last exercise requires strength as well as flexibility. Ease your way up to the deep end of the pool. Face the poolside and place your arms above your head in line with the shoulders. Press down with your hands on top of the poolside, pulling your chin and then your upper body out of the water until your hips are level with the poolside (*see* fig. 3.13). Now allow your body to ease back to its starting position in the water. Do this four or five times to get the feel of the last phase of the pulling movements in freestyle and butterfly.

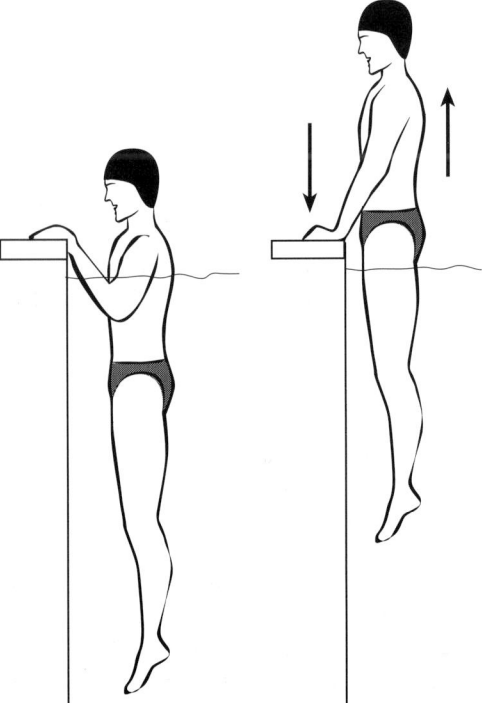

Figure 3.13 Pool press-up

Building into the training session

The early part of this book emphasises the importance of a gradual introduction to swimming exercise. This not only holds good for the approach towards a monthly or annual programme, but is also important in every individual session. There are few benefits to be gained from diving in off the poolside and swimming flat out for 50–100 m at the start of a session. Try to treat your body like a car; it needs to warm up in order to perform at its best. Long, easy swimming, working at what you consider to be 50% of your maximum, is much more preferable. Concentrate on stretching and streamlining at this stage in your warm-up.

This is also a good time to become accustomed to the water and air temperature as well as the pool conditions: for example, whether the pool is busy, whether there are lanes for you to swim in, or whether the water level means that you are swimming through choppy water. Also, avoid swimming soon after eating (*see* also pp. 85–95). When you start swimming, try to feel your hands pulling right the way through the movement. Aim to breathe out fully before taking the next breath. These are small tips that can help to encourage you to relax at the start of your swimming session and to avoid early strain.

Loosening off following training

The loosen-off or cool-down period is just as important as the warm-up. The main reason for the swim-down is so that all the body systems can regain their pre-training state. Blood needs to be returned to the heart in order for it to help in the removal of waste products such as lactic acid. Generally, lactate can be more rapidly removed when the muscles are working at a low intensity.

Lactic acid occurs naturally in the body as a by-product of exercise (*see* also p. 53). It builds up when the muscles are tired or fatigued, and is brought about during the breakdown of the carbohydrate glycogen, when insufficient oxygen is available to the body. During the cool-down, muscular contraction brings about a squeezing effect on the veins, pushing venous blood back to the heart at an increased rate. At this point excess lactate is removed and metabolised by cardiac muscle fibres.

Just like the warm-up, your loosen-off period also has psychological benefits, helping to relax the mind and remove feelings of stress by the time you leave the water. This will promote a feeling of wellbeing at the end of your training session.

When planning your session, try to allow at least five minutes at the end to loosen off. This period will allow you to ease down, get rid of any carbon dioxide from your lungs and clear as much lactic acid from the rest of your body as possible. The longer and harder your session, the more time you need to fully loosen down. Most people find that their loosen-down will depend on the time they have available – but try not to skimp on it.

Loosen off with some easy freestyle or breaststroke (5–6 lengths), or by swimming legs-only very easily with the face placed in the water from time to time. All three of these will allow you to breathe out into the water, thus clearing the lungs. Arm recovery movements can be fairly floppy and the pull does not need to be strong. Hopefully you will have worked hard but won't leave the pool feeling like a wreck.

Part II
Swimming for fitness

4 The strokes revisited

Easing your way back to fitness

The first session is the most difficult part of any swimming programme. Go along prepared to feel a little stiff afterwards. You are bound to feel a little stiff after each session but the level of stiffness will soon ease. If you are a little older, try to account for this in your planning by building up gradually. As mentioned in Chapter 1, if you can swim with a friend or as part of a group this can really help to break down early barriers. To help record your improvements and achievements, buy a simple diary that you can use as both a log of your swimming sessions and a diary for future planning.

Gradual increases in levels of intensity (*see* p. 54) should be the cornerstone of your swimming during the early months. Try to work at your own rate and bear in mind that sometimes you won't improve at all. You may stay at the same level or go back slightly before moving forwards to the next plateau. Your swimming actually becomes an act of faith as well as a matter of scientific and artistic approach. You have to believe that what you are doing will be beneficial in the long run. This chapter takes you through your first sessions in the pool, before brushing up on your stroke technique, practising your breathing and introducing you to stroke-counting.

The first session

Be prepared to ease your way back in with some very simple exercises, even if you have previously swum at quite a high level.

Normally you would start your session with a few stretching exercises on the poolside (*see* also pp. 23–7) but on this first occasion you can stretch in the water. Before you get into the water, take your pulse (*see* p. 18). After the session, you might want to record this in your swimming diary for future reference.

Then slide into the water off the pool deck. Avoid diving in the first time, since this almost suggests having to swim fast as soon as you leave the poolside. During this first session, you need to emphasise ease of movement. As you slide in, try to build up a mental picture that this is how you want to swim – you want your movements to be slippery, oily and fish-like when you start. Imagine that you are going to try to cut through the water with all your movements, and that you are going to move the water with a steady force that doesn't cause the water to splash. The last thing you want is heavy, over-emphasised actions that move your body all over the place in the water. These early mental pictures may seem fairly trivial but they will focus the mind on exactly how you are going to approach your swimming programme.

Then, from a standing position, push off from the bottom of the pool, stretch your arms together out in front of you and just glide (*see* fig. 4.1). Do this a few times with

Figure 4.1 Front glide from standing

your face in the water between your arms. Perhaps you had forgotten what it feels like to be back in a pool: this movement will help you to get used to the feeling of weightlessness and of having your face in the water, breathing out. Remember, there is no hurry at this stage to get swimming. Acquainting yourself with the water is just as important.

After doing this a few times you can try swimming some easy strokes. These would normally be freestyle or breaststroke, but you might want to simply keep your hands stretched out together in front of you and to kick legs-only on either stroke with your face in the water. Slide your hands into the water instead of 'crashing' them through the surface. Try to stretch out on the strokes and really try to feel the water as your hands pull. The hands will tend to make sculling movements. Remember that at a certain point in the stroke – whatever that stroke is – you will keep the hand fixed in one plane while you pull your body past that fixed position, a little bit like watching a boat being rowed from one side. The efficiency of the sculling movement is therefore important.

Take a break and then try kicking a length very steadily with your arms out in front of you. Then take another break and swim full stroke for a length. Try this about six times in all.

In order to get used to using the water as efficiently as possible, stroke-counting is a handy way to start. In the first instance, it is much easier to count the number of strokes per length when you are moving slowly than when you are moving fast. Stroke-counting is covered in more detail on pp. 50–1 but for now, literally count the number of strokes it takes you to swim the length. Take a rest for about a minute at the end of the pool and try to do one less stroke on the way back. You might want to do this for half a dozen lengths and then record the results in your diary later, as they will set standards for the future.

If you are not too stiff, you might want to follow this up by working on the efficiency of your push-off or glide (*see* fig. 4.1 above). This basic skill is often overlooked by swimmers. Remember that it is faster and saves more energy to push off the wall further and more efficiently than it is to push a smaller distance and to swim to the same point. The push-off also determines how streamlined your body will be during the first part of the length. For swimmers at all levels, it is important to get it right and to extend the glide as much as possible.

There are two handy hints. First, start from a depth on the wall of about half a metre under the water, where the water is less disturbed. Second, keep the hands close to one another, squeeze the elbows, point the toes and stretch so that you arrow your way through the water more effectively. Practise this as much as possible; it takes time to find the best position for you.

Following this, loosen down with some easy, very relaxed swimming over about four lengths and that will be sufficient for this session. Keep the first few sessions at this level so that you can get used to the water and avoid too many early aches and pains. Eventually your body will adapt to increasing levels of exercise, but the intensity of your sessions needs to be built gradually. If you fail to consider your body in this way, it could prove unproductive and demoralising.

Revising and correcting stroke technique

Now that you've made the initial breakthrough and are back in the water, time spent brushing up on your strokes will help to keep you on the right track. It is important to get into good habits from the start as faults tend to multiply as swimming becomes more intensive. Remember, speed has a direct relationship with stroke efficiency, not energy expenditure. One of the great difficulties in returning to a fitness programme of this nature lies in trying to build up a mental picture of what your strokes actually look like. Many people cannot remember what their technical faults were when they swam in the past; this is made harder by the fact that you can't see yourself while you are swimming, which is why exercising with a partner or in a group is of such value. If, however, you are swimming on your own and find it hard to visualise your own strokes, the following section offers some useful tips. It does not claim to be comprehensive but assumes that you have already reached a certain standard in your swimming – for example, the ability to swim 20–30 lengths in the past. There are many books that cover stroke technique to a high standard, and if you feel you would like to examine this in detail then the Amateur Swimming Association at Loughborough has a comprehensive publications department. If you are also interested in brushing up on your starts and turns, see Chapter 14.

Focus on your technique

Concentrate on the basics – a good push-off; completing each stroke before going into the next one; using the neck and head to streamline the body and make it flatter on the surface of the water.

Freestyle

Freestyle, or front crawl, is the fastest of the strokes (*see* fig. 4.2). The important thing to bear in mind at this initial stage is streamlining. Any undue lateral movement is going to cause an opposite reaction (*see* p. 5), which will mean that the body snakes from side to side.

Try to imagine that you are swimming down a tube a little bit like the London Underground but on a much smaller scale. The diameter of the tube is about 1 m and your main aim in all the movements is to avoid touching the side. In order to manage this, the elbows need to be bent and held perpendicularly during the recovery of the arm. This can be achieved by aiming to show more and more of the armpit as the arm is recovered. The fingers need to be relaxed as they face down towards the water's surface. When pulling under the water, the hands need to press back towards the stomach and then on towards the upper legs.

Swimmers employ a number of different rhythms for freestyle. (*See* also pp. 49–50 for tips on breathing.) These rhythms are governed by the number of leg-kicks for each arm cycle. Generally, six leg-kicks to each complete arm-cycle – i.e. completion of 360 degrees of movement by both arms – are used when a swimmer wants to swim at speed with a longer arm stroke. If you want to swim over a longer distance, a strong six-beat kick is too tiring to maintain and most people will revert to a four-beat, two-beat or a two-beat kick with a cross-over (where the legs move laterally to the side but do not complete a downward movement).

The two-beat kick consists of a downward kick by one leg as the opposite hand begins its pull. For example, the right hand sinks and sculls in the water to a point where it catches hold of the water at the start of the pull. At this point, the left leg is driven towards the bottom of the pool, partly as a form of balance and partly for propulsion. The opposite movements occur when the left hand enters.

The catch, hand speed and hand pitch

Good swimmers let their hands enter the water steadily without splashing them through the surface. There is a short period when the hands settle before really purchasing on the water. The point where purchase is made is known as the catch.

The swimmer should aim to increase the speed of his hand during the propulsive part of the pull – i.e. in the period immediately following the catch. When hand velocity has reached its maximum, it then needs to change direction. If it fails to change direction, slippage follows and a lack of purchase sets in.

The pitch of the hand should be constantly altered to determine the best position to create maximum lift propulsion. Highly skilled swimmers will move their hands throughout the stroke to avoid drag, and in freestyle and butterfly tend to enter their hands at an angle with their thumb and first finger leading. The hand is then rotated at the wrist throughout the pull until the little finger increasingly falls into line horizontally with the rest of the wrist. This whole movement is also facilitated by rotating the forearm so it makes part of the pull.

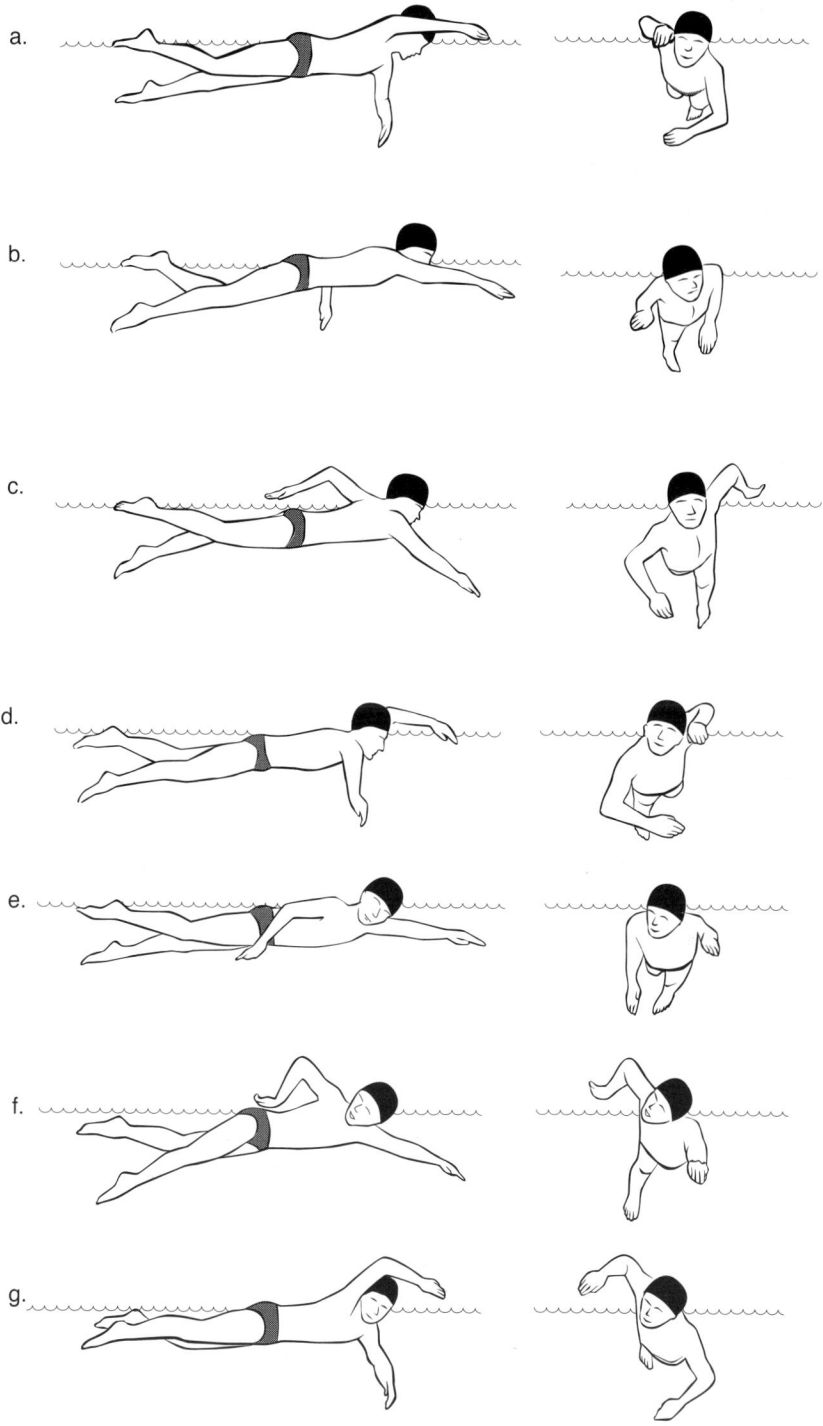

Figure 4.2 Freestyle stroke sequence

The four-beat kick can involve a 'cross-over' of the legs. As with the two-beat kick, there are two downward movements; but there are also two downward involuntary kicks, which are made as a cross-over so that during the downward movement, one leg-kick crosses at the knee of the other. The reason for this involuntary movement is simply to balance the body and counteract any lateral body movements brought about during the arm-cycle either by the arms, or by excessive breathing movements. For the purposes of fitness training, four or two leg-kicks for each leg-cycle are sufficient.

Key skill points

Body position
- There will be a certain amount of body roll around the lateral axis.

- Keep the hairline on the surface when the head centres to the front.

- When turning the head to breathe, keep the nose on the surface.

Arms
- Bend the elbows to 90 degrees, with the fingers pointing towards the water, during recovery.

- The hand enters at a 45-degree angle.

- Accelerate the hand during the pull.

- Extend the hand until the arm is almost straight before beginning the pull.

- Pull *under* the body.

- Complete the pull back to the hips before recovery.

Legs
- The kick emanates from the hips.

- When kicking down, keep the legs as straight as possible.

- When kicking, try to feel as though you are shaking the feet off.

- Try to keep the legs under the surface. Restrict the kick so that just the heels break the surface.

> ## Some common problems
>
> ### Arms
> Problem – your elbows drop when your hand enters the water.
> Tip – try to pull with the forearm as well as the hand.
>
> Problem – your elbows are bent but your hands and lower arms still feel too high during the recovery.
> Tip – aim to scrape the fingertips lightly along the surface of the water during the recovery.
>
> ### Legs
> Problem – your legs tire very quickly when swimming the stroke.
> Tip – this may be caused by breathing rather than the legs themselves. Make sure that you exhale all used air at the end of each arm-cycle.
>
> Problem – your legs drop too low in the water.
> Tip – if you are having difficulty in keeping your legs high enough, drop the head a little lower when it comes to the front, by looking directly down.

See pp. 59–60 for freestyle drills.

Breaststroke

Breaststroke was the first stroke to be swum in this country. While it is the slowest of the four competitive strokes, it is probably also the most relaxing. It particularly suits fitness swimmers who are exercising in busy public pools, as it allows a good view of other people in the water (*see* fig. 4.3).

Breaststroke is basically comprised of a series of sculling movements, with the swimmer trying to part the water with his hands in order for his head and body to pass through. The stroke begins with the legs straight; these then bend at the knees, with the heels lifted towards the backside. The feet fan out so that the soles face backwards in preparation for the kick. When the kick takes place, the feet move circuitously, the toes staying curled. The heels are brought together and the toes point at the last moment to produce a whipping movement.

During the pull, the arms stay in front of the shoulders, and the hands in front of the face. The head is lifted at the end of the outward scull so that the swimmer can take a breath, with the exhalation taking place as the arms are straightened in front of the head during the kick.

Key skill points

Body position
- Your body needs to be in a straight line once in every arm-cycle – i.e. when the hands are stretched out in front at the end of the recovery.

- The shoulders are shrugged as the hands cup in front of the body.

- The arms really stretch out in front as the feet kick.

- Never move the head from side to side.

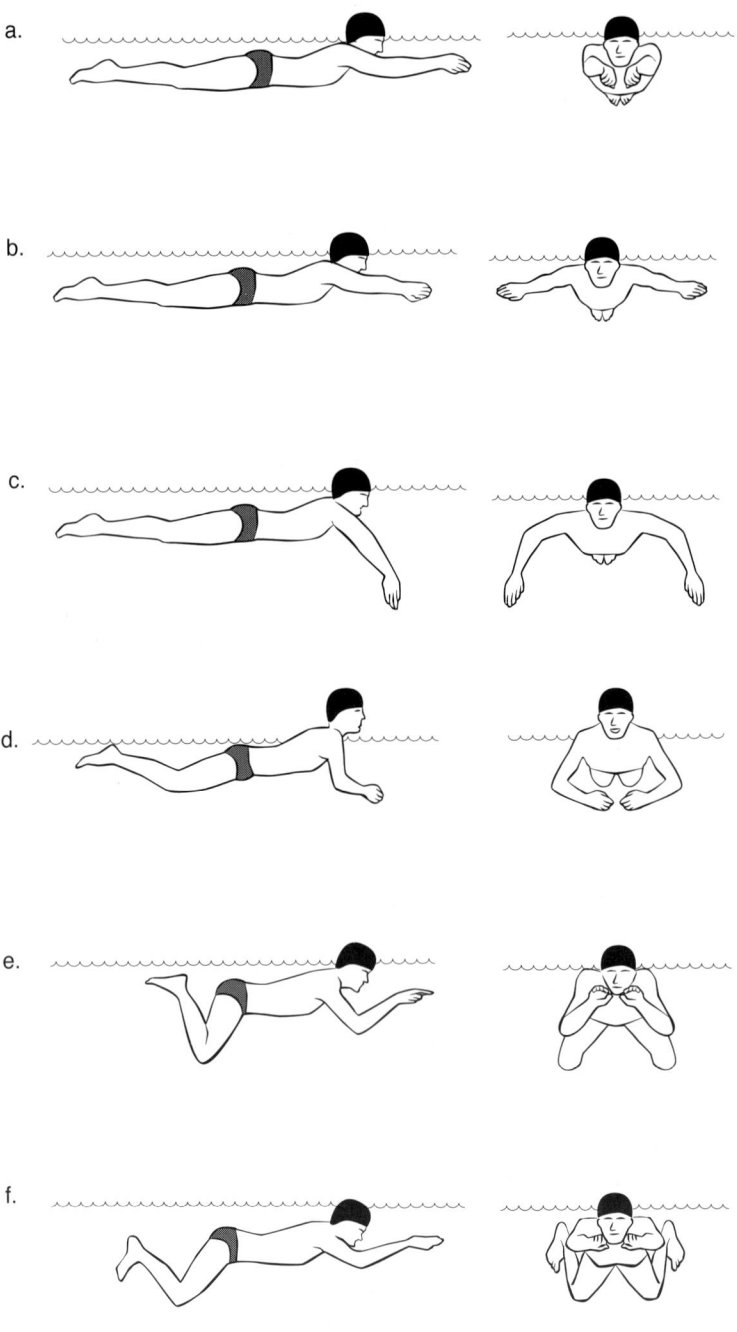

a.

b.

c.

d.

e.

f.

Figure 4.3 Breaststroke sequence

Arms

- Your hands scull out and scull in.

- Keep your elbows in front of your shoulders.

- The elbows should be higher than the hands throughout the stroke.

- The recovery movement of the arms results in a strong, downward follow-through from the shoulders and upper body.

- Arms pull before the legs start to kick in each arm-cycle.

- Your feet should not break the surface of the water.

Legs

- Move your legs simultaneously with your arms.

- Keep your thighs together.

- Rotate your feet through as close to 360 degrees as possible, with the surface of the feet facing the water during the main propulsive phase.

- There is a stronger emphasis on the kick as a propulsive force than in the other strokes.

Some common problems

Arms
Problem – you have difficulty in recovering the arms quickly.
Tip – try to tuck the elbows into the ribs at the end of the pull and keep the hands in front of the face. Avoid pulling the elbows too far back under the body during the pull.

Breathing
Problem – the water often goes up your nose when you stretch your arms out in front of you.
Tip – start to breathe out before your face goes under the water.

Legs
Problem – you have difficulty in kicking because your toes become pointed.
Tip – curl the toes as soon as you lift your heels to your backside.

Problem – your legs seem to act as a brake on the movement of the body through the water.
Tip – when preparing the legs to kick, lift the heels high towards your backside and the surface, thereby avoiding lifting the knees under the body.

Body position
Problem – your legs drop down too far.
Tip – lower the face and look at the bottom of the pool as the arms are recovered and straightened in front of the face.

See pp. 60–1 for breaststroke drills.

Backstroke

Backstroke, or back crawl, was introduced in the third Olympic Games in 1904, underlining its increasing importance as a stroke during the 1890s (*see* fig. 4.4). It remains an important stroke today, although the way in which it is swum has changed considerably. Now, the best backstrokers rely on a strong leg-kick, with the arms being driven back deep behind the head to increase the range of their pull. In order to achieve this, it is important to roll at the shoulders while keeping the head and the central vertical axis of the body as still as possible.

Backstroke is a bit like rowing a boat. The hands start pulling from a position at arm's reach in front of the head. They pull until they 'fix' on the water almost in line with the shoulders, and then push the body past this fixed position. This action is then replicated with each arm-stroke.

In a similar way to freestyle, the legs can kick at the rate of six, four, two or two beats with a crossover movement to each arm-cycle. Again, a sprint version of backstroke normally calls for a six-beat kick, while someone wishing to conserve their energy will look for just two kicks to each arm-cycle. If you want to swim good backstroke, think about holding your head still enough to balance a glass of water on it while you are performing the stroke.

Key skill points

Body position

- Keep your head steady throughout the stroke.

- Tuck your chin into your chest slightly, so that water does not run over the top of your head on to your forehead.

- The arms should enter between 1 and 2 o'clock, and between 10 and 11 o'clock.

- Aim to keep the hips reasonably high in the water.

- The level of the water should be just beneath the level of the chin and just over the ears.

Arms

- Lift the shoulders prior to recovering your arms over the water.

- Lead the recovery with your little finger; the hand should enter the water little finger first.

- Keep your arms straight on the recovery.

- Accelerate your hand at the end of the pull by pressing back towards the feet.

- Before pulling, drive your arm 35–50 cm back behind the head.

- The pull should comprise an elongated 's' shape.

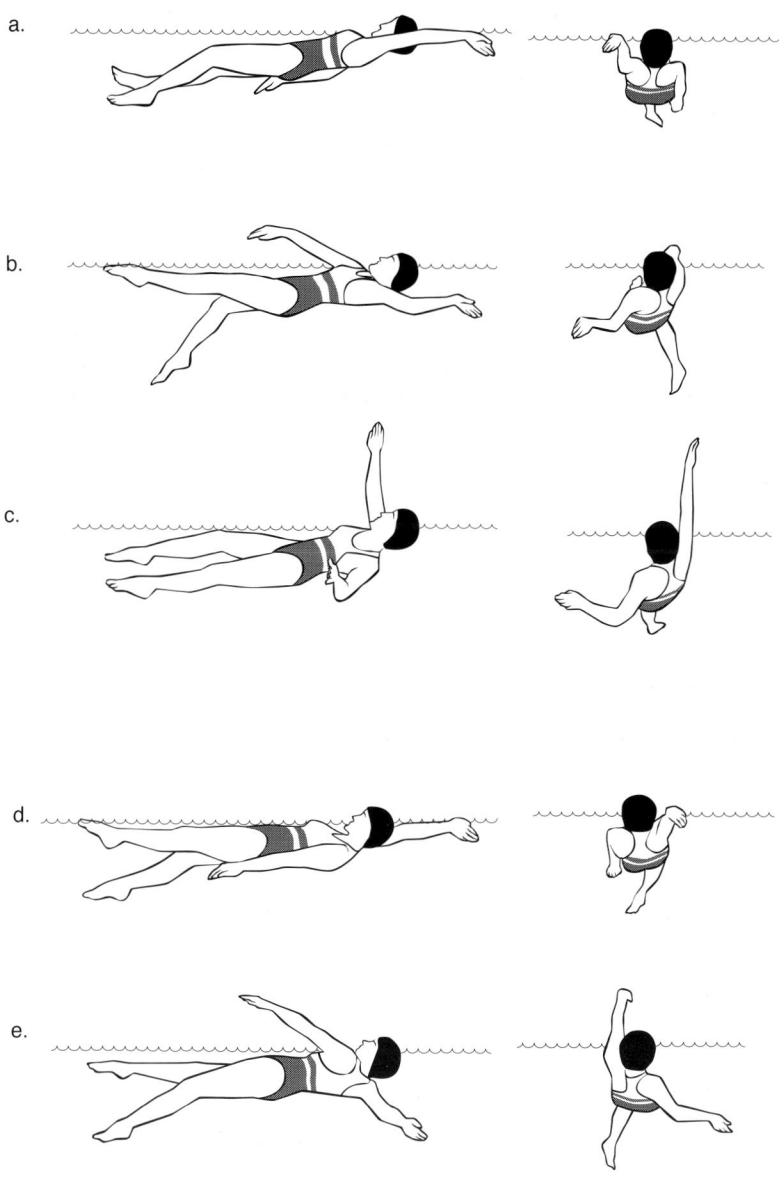

a.

b.

c.

d.

e.

Figure 4.4 Backstroke sequence

Legs

- Keep your knees under the water.

- Relax your feet, but point your toes at the end of the upward kick.

- Your knees should be straight on the upward kick and bent on the leg recovery.

- The legs act as both balancing agents and important propulsive agents through a series of small, rapid kicks.

Some common problems

Arms

Problem – water runs into your face off your arms each time you recover them over the water.

Tip – lead the recovery with your little finger and turn the palm of the hand slightly outwards as you lift your hand free of the water. This presents a 'cleaner' surface as you bring the arms over.

Problem – when you pull, your legs seem to move sideways instead of just up and down.

Tip – when your arm is level with your shoulder during the pull, push with your hand straight towards your feet.

Breathing

Problem – you find your head rolls sideways under the water.

Tip – think about keeping your central axis steady. You can achieve this by fixing your eyes on a line on the pool ceiling.

Legs

Problem – your legs tire very quickly.

Tip – you should not only reduce the strength of the kick, but also concentrate hard on breathing out once or twice in every arm-cycle. Most people breathe in on one arm and out on the other. Getting rid of carbon dioxide from your lungs helps.

Problem – your leg-kick is very weak.

Tip – concentrate hard on pointing the toes on the up-kick, so that the leg is straight at the end of the kick. Also, keep the knees under the surface.

See pp. 61–2 for backstroke drills.

Butterfly

Butterfly is the most recent of the competitive strokes, being introduced in the 1930s (*see* fig. 4.5). It will take you a number of weeks to work up to using this stroke as part of your fitness programme, but it is covered here in order to complete our short review of the strokes. Just as breaststroke reminds you of a frog, and freestyle and backstroke of a water-boatman, butterfly was referred to as 'butterfly dolphin' during its early years because of the similarity of the up-and-down movements to those of a dolphin.

The rhythm of the stroke is very important, and the most proficient swimmers aim to kick at either end of the pull. The weight of the head, coupled with the fact that both arms are simultaneously above the water for much of each stroke-cycle, can make the whole stroke very tiring. In order to facilitate these movements, try to get the timing right and avoid carrying the weight of the head out of the water for too long. You can work on this by following the 'two head before' rule: your head should go into the water before your arms enter, and come out of the water before your arms exit.

The best way to get back into swimming butterfly is to lengthen the whole stroke out. Start by kicking legs only under the water with your arms straight out in front of you, making long, easy, up-and-down kicking motions. Eventually you can add the arms. When you start using the arms, avoid continuous rotation – introduce the stroke steadily by recovering the arms, holding them out in front of you before you pull and then by adding an extra kick.

Key skill points

Body position
- Keep your chin on the surface when breathing in, to flatten out the overall movement.

- Roll your shoulders as your hands enter the water.

- Your heels should be the only parts of your body to break the surface.

Arms
- Lift your elbows slightly as your hands enter.

- Ensure that your hands enter in line with your shoulders and, in pulling back towards the stomach, make an hour-glass shape.

- Stretch out as your hands enter.

- Make the pull back towards your stomach and eventually towards your hips.

Legs
- Straighten your legs at the end of the kick.

- Try to kick at the start and end of the pull.

- Your ankles should be relaxed.

- Drive the hips close to the surface with a strong downward kick.

- Ensure that only the heels break the surface.

- Bend your knees in order to commence the downward thrust of the feet.

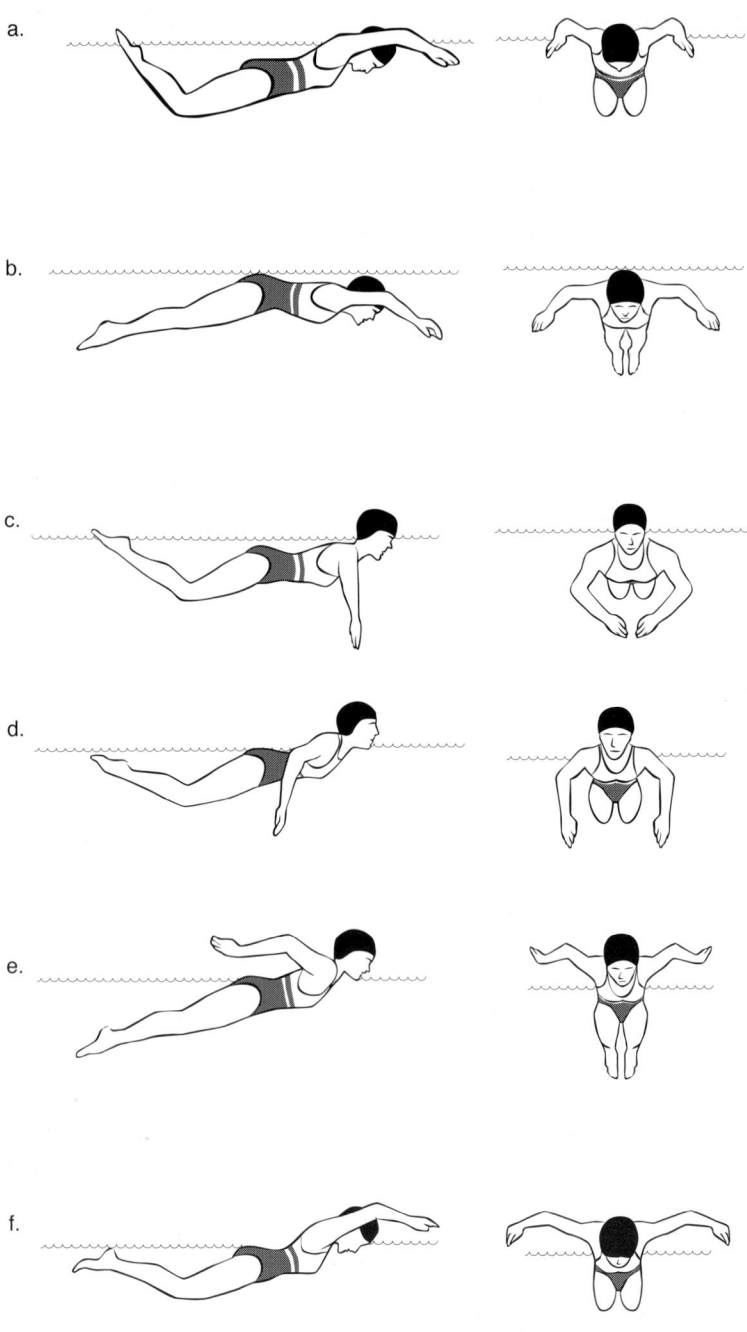

Figure 4.5 Butterfly stroke sequence

Some common problems

Arms
Problem – your arms hit the surface of the water as they are recovered.
Tip – try turning your hands to face outwards and then down just as they are
about to enter the water. If your hands face down during the recovery, this
encourages your elbows to catch the surface.

Problem – you find it difficult to clear your arms from the water at the start of
the recovery.
Tip – drop the head a little lower by looking back towards your feet under the
water. 'Explode' your exhalation and flip your fingertips at the end of the
stroke.

Breathing
Problem – you swallow water at the start of the arm recovery.
Tip – press back much harder at the end of the pull and kick hard to ensure that
your chin clears the surface.

Legs
Problem – your legs drop the whole time.
Tip – try looking under the body during the pull.

See pp. 62–3 for butterfly drills.

Breathing exercises

Breathing is often a neglected area in swimming, generally because the face is underwater so that faults are difficult to identify and correct. However, breathing exercises can help to improve stroke control, timing and streamlining, as well as bringing about a certain amount of conditioning.

In order to be able to breathe properly on any stroke, you need to balance the pressure of the water outside with the air pressure inside your nose – while bearing in mind that you always exhale through your mouth. Many people either take in too much air or not enough. Another common fault is to let air out too early or too late in relation to when the head moves back to the centre line.

The introduction of breathing exercises at an early stage in your fitness programme is a good way of combining many of the fundamentals that will form the background to your training when you are much fitter. By experimenting, you will be able to build the breathing pattern that suits you best, giving time and thought to the correct breathing pattern. Here are some of the ways you can experiment with freestyle breathing, of which there are many variations.

Freestyle breathing exercises
• Start by attempting bilateral breathing: this involves breathing every three strokes, alternating a breath to the left with a breath to the right. Bilateral breathing has the advantage of helping the body to keep on a more even keel while swimming the stroke, the head remaining on the centre line for a longer period of time. The total stroke is therefore more balanced.

- Now try taking a smaller breath than normal, and then blow the air out in a steady stream starting from the time the face re-enters the water through to the point where the face turns up to take the next breath. On the next length, take a larger breath than normal and repeat the exercise.

- Take another smaller breath and let the air trickle out naturally. Let the trickle start when it feels natural to you. Again, repeat this with a larger breath.

- Take a smaller breath once more and explode the air out when it feels comfortable to exhale. Repeat this on a larger than normal breath.

- Take a small breath again and breathe out hard when your nose reaches the centre line of your body. Then experiment with this on a larger than normal breath.

- On the next small breath hold your air in longer than normal and then expel it, somewhere between when your head reaches the centre line of your body and when you turn your head to the side to breathe again. Again, follow this with a larger than normal breath.

- Finally, take your last small breath and try breathing out at the mid-point between taking your breath and your head reaching the centre line. Follow the same pattern on a larger than normal breath.

Now try all of the above combinations with a normal sized breath. Which one feels the best to you? Breathing – its timing and volume – is very individual: a technique that is comfortable to one person is not necessarily comfortable to another. You may even want to devise your own breathing pattern to determine what feels good to you. (*See* also breath control swims on p. 56.)

Stroke-counting

One way of really building up your technique is by stroke-counting. This helps to ensure that you get the best out of every stroke you make by emphasising its length and completion. In essence, if you are moving efficiently, you will be able to fix your hand in one plane while pushing your body past that point.

A good way to start your stroke-counting is by trying it over single lengths. Begin with freestyle. A person of average height has a stroke span of about 1–1.5 m for each arm cycle. Allowing for a push-off of about 3 m, your aim should be to swim around 20 strokes for your first swim in a 25 m pool (although of course, this will depend on your height). Time yourself on the pool training clock. When you have finished, make a note of both the number of strokes and the time.

Now, make the same swim and attempt to reduce the number of strokes by one while maintaining the same speed. Attempt this several times. When you feel you have reached as few strokes as you are going to be able to manage at that speed, try dropping your time by two seconds and compare the number of strokes. Try hard to maintain the same technical efficiency while reducing your time. This may all take a little concentration, because it is difficult to be certain that you are going faster until you finish. Nevertheless, it all concentrates the mind on maximising every stroke made.

Stroke-counting can be done when you are warming up, swimming a set or swimming at speed, and is applicable to all four of the main strokes. Keep a note in your training diary of what your stroke-count is for any given part of your session, and constantly attempt to improve on your best.

In all strokes, there are certain parts of the arm action in which the hands pull or 'fix' on the water. These are seen as sculling movements. There are other points in the propulsive phase of the arm stroke where the hand paddles to the next pulling phase. These are almost like set-up phases, where the hand and arm are positioning themselves for the next body-hauling section. Stroke-counting can help to make both the pulling and sculling phases more efficient by making the swimmer more aware of where his hands are and what they should be doing next. This is achieved by trial and error as much as anything else, because the most efficient stroke technique differs from swimmer to swimmer. Chapter 5 describes some stroke drills, a number of which can be used to help reduce your stroke-count – especially those supported by long glides (such as catch-up freestyle, freestyle with a long, exaggerated push-through; glide breaststroke; shoulder-lift backstroke; and dive butterfly).

Types of training

Swimming training can be split into three types:

• long, continuous swims

• interval swims

• short, explosive swims.

All training programmes are written around these three main elements.

The long swims are further split into two areas – fartlek or 'speed play', and locomotive swimming. Fartlek normally involves swimming over longer distances at varying speeds, although the whole swim should never be exhausting. With locomotive training, the swimmer alternates fast and slow efforts but in a gradual way – e.g. 25 m slow, 25 m fast, 50 m slow, 50 m fast, 75 m slow, 75 m fast, 100 m slow, 100 fast and so on. This type of swimming can include any ratio of lengths using the same format. Interval swimming is another term for repetition swimming, and involves taking a break between the allocated lengths. Short, explosive swims address anaerobic work (*see* below). This chapter outlines the varioius training methods used by swimmers, shows you how to monitor your performance and then gives you a wide range of drills to fine-tune your stroke technique before providing some ideas on training in a group and also on your own.

The three energy systems

To understand how long continuous, interval and explosive swims work, it is useful to understand the different energy systems employed – bearing in mind that these are complimentary and can overlap.

Energy is produced by the splitting of a chemical substance called ATP (adenosine triphosphate), which is formed in all the cells of the body as a result of the breakdown of nutrients or 'fuels' – carbohydrates, fats and proteins (*see* Chapter 9). The energy production process can happen *anaerobically*, i.e. in the absence of oxygen, or *aerobically*, requiring the presence of oxygen. The body can only store a limited amount of ATP, and this is used up within a few seconds of exercise (*see* below): therefore, it must be continually re-made.

There are three ways in which your body can re-make ATP while you are exercising. The first two are anaerobic, and the third is aerobic. Aerobic swims are made at a slower pace and the oxygen required can be called upon as the exercise takes place.

(1) The first system – known as the ATP–PC (phosphocreatine) system – can only provide energy for about 5–10 seconds of exercise when the body is working at its maximum. Elite athletes can run 100 metres in 10 seconds, but in swimming you will be lucky to cover more than 20 metres in that time, even if you are among the best.

(2) After this initial period of high-intensity activity, the second system – known as the anaerobic glycolytic or lactic acid system – comes into play. This system can take the body through a further period of intensive exercise, lasting for up to 90 seconds, and involves ATP being replaced by energy from glycolysis – or the breakdown of muscle glycogen to single units of glucose. This process is performed anaerobically (without oxygen), and lactic acid forms as a by-product. The build-up of lactic acid in your muscles can leave you feeling exhausted and you won't be able to maintain your pace for very long.

(3) The third and final system comes into play beyond this initial 90 seconds of exercise and is known as the aerobic system. This system requires the presence of oxygen to breakdown carbohydrates (by glycolysis) and fat (by lipolysis) to generate ATP. Aerobic glycolysis provides the energy for swims of longer duration and uses carbohydrates stored as muscle glycogen.

Figure 5.1 shows the contribution of each of the above energy systems to a 100 m event.

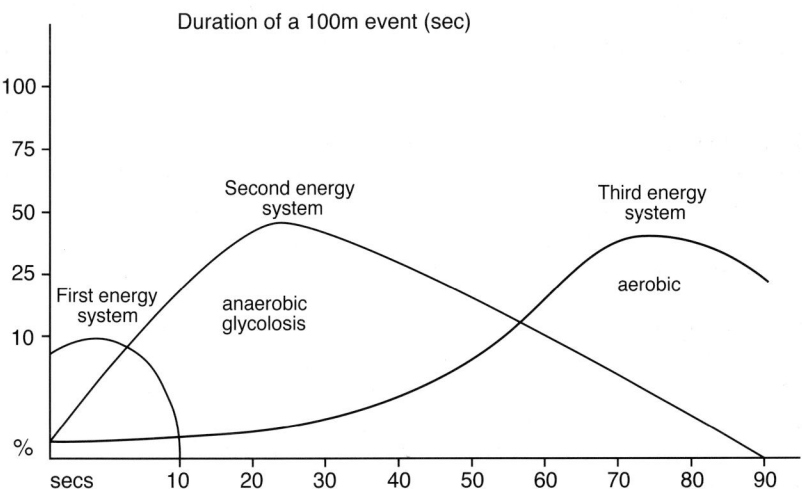

Figure 5.1 Energy systems employed during a typical 100m event

Developing swimming endurance

Endurance is a key component of swimming fitness. Speed often comes after a base of endurance has been established. Generally, the best way to develop stamina for swimming is through swimming training itself.

Endurance training can be divided into four main areas.

Easy to moderate swimming

Aerobic swimming undertaken at an easy to moderate pace – i.e 50–60% of maximum heart rate (MHR) – is suitable for anyone easing into a training programme. You should be slightly breathless at the end of each of these swims but still be able to talk. During your re-introduction to a swimming programme, all your swimming should be done at this level. Later, when you are fitter, you will use such swimming for warm-ups and swim-downs (*see* also Chapter 11). Long, steady swims aiming for a heart rate of 130–140 bpm help the body to burn off fat through a process called lipid metabolism.

Moderate to high-intensity swimming

Working at 70–80% of your MHR is still primarily endurance work. You will find that your body can remove the lactic acid as you swim and so should not be totally exhausted. When you gain a reasonable level of swimming fitness you should aim for 70% of your training to be done at this level.

High-intensity aerobic training

This is peformed at 80–90% of your MHR, and should be avoided if you have any conditions likely to be affected by this level of intensity and also for the first three to four months of your programme – although you should eventually aim to devote 10% of your training to this level. Your efforts will be such that you are out of breath, your arms ache when you pull and you need a reasonable rest to recover from each repetition or swim that you make. Most swimmers try to introduce this type of training towards the back end of their sessions.

Anaerobic swimming

This refers to efforts made at a much more intense level, more than 90% of your MHR. Basically, you are sprinting; pain increases as lactic acid builds in your muscles and oxygen debt sets in. If you are swimming at this level, you will need to take increasingly long rests between repetitions.

Table 5.1 summarises the energy systems for a young fit Masters swimmer (aged 19–30 and able to swim 5000 m or more per session).

Table 5.1 Energy system

Target heart rate	% of MHR	Speed	Energy system employed
120–140	50–60	Fairly easy	Aerobic
150–160	70	Moderate	Aerobic
170–180	80	Fast	Anaerobic threshold
190–200	90	Nearly flat out	Anaerobic glycolytic
over 200	100	Flat out	ATP–PC

Repetition or interval swimming

Once you have begun swimming regularly again and have improved your level of swimming fitness, there are various types of repetition swims that you can try.

Interval swimming

Interval swimming – referred to also as controlled interval swimming (CIS) – first came into the sport via athletics. It requires the swimmer to complete a sub-maximal set number of swims, all of the same distance, with the swim and rest amounting to the same amount of time for each repetition. The amount of rest you take is therefore predicated on the amount of time your repetition took. For example, if you were swimming 6 repetitions of 100 m freestyle on 2 minutes, your first swim might take 1 minute 35 seconds, leaving you with a 25-second rest. Your second swim could take 1 minute 25 seconds, leaving you a 35-second rest, and so on. These swims can be grouped to fit in with the energy systems discussed above. In other words, four swims of 100 m with 10 seconds rest will address aerobic conditioning because they would be performed at a lower intensity, while four swims with 2 minutes rest will clearly involve greater speed and physical intensity, thereby addressing anaerobic conditioning.

> **Terminology**
>
> CIS is normally expressed as swims being made 'off', 'at' or 'every' period of time. For example, four swims of 100 m aiming at a longer rest would be '4 × 100 m off 3½ min', while four swims aiming at a shorter rest would be '4 × 100 m off 2 min'. This would clearly depend on each individual's speed and the stroke involved.

Descending or reducing repetitions

These repetitions are very popular with competitive swimmers, as they provide a focus on continuous improvement. The swimmer follows the pattern of CIS but aims to swim progressively faster for each repetition.

Regressive repetitions

By comparison, regressive repetitions are rarely used. You may, however, want to introduce them into your training programme to help create levels of speed awareness. With regressive swims, you make your fastest effort first and your slowest last.

Negative splits

Here, you swim the second part of your repetition faster than the first. Negative splits – or 'bringing things back harder' in coaching parlance – can be used for any type of repetition, not just CIS, and are a good way of teaching yourself pace and encouraging a balanced swim in terms of speed.

Broken swims

These are quite different from CIS. The swimmer completes a set number of repetitions but takes an extra and consistent break in order to let the heart rate drop slightly. If we take the example of 4 × 100 m off 3½ min, each of the 100 m swims would be further broken by a rest at 50 m. Broken swims are often made over slightly longer distances, although the breaks should be kept consistent throughout the repetitions – both in terms of the length of the rest and the point at which it is taken. Broken swims work particularly well if you are training seriously to take part in a Masters competition. During the tapering phase (i.e. the phase when you are easing back for competition – *see* p. 137), they help to sharpen up pace and improve times. This is both a physical and a psychological benefit.

Alternating swims

Alternating swims are a way of breaking up the training to make it more interesting. The swimmer alternates two completely different types of swims: for example, 5 × 200 m freestyle alternating with 5 × 100 m breaststroke.

Mixed swims

These are a further way of adding variety to your sessions. For example, you might be swimming 4 × 200 m freestyle off 4 min. After the second 200 m repetition, you could add in 6 × 25 m breaststroke off 1 min.

Over-distance swimming

This consists of a small number of long repetitions at a medium to slow pace. The idea is to concentrate on technique and build a base level of cardiovascular fitness.

Standard rest swims

Not all repetition swims have to be made so as to integrate the time of the swim and the rest into a controlled interval. You could also take a standard rest between each swim – for example, 4 × 100 m freestyle with 10 sec rest.

Breath control swims

The aim of breath-holding swims, sometimes also known as *hypoxic* training, is to teach you how to make better use of the available air. To do this, you simply take fewer breaths per length than normal, although as a training technique it is only relevant to freestyle. The lungs are very elastic and can take in a considerable amount of oxygen, but often, very little of this is used. Improving oxygen uptake through training will in turn delay the onset of oxygen debt and so enable you to swim for longer before fatigue sets in.

This form of training puts the body under pressure by asking it to work without sufficient oxygen. The aim is to create more red blood cells to aid the absorption of oxygen from the lungs and improve cardiovascular efficiency. Not only does it build breath control, it is also useful for those who want to race – since it will teach you to keep your head to the front as well as down at the end of the event.

Here is how you might go about your hypoxic swimming. Swim 200 m freestyle. For the first 50 m, breathe every arm cycle; for the second 50 m, breathe every second arm cycle; and so on until you reach four arm cycles (8 arm pulls). This is probably the maximum you want to do until you get used to this system of swimming. After a bit of practice, you will be able to work on even longer arm cycles to each breath. *See* also the breathing exercises on pp. 49–50.

High-quality sets

These are also known as *fast interval sets* and are designed to put the swimmer under maximum pressure. They feature longer rests but your efforts are made at maximum speed – normally somewhere between 8 and 12% slower than your best time for that distance. You would normally start the set with time targets in mind. These types of swims are useful for building up speed and working the fast twitch muscle fibres that are responsible for sprinting. High-quality sets very quickly deplete body reserves, and too much of this type of training before you compete can be debilitating. There is therefore a fine line between these sets being beneficial and detrimental to your fitness training. You will need to work towards high-quality sets over a period of time by first working on swims that are less tiring.

Measuring your performance using your heart rate

Measuring your heart rate after each repetition is a useful guide to how you are progressing. For example, if you replicate a set of swims made in a previous swimming session and find your heart rate has dropped, you are likely to be on the right track.

Here is a simple way of measuring your performance. We will take a set of swims, for example, 5 × 200 m backstroke off 4½ min. There is a reasonable amount of rest and the swims are of moderate intensity. Using a HRM, try to maintain a heart rate of 140 bpm. See how fast you can go for each 200 m effort while still maintaining that same heart rate. With each swim, try to go a little faster while keeping your heart rate in the range of 135 to 145 bpm.

The key to achieving this is by really focusing on your stroke efficiency – counting your strokes and attempting to reduce the number that you take for each length. Go back to your very first initiatives when starting your swimming programme. Concentrate hard on lengthening your push-off from the wall, making it as efficient as possible, and work on your breathing too. In doing all this, you end up with the matrix illustrated in figure 5.2, in which you should try to hold all the variables except speed.

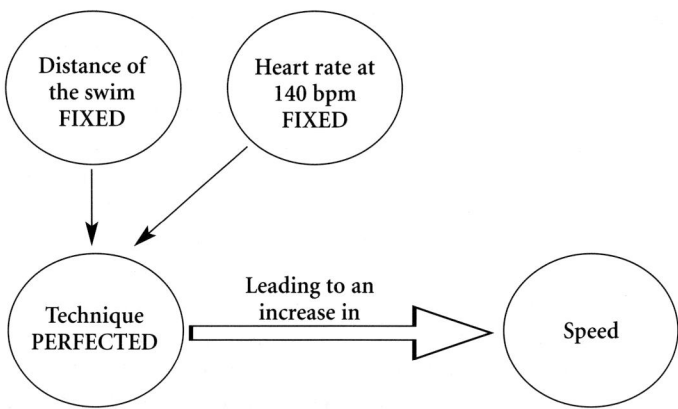

Figure 5.2 How speed improves

Which energy system(s)?

Table 5.2 summarises the various training methods and how they fit in with the energy systems described earlier in this chapter.

Table 5.2 Energy system(s) employed for various training methods

Training method	Target heart rate (bpm)*	Typical swim	Typical rest	Energy system employed
Fartlek	120–140	100 m and up		Aerobic
Locomotive	120–140	4 × 300 m	20 sec	Aerobic
CIS	140	6 × 100 m	Off 1 min 45	Aerobic
Descending	140	4 × 200 m	Off 3 min 30	Aerobic
Regressive	140	4 × 200 m	Off 3 min 30	Aerobic
Negative	160–170	4 × 200 m	Off 4 min 30	Aerobic/anaerobic
Broken	160–180	4 × 200 m + 10 sec at 100's	Off 4 min 30	Aerobic/anaerobic
Alternating	140	4 × 200 m backstroke with 4 × 50 m butterfly	10 sec	Aerobic
Mixed	140	4 × 300 m split with 6 × 25 m at 2nd 300	20 sec	Aerobic
Over-distance	140	3 × 600 m	1 min	Aerobic
Standard rest	140	8 × 150 m	15 sec	Aerobic
Hypoxic (breath holding)	180–200	4 × 100 m breathing every 6 strokes	Off 3½ min	Aerobic/anaerobic
High-quality cruise	200–220	4 × 100 m	Off 3½ min	Anaerobic

*The bpm are averages, but will change according to your age (see p. 19).

Stroke drills

There are literally hundreds of drills that can be used in swimming. These can either be incorporated into your programme to make your training more interesting, or to concentrate on and improve stroke technique. If you know that you have certain technical faults – perhaps your training colleagues have made you aware of these – then focus on the drills that will help to put them right.

None of the drills are particularly simple, and it will take a little practice before you can manage them. I expect you can think of or have seen many more varieties, so do not be afraid to experiment.

Freestyle

- Freestyle with the shoulder brushing the ear during the recovery.

  Benefit – develops flexibility.

- Freestyle entering the hands with a small, pre-entry hesitation.

  Benefit – helps concentration on the hand entry.

- Full stroke with clenched fists.

  Benefit – the closure of the fists encourages the swimmer to utilise his forearms and wrist during the pull.

- Single-arm freestyle – this takes place with the shoulder (same side as the single arm) against a pool wall or lane rope.

  Benefit – encourages the employment of a high elbow, as the swimmer is prevented from recovering the arm too laterally.

- Catch-up freestyle – in this well-known drill, one arm enters the water and then pauses while extended in front of the head. The other arm meets it in front of the head so that the hands are parallel. The first arm is pulled as soon as the two hands become parallel in front of the head. The cycle is repeated on the other arm.

  Benefit – makes the swimmer aware that he needs to feel his way into the catch before pulling.

- Monkey swimming – every time the arms are recovered during the stroke, the fingertips touch the armpit (same fingers, same-side armpit) before stretching out in front of the head and entering.

  Benefit – encourages a high elbow position during the recovery.

- Water-polo front crawl – the swimmer's head is kept out of the water during the stroke. The pull is slightly longer and made right through to the end of each stroke.

  Benefit – this is particularly good for sprinting because the body is high in the water and the legs have to work very hard to keep the body there.

- Freestyle with a long, exaggerated push-through towards the feet. The swimmer aims to straighten the arm at the end of the pull.

  Benefit – the swimmer learns to maximise each pull.

- Single-arm freestyle, with the arm not being employed stretched out in front at the entry position.

  Benefit – concentration on one arm helps the swimmer with hand entry and position of the pull.

- Bilateral freestyle – the sequence of swimming is to breathe to one side, swim three strokes and breathe on the other side.

  Benefit – helps to balance out the stroke, and encourages the swimmer to keep a better balanced position by positioning the body on the centre line for a longer period per arm cycle.

- Hand flick at the end of the pull – the swimmer pushes his hands well past his hips and over-emphasises the final push of the palm of the hand towards the pool roof.

  Benefit – enables the swimmer to really concentrate on completing the pull.

- Finger-scrape – the fingers scrape the surface of the water as the arms recover.

  Benefit – encourages a high elbow recovery and keeps the hands close to the surface.

- Freestyle legs with the arms crossed behind the body and the head in the water.

  Benefit – increases resistance and encourages the swimmer to work the hips up towards the surface by driving harder with the legs.

- Freestyle legs with the arms crossed in front of the head and the hands, interlocked.

  Benefit – strengthens the legs and encourages the swimmer to build a streamlined position while working the legs.

Breaststroke

- Single-arm breaststroke – the swimmer pulls with the left arm and then kicks, pulls with the right arm and kicks, and then pulls with both arms and kicks. There are several variations on this drill, in which the number of arm pulls on each arm can be increased before changing to the other arm.

  Benefit – encourages the swimmer to concentrate on the sculling action of the hands and getting the right arm positions.

- Breaststroke kick on back.

  Benefit – feet get used to rotatory action.

- Dolphin-kick (butterfly leg-kick) drill – the swimmer makes four normal pulls with a dolphin kick and then four normal pulls with breaststroke leg-kick.

  Benefit – builds the feeling of following the arm recovery with shoulder and hip rotation.

- One pull and then three kicks.

  Benefit – encourages the swimmer to lift his heels closer to the surface during the kick.

- Three full strokes breaststroke followed by three kicks underwater.

  Benefit – the swimmer finds there is greater pressure on the ankles during the kicking phase and builds greater resistance.

- Seahorse breaststroke – the swimmer rises higher than normal at the end of his arm pull. He lifts his head and shoulders higher than normal to breathe in. The arm pull is made very wide and the arms shoot through together when recovering, again in an exaggerated manner. Instead of swimming with breaststroke legs, the swimmer swims with a dolphin kick.

  Benefit – this encourages the swimmer to develop a more powerful early body position.

- Glide breaststroke – this requires a normal stroke, but each time the hands stretch out in front the swimmer pauses for a period of two seconds.

  Benefit – this encourages the swimmer to complete the stroke and lengthen out.

Backstroke

- Double-arm, final phase of the pull – the swimmer swims with his normal backstroke leg action. While kicking, he lifts both arms at the same time until they are in line with the shoulders. He then makes a double final phase of the pull to the hips.

  Benefit – discourages pulling with the arms straight at the end of the pull, because it is difficult for the swimmer to pull with both arms straight at the same time.

- Shoulder lift backstroke – the swimmer works with arms and a normal leg-kick. The arm being used is recovered over the water using an exaggerated lift of the shoulder. The other arm stays by the hips. Eventually the other arm is used.

  Benefit – develops good shoulder roll and recovery position.

- Double-arm backstroke – the swimmer kicks normally but recovers both arms together over the water.

  Benefit – encourages the swimmer to perform the first part of the pull correctly, and to achieve a deep pulling position behind the head.

- Pull and pause – the swimmer swims normal backstroke. On completing each arm pull, he pauses before pulling as two extra kicks are made.

  Benefit – gives the swimmer time to obtain a good entry position and builds awareness of the position of his 'catch', i.e. when his hands fix on the water.

- Left arm, right arm, both arms – the swimmer changes the normal pattern of the arm stroke while maintaining a regular kick.

  Benefit – helps the swimmer to concentrate on a better entry position.

- Kick with arms above head – the swimmer extends the arms above the head, keeping his fingers and hands together while locking the elbows.

  Benefit – overloads the leg action and makes the swimmer kick harder to drive his body to a higher position in the water.

- Kick with hands on head.

  Benefit – a further drill which overloads the legs.

Butterfly

- Leg action on back with arms straight out in front – the swimmer locks the elbows by straightening the arms and interlinking the hands.

  Benefit – enables the swimmer to build up the legs and to watch his kicking technique from time to time.

- Leg action variation – the swimmer makes a breaststroke arm pull followed by a butterfly leg-kick. He then completes a full stroke cycle on butterfly. The combination of these two variations can be made 2, 3 or 4 at a time.

  Benefit – develops feel for the water in the arm stroke, encouraging outward sculling movements.

- Full stroke while attempting to get the hands to touch one another in front of the head prior to entry.

  Benefit – encourages a longer entry at the front part of the stroke and calls for increased flexibility.

- Butterfly catch-up – the swimmer kicks with a single-arm catch-up. One arm stays in front on the water's surface, while the other arm recovers and meets it in front of the head.

  Benefit – again, helps with the outward and inward hour-glass, sculling movements, and encourages a good 'catch' before pulling back towards the hips.

- Dive butterfly – the swimmer makes three or four kicks at the end of each arm stroke. In order to do this, he drops down under the surface.

  Benefit – as well as being good for developing the leg-kick, gets the swimmer used to kicking with increased water resistance.

- Lateral butterfly kick – the kick is made to one side with one arm by the swimmer's side and the other arm stretched out in front along the surface.

  Benefit – builds up the kick with increased water resistance around the hips.

- Butterfly legs with the hands clasped behind the back.

  Benefit – develops the use of hips and upper legs.

- Butterfly with head above water.

  Benefit – helps to strengthen the legs.

- Alternate left arm, kick; right arm, kick; both arms, kick.

  Benefit – enables concentration on hand entry and position of pull underwater.

- Single-arm butterfly – one arm is kept out in front under the surface while the other one moves normally. One length is swum on the left arm, the next on the right. Breathing takes place to the side.

  Benefit – enables the swimmer to work on his hand entry.

- Prone butterfly – the swimmer lies on his back and swims butterfly upside-down.

    Benefit – enables the swimmer to watch and correct the position of the legs.

Working as a group

Despite the fact that most people have their heads under water for much of the time when swimming, it is still a great social sport. Unfortunately, friends who want to start swimming at the same time as you don't grow on trees, so you may well have to find out if a group of recreational swimmers meets at a certain time at your local swimming pool – or better still, find out when adult lane swimming takes place.

Making your training programme more interesting

Human beings are great creatures of habit, and there is no harm in the group chain swimming – in other words, following one another up and down the lanes – in the same order. This will enable you to measure how quickly you are swimming compared to the norm. However, here are a few ideas to break up any training boredom.

Head-to-head kicking

Work with a partner. Start in the middle of the pool, facing one another. Each partner holds one end of the float and kicks. The object is to move forwards yourself while forcing your partner back. This generally works best on freestyle legs.

Pulling your partner

Start at the end of the pool with a pull buoy between you legs. Your partner holds your legs while you swim arms-only for the length. You then change round so that your partner tows you.

Swimmer shuffle

A group of you swim as hard as you can over one length. At the end of the length, shuffle your starting order so that the slowest is in lane 1 and the fastest is in lane 6. Repeat the exercise, shuffling your order again on the same basis. This continues until the end of the series of swims has been completed.

Last swimmer in

A similar series of sprint swims is made. At the end of each length, the last swimmer drops out. This continues until an eventual winner is found.

Group fartlek

You need four or five people swimming in a chain in one lane for this activity (four is the optimum number). You all swim the same distance, for example 400 m, setting off one by one about three seconds apart. After the first length, the first three swimmers slow down and allow the last swimmer to sprint past. This process will generally take a length. The swimmer who has overtaken the others reaches the front and then slows down himself; the newly established last swimmer then repeats the exercise. This continues until everyone has completed their sprint length and the whole process begins again.

Opposite-end sprints

You will need to work with a partner. Each swimmer sprints a length on the same stroke, starting simultaneously from opposite ends of the pool. The object is to finish your length faster than your partner. As you pass one another you can gauge how well you are doing by judging how far this takes place from the halfway mark on the lane ropes.

Catch-up

The above exercise can be replicated with continuous swimming, the partners swimming as part of a chain aiming to catch one another. This can be extremely tiring if there is just two of you! It is therefore best attempted when there are about 10 of you in the chain. The process of slowing down, speeding up or overtaking other swimmers in the lane not directly associated with you and your partner, makes for greater excitement and makes the exercise less exhausting.

Solo swimming

Although group swimming can be more motivating, many of you will train on your own, so here are a few useful tips.

- If you are joining an adult training lane, try to make sure that you enter a lane of similar speed.

- Swimming in the slipstream of the swimmer in front (i.e. swimming in water that has already been disturbed) is much less tiring than swimming in normal water.

- Regular use of the pool clock, so that you are thoroughly familiar with its face, is important. A pool clock can look completely different when you finish an exhausting length and lift dripping goggles from your face. Make timing simpler by always setting off at the top of the clock – i.e. on 60 – or at the bottom on 30. It becomes difficult to remember where on the clock you started when you are tired.

  An alternative is to use a digital watch or a heart-rate-combined watch which is waterproof. Such watches normally tell you when to start your swim and how long your rest interval should be based on the pace at which you swam your last repetition. If you do need to use the pool clock, try to encourage all the other swimmers in your lane to set off at five-second intervals. Reducing swims (*see* p. 72) help you to get used to using the clock.

Pacing

You should aim to practise race situations once every two weeks. A good way to practise pace is to concentrate on maximising speed during the first half of your swim whilst maintaining minimum effort. During the second half, try to keep stroke count low and stroke efficiency high.

6 Land conditioning

A land conditioning programme can both support and enhance what you are doing in the water, and is advantageous for a variety of reasons:

- you may find it difficult to get to the pool on a regular basis, but have a gym nearby or can train at home

- your colleagues or coach tell you that you are quite stiff in the water and hence some flexibility work would not go amiss

- you know that you are not as strong in the water as you should be, and therefore a strength programme on land could help to increase power

- you lack the motivation to constantly swim lengths to get fit, and so add land conditioning for variety.

Nearly all of the endurance required for swimming can be built up in the water, although running in the early part of the season can be beneficial. However, very little muscular strength can be gained by swimming alone, so that land conditioning is a necessity for increased power. As far as flexibility is concerned, this is best developed in the water itself – the benefit of flexibility work on land lies in the extra resistance it can offer (*see* below).

Flexibility

Why should swimmers bother with flexibility work? Apart from its importance to your general health and comfort, the main reason is that it helps to increase the range of motion (ROM) of muscles and joints. As the range of limb movement increases, so the efficiency of the stroke is improved. In theory, the amount of drag should similarly be reduced because of the swimmer's ability to overcome resistance (*see* also Chapter 1, pp. 4–5).

Broadly speaking, stretching can be either *static* or *dynamic* (moving). In static stretching, you take a part of the body to the point at which a stretch is felt. You then hold that position – usually for 15–30 seconds – during which time the muscle gradually relaxes. The stretch should be released slowly to allow a gradual release in tension. Always ensure that you are fully warmed up and in a comfortable position for this type of flexibility work: kneeling and single-leg standing should generally be avoided. Dynamic stretching involves movement, and so must be carried out gently and progressively to avoid injury: a good example is circling the arms, as described on p. 24.

While stretching can be done individually, it is sometimes more effective when carried out with the help of a training partner. Since your partner can encourage a greater stretch than you would be able to achieve alone, take great care with this kind of work, and always ensure that the person being stretched gives continuous feedback. Whatever type of flexibility work you are doing, build up steadily and gradually increase the range of movement without pain. Some sample stretching exercises are given over the following pages and are intended to help you improve your flexibility over time. Please note that several exercises are for more advanced swimmers and should not be attempted unless or until you have built up your general programme and flexibility to a good base level.

Measuring your flexibility

When you start your training programme, it's useful to measure your flexibility so that you have a means of assessing any progress made – as a result of both swimming itself, and your land conditioning work. You can record the results in your training diary (*see* pp. 110–11).

Shoulders

The ability to flex and extend the shoulders is paramount in all swimming strokes. In backstroke, for example, increased flexibility can help you drive your hands deeper into the water behind the head after the hand entrance and prior to the pull. The capacity to hyperflex the shoulder is of value in increasing the range of movement in the pull. Here is a quick way of measuring your shoulder flexibility so that you can test yourself from time to time:

Shoulder flexion

Lie on the floor with your face to the ground and your arms extended above your head, hands locked together (*see* fig. 6.1(a)). Then, while keeping your chin on the floor and the fingers of your hands locked throughout, lift your hands as high as they will go. Keep the movement slow and gentle. Get a partner to measure the distance between your hands and the ground: this is your baseline for the future, as you will look to increase the distance during your fitness programme.

Figure 6.1(a) Measuring shoulder flexibility – shoulder flexion

Shoulder extension

This is another easy measurement (*see* fig. 6.1(b)). Stand up straight and stretch your hands back as shown below, keeping your arms as much in line with the shoulder as possible. Your partner then needs to measure the distance between your two hands.

Here are some exercises to aid shoulder flexibility.

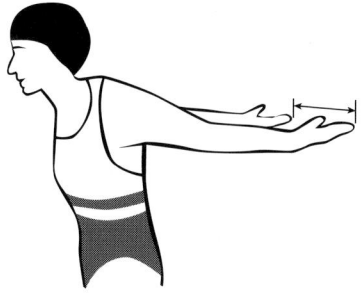

Figure 6.1(b) Measuring shoulder flexibility – shoulder extension

- Hold a towel, with both arms in front of you by your thighs. Keeping your arms straight, bring the towel in a controlled fashion through 180 degrees and over your head so that it comes to lie behind your buttocks (*see* fig. 6.2 (a) – you may need to move your hands further apart to complete this motion). Then bring it back over your head to the starting position. Do this several times. Slowly, as you become more flexible, you will be able to move your hands closer together along the towel.

- Lying on a bench as shown (*see* fig. 6.2 (b)), get a partner to hold your elbow and wrist as you mimic a high elbow recovery on freestyle. Your partner then very gently pushes your elbow in towards the centre of your back. Hold the stretch for 15–30 seconds, then relax. Repeat on the other side.

- Lying on the floor face-down, place both hands in the small of your back. Your partner kneels at your head as shown (*see* fig. 6.2 (c)), and takes hold of the outer part of your elbows. They then lean backwards, gently pulling your arms inwards and upwards. Hold the stretch for 15–30 seconds, relax and repeat.

- Stand, placing your right hand behind your head on your right shoulderblade as shown in fig. 6.2 (d). Press gently and steadily with your left hand on your right elbow, so as to move your right hand as far down your back as possible. Keep your back straight, your shoulders down and face forwards throughout. Hold for 15–30 seconds then relax. Repeat on the other side.

- To extend the previous exercise, place the palms of your hands behind your head and on opposite shoulder blades (effectively, the arms cross at the forearms). Gently stretch the fingers of both hands as far down your back as possible, as in fig. 6.2(e).

- Standing upright, with your arms out to the side in line with your shoulders (*see* fig. 6.2 (f)), try to move your hands backwards using a series of small, *controlled* bounces. Then try the same exercise but with your arms straight up above your head.

- Finally, try single-arm circles through 360 degrees in both directions. Throughout the exercise, stand up straight and face forwards. Keep your arm close to your

Figure 6.2(a)–(f) Improving your shoulder flexibility

head, and don't let the shoulders lift. Repeat on both sides and in both directions. Then change to backward and forward circles with both arms – make the movements in this exercise a little slower so that the shoulders almost scrape together. Then, bend forwards slightly and copy butterfly arms movements, swinging the arms a little more vigorously. These circling exercises are illustrated in Chapter 3, p. 24.

Feet and ankles

Ankle and foot flexibility is essential for swimming. Flexibility in the ankles increases the extension of the feet, enabling a larger range of movement in all strokes – and particularly in backstroke and breaststroke, where the leg action plays an important part. In addition, this flexibility enhances the propeller-like movement so necessary to create lift force.

Here is a quick way of measuring your ankle flexibility so that you can test yourself from time to time. For all ankle measurements, you will need to carry out the following preliminaries. Take a large proctrator and an A3 piece of paper. Place the proctractor over the paper and mark in the degrees in pencil. Then stick the paper to a wall, so that it touches the floor.

Plantar flexion

Sit on the ground with your legs outstretched so that your feet are adjacent to the paper on the wall. Keeping your ankles together, point your toes and press them down towards the ground (*see* fig. 6.3(a)). Get a partner to measure the number of degrees through which your toes move – from a position where they are curled up towards the body to when they are pointing towards the ground.

Dorsi flexion

In the same position, start with your feet relaxed and hanging loosely. Then curl your toes up towards you as far as possible (*see* fig. 6.3(b)). Once again, ask your partner to measure the degree of movement achieved.

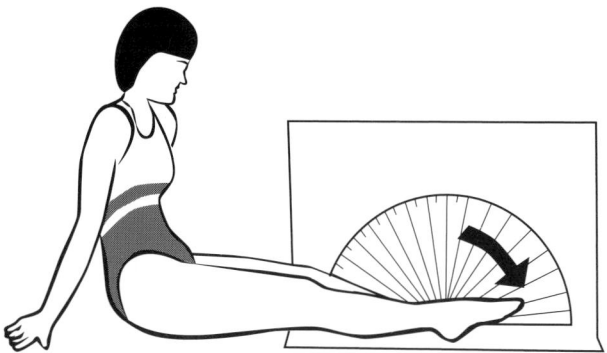

Figure 6.3(a) Measuring ankle and foot flexibility – plantar flexion

Figure 6.3(b) Measuring ankle and foot flexibility – dorsi flexion

Eversion and inversion
Remove your paper from the wall and place it on the ground (*see* figs. 6.3(c) and
(d)). Sit on the floor so that the heel of your foot is placed over the centre point of
your protractor layout, i.e at 90 degrees. Keeping your heel on the centre point and
on the ground, stretch your big toe as far outwards as you can (eversion) and then as
far inwards (inversion). For each movement, hold the position while a partner
measures the angle your ankle makes to the protractor.

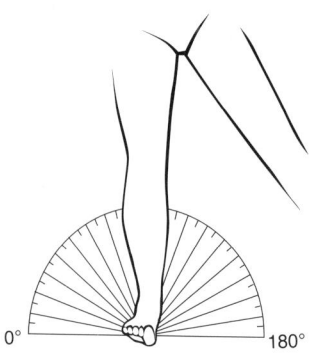

*Figure 6.3(c) Measuring ankle and
foot flexibility – eversion*

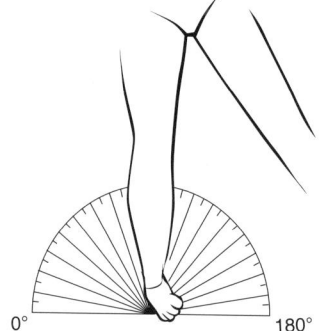

*Figure 6.3(d) Measuring ankle and
foot flexibility – inversion*

Here are some exercises to aid ankle flexibility, all of which are static in nature. Each of these exercises is illustrated on pp. 72-3 overleaf.

- Sit with your legs outstretched and straight at the knees. Hook a towel over your toes and pull the toes towards your body (*see* fig. 6.4(a)). Hold for 15–30 seconds, relax and repeat.

- Stand on one leg and loop the towel over your raised foot. Pull the towel and the foot so that the sole is squeezed to your backside (*see* fig. 6.4(b)). Ensure that your knee is pointing downwards, your legs are pressed together, and avoid hollowing your back. Repeat on the other side.

- Kneel on the ground with your toes pointed rather than curled. Place a towel under your feet for cushioning. With your hands placed on the ground on either side of your shoulders to provide balance, and your chin forwards, carefully rock back, extending the toes (*see* fig. 6.4(c)).

- Sitting with your legs outstretched and straight, feet together, point your toes towards the ground. Then, rotate your feet so that your big toes face in to one another (*see* fig. 6.4(d)).

- Remaining in the same position, keep your heels on the ground and fan your feet outwards so that your little toes are 'trying' to meet the ground (*see* fig. 6.4(e)).

- Now stand with your heels together and your feet facing outwards. Bend your knees as shown (*see* fig. 6.4(f)), keeping your back straight and head up. Hold for 15–30 seconds then relax and repeat.

- Lie on your front with one elbow in front stabilising you in an upright position. Bend one leg up and reach to hold the toes of one foot in the crook of your elbow on the same side. Pull your foot gently towards the small of your back (*see* fig. 6.4(g)). Hold for 15–30 seconds then change feet. This exercise also stretches the quadriceps muscle at the front of the thigh.

- Standing, lean and reach forwards against a wall with your arms straight. The legs also stay straight. Keep the soles of your feet flat on the ground and gradually move your feet back so as to stretch the ankles and the calf muscles (*see* fig. 6.4(h)).

- Sit facing another swimmer, both of you with your legs slightly apart. Holding the heel of your partner's foot in one hand and the toes in the other, gently press their toes outwards towards the ground (*see* fig. 6.4(i)).

a.

b.

c.

d.

e.

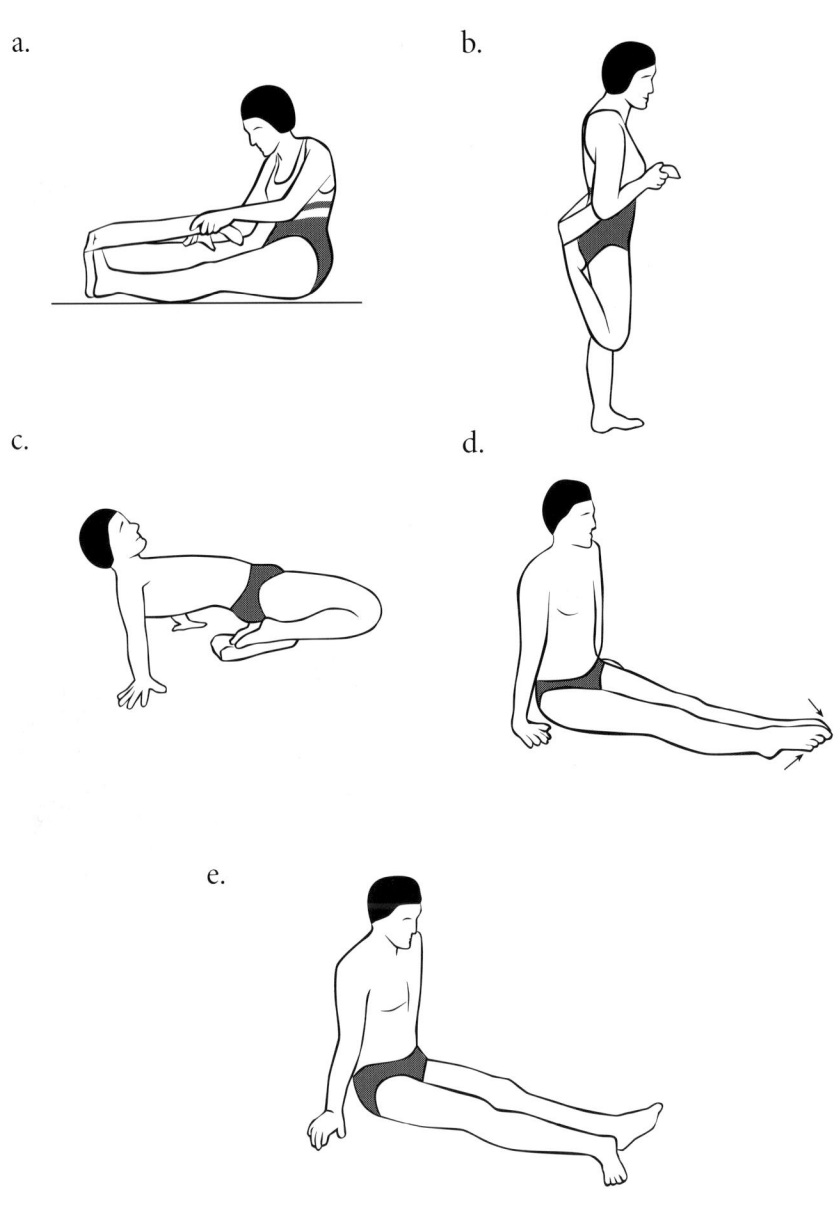

Figure 6.4 (a)–(e) Improving ankle and foot flexibility

f.

g.

h.

i.

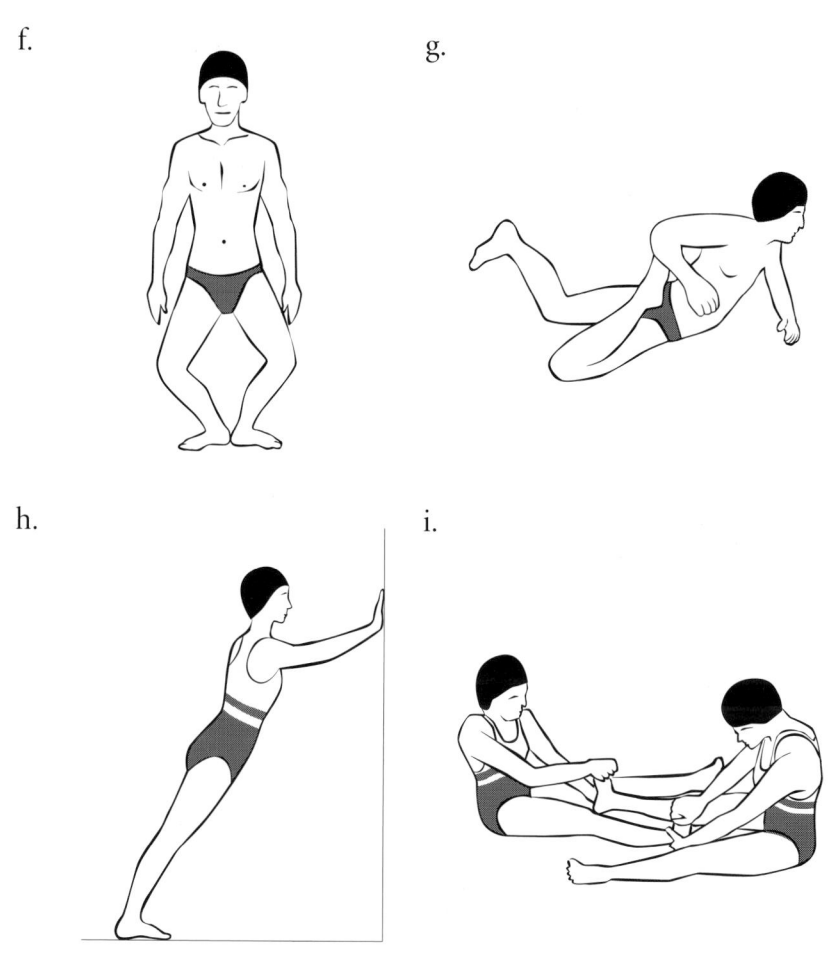

Figure 6.4 (f)–(i) Improving ankle and foot flexibility

Trunk and hips

In swimming, reasonable flexibility of the trunk and hips is important for general body position – and that of the hips aids hip rotation. There are no handy hints for measurement as there are for the shoulders, feet and ankles, but here are one or two useful exercises that you may wish to try. (These exercises are illustrated on the opposite page.)

- Sit on the ground with one leg outstretched. The other leg is bent, with the sole of the foot positioned against the inside of the outstretched leg (*see* fig. 6.5(a)). Bend forwards slowly from the hips, keeping your back straight, while reaching towards the foot of your outstretched leg. Hold for 15–30 seconds then relax. Repeat on the other side.

- Lie face-down on the ground. Hold your ankles as shown in fig. 6.5(b), with your toes pointed. Keeping the head up, *gently* rock backwards and forwards, pushing your hips downwards to achieve the stretch. (Take care if you have any problems with your back or neck.)

- Sit on the floor with your knees out and the soles of your feet together. Clasp your hands around your feet and gently pull downwards, aiming to place your forehead on your feet (*see* fig. 6.5(c)). Hold the stretch for 15–30 seconds, relax and repeat.

- Now lie on your front, with your hands on the ground by your sides, fingers facing forwards. Keeping your feet on the floor, push upwards and slowly arch your back – first up on to your elbows and then, for a more intense stretch, up on to your hands as illustrated in fig. 6.5(d). Hold for 15–30 seconds then relax. Follow this by placing your hands together behind your back and arching once again; then with your hands on either side of your head and your elbows back. Keep the feet firmly on the floor throughout.

As alternative forms of flexibility work, both Pilates and yoga – where breath control forms part of the programme – should be considered.

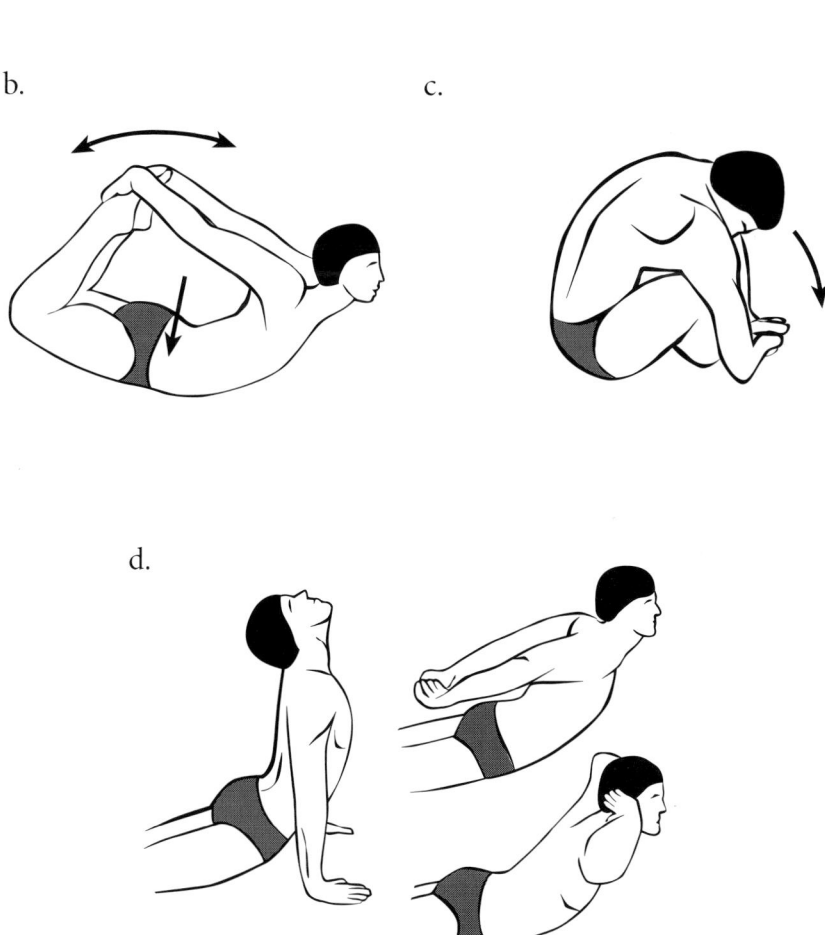

Figure 6.5 (a)–(d) *Improving trunk and hip flexibility*

Strength training

While muscular endurance improves through swimming, strength is something that cannot easily be developed in the water. A weight training programme, supported by a diet rich in carbohydrate and protein (*see* also pp. 85–95) can help build muscle tissue and make your swimming more powerful. Again, if you have recently embarked on a training programme, build into the strength training part gradually. The best way of breaking yourself in is to concentrate initially on endurance-based work – i.e. more repetitions with a lighter weight, rather than power work (a small number of repetitions with a heavy weight). Gradually, you can change the balance between the two. The number of repetitions and weight lifted will determine the degree of endurance and strength benefits that you will receive. As a guide, at first you need to select weights that will allow you to perform between 10 and 20 repetitions fairly easily, and to spend the first three to four weeks on endurance-based weight training.

Weight training in general can be split into free and fixed weights. Fixed weights are normally found at sports centres and swimming pools, and are easier and safer to use. However, many people find it more convenient to carry out their strength training from home, and so tend to use free weights.

Which muscles?

When strength training for swimming you need to concentrate on two things:

- exercises that focus on the muscles or muscle groups used to propel your body through the water

- exercise that reflect the movements used in swimming.

Table 6.1 summarises the main swimming movements, the body parts involved, the muscles used and appropriate exercises, whilst Table 6.2 lists a variety of exercises appropriate for each stroke. Select about six or seven for each session, including some aimed at your abdominals as well. Figure 6.6 also shows where the main muscles are located.

Table 6.1 Swimming muscles

Movement	Body part(s) used	Major muscles used	Sample exercises
Downsweep of arms – from over the head towards the hips – and upsweep	Shoulder	• Pectoralis major (chest) • Latissimus dorsi (back) • Trapezius (upper back) • Rhomboids (upper back) • Deltoids (shoulder)	• Lat pulldowns • Pullovers – bent arm and straight arm • Bench press • Chins • Rows – upright, seated and bent-over
Inwards sweep of arms	Shoulder	• Pectoralis major (chest) • Biceps brachii (upper arm) • Brachialis (upper arm) • Brachioradialis (forearm) • Subscapularis (upper arm) • Teres major and minor (upper back)	• Lying lat raises • Side pulleys
Flexion and extension of arms	Elbows	• Triceps brachii • Biceps brachii	• Triceps kickbacks • Triceps press • Biceps curls
Fixing hands on the water when pulling	Wrist	• Flexor carpi ulnaris (forearm) • Palmaris longus (forearm) • Flexor carpi radialis (forearm)	• Wrist curls
Downwards kick in freestyle and butterfly, upwards kick in backstroke, and knee extension in breaststroke	Hips and knees	• Quadriceps (front of thigh) • Hip flexors (psoas major, iliacus and pectineus)	• Leg extensions • Leg presses • Half squats
Upwards kick in freestyle and butterfly, downwards kick in backstroke, and knee flexion in breaststroke	Hips and knees	• Hamstrings (back of thigh) • Gluteus maximus (backside)	• Leg curls • Leg presses • Half squats

Table 6.1 continued

Movement	Body part(s) used	Major muscles used	Sample exercises
Inwards sweep of legs in breaststroke	Hips	• Adductors (inner thigh)	• Adductor machine
Trunk stability during strokes and kicks	Abdomen and lower back	• Rectus abdominis (trunk) • Obliques (side of trunk) • Erector spinae (lower back)	• Abdominal curls • Oblique curls • Back extensions

Adapted from Costill, D. L. et al (1992), *Swimming* (Oxford, Blackwell Science), pp. 162–3.

Table 6.2 Which exercise, which stroke?

Stroke	Exercise	Benefits
Freestyle	Pullover; triceps press; bench press; row; wrist curls; shoulder press; lat pulldown	Arms
	Bent-over rowing; calf raise; jump quarter squats; leg press	Legs
Breaststroke	Triceps press; bench press; row; wrist curls	Arms
	Calf raise; jump quarter squats; leg press; adductor machine	Kick
Backstroke	Pullover; triceps press; wrist curl; sideways lat raise; lat pulldown	Arms
	Calf raise; jump quarter squats; leg press	Kick
Butterfly	Pullover; triceps press; bench press; wrist curls; shoulder press; lat pulldown	Arms
	Calf raise; jump quarter squat; leg press	Legs

Superficial muscles

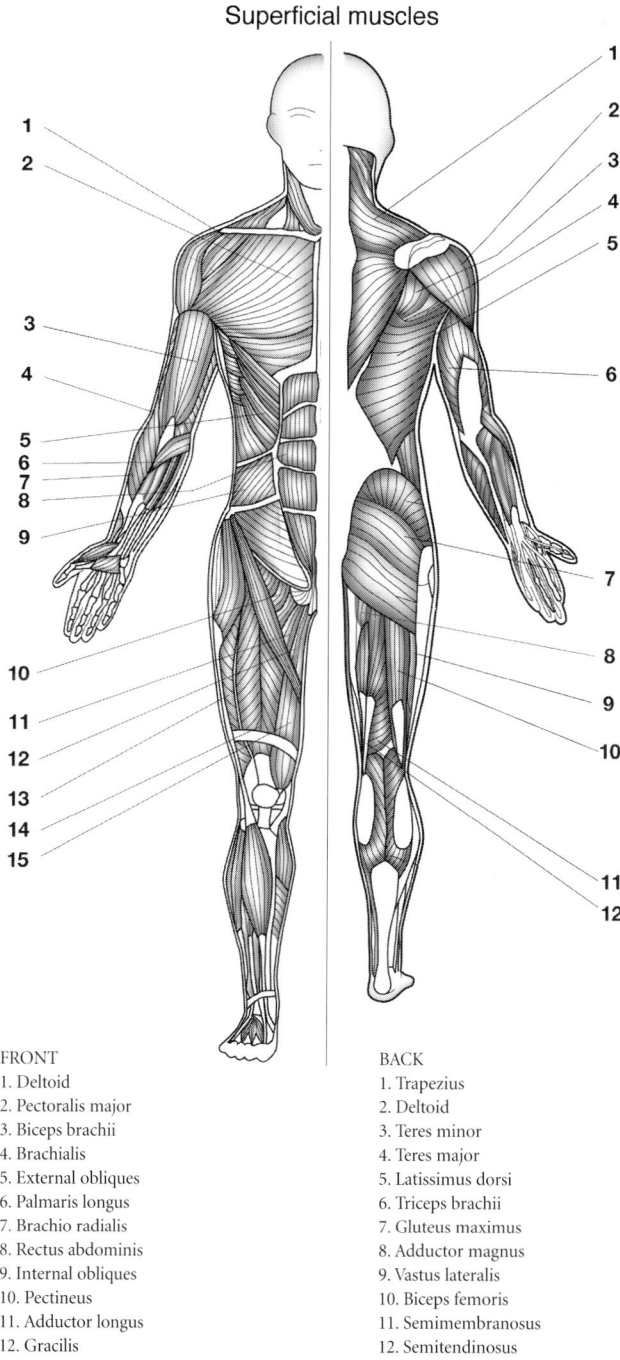

FRONT
1. Deltoid
2. Pectoralis major
3. Biceps brachii
4. Brachialis
5. External obliques
6. Palmaris longus
7. Brachio radialis
8. Rectus abdominis
9. Internal obliques
10. Pectineus
11. Adductor longus
12. Gracilis
13. Vastus lateralis
14. Rectus femoris
15. Vastus medialis

BACK
1. Trapezius
2. Deltoid
3. Teres minor
4. Teres major
5. Latissimus dorsi
6. Triceps brachii
7. Gluteus maximus
8. Adductor magnus
9. Vastus lateralis
10. Biceps femoris
11. Semimembranosus
12. Semitendinosus

Figure 6.6 Major muscle groups used in swimming

Using weights – some basic guidelines

As far as technique is concerned, there are a few important, common-sense points to bear in mind:

- always warm up with light exercise that raises the heart rate before going into any weights session
- do not try to lift a weight which is clearly too heavy for you
- build up steadily towards a weight through a series of sets of increasing weight
- when lifting and lowering any weight, try to make the movements as steady as possible. Avoid jerky movements and any undue strain which will result if a heavy weight pulls muscles out of position too rapidly
- breath out on exertion, and never hold your breath
- if you are using free weights remember to keep your head up and your back as straight as possible so that you don't arch it.

Swimming exercises

It is not possible here to prescribe a set of weight training exercises that simulate exactly the movements involved in a swimming stroke. The figures below are examples of only one common leg and arm exercise that are beneficial for a particular aspect of each stroke. Many of the exercises use free weights, but can be replicated using fixed weight machines in the gym (the leg extension, leg press, lat pulldown all require the availability of such machines).

Freestyle – arms

Triceps press

Starting position: this exercise can be tried kneeling – on a cushion or towel as illustrated – standing, or lying on the floor or bench with your knees bent to help protect your back. Gripping the bar with your hands about 12 inches apart, hold it straight over your head, elbows extended and palms forwards as shown.

Instructions: carefully lower the barbell by flexing the elbows. Keep your elbows up and still as you do so. Return to the starting position as you exhale, ensuring that your back does not arch as you do so.

Freestyle – legs
Calf raise

Starting position: with your shoulders under the pads of the machine, stand on the block with your heels hanging off the edge. Your feet should be hip-width apart.

Instructions: rise up on your toes, hold the position briefly then lower your heels back down again, as far as they can go without overstretching the calf muscles. Repeat, keeping your legs straight and lower back flat throughout.

Breaststroke – arms
Bench press

Starting position: lift a barbell or dumbbells to your thighs (remember to keep your back straight and your head up) and sit on a bench, with the bar resting on your lap. Lie flat on the bench as shown, and roll the bar towards your chest. Grip the bar with your hands just slightly wider than shoulder-width apart.

Instructions: push the weight straight up above your chest and then bend your elbows to slowly lower it again. As soon as the barbell reaches your chest, repeat the exercise, exhaling as you push the weight upwards.

Breaststroke – kick
Inner thigh raise – adductors

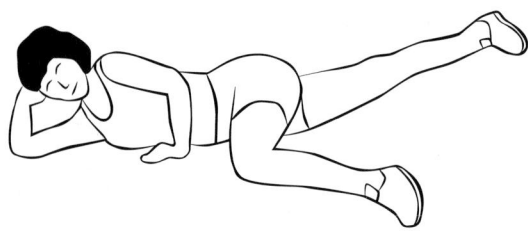

Starting position: lie on your side, with your head resting on your lower hand and upper arm resting on the floor for support. Bend your upper leg, resting it on the floor as illustrated, and exhale as you slowly lift the lower leg as high as you can.
Instructions: Keep your abdominals pulled in tight, your back straight and the foot flexed and parallel to the floor throughout. Do the required number of reps and repeat on the other side. Use ankle weights to increase the intensity of the movement, paying particular attention to your form if you do.

Backstroke – arms
Pullover

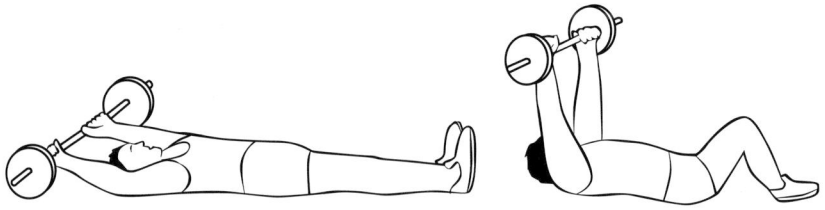

Starting position: lie on your back with your knees bent – either flat on the floor or using a bench (flat or inclined) – holding a barbell with your arms outstretched behind your head as shown. Make sure your lower back remains in contact with the floor or bench at all times.
Instructions: keeping your arms straight, lift the weight smoothly in an arc from behind your head down to your thighs. Return the weight to the starting position and repeat. This exercise can also be performed with dumbbells.

Backstroke – kick
Leg extension

Starting position: sit on the leg extension machine and hook your feet under the pads as shown. Ensure that your lower back and thighs are fully supported, and hold on to the side-bars (or side of the seat) for balance.

Instructions: slowly straighten your legs. When you reach the top of the movement – i.e. when your legs are fully straight – hold that position briefly and then lower the weight back down in a controlled fashion. You can also do this exercise one leg at a time – although obviously using a lighter weight.

Butterfly – arms
Lat pulldown

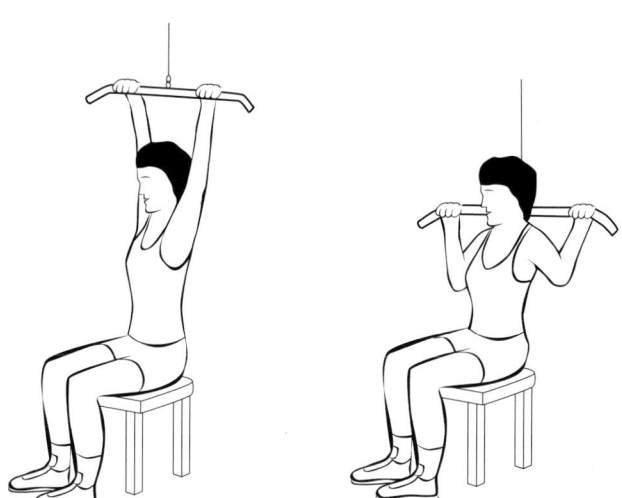

Starting position: sitting down at the lat pulldown machine, reach up and hold the bar at slightly wider than shoulder-width apart. Your feet should be flat on the floor and hip-width apart.

Instructions: bend your elbows and smoothly pull the bar down behind your neck. Hold that position briefly before returning the bar to the starting position. Breathe out as you pull down, and hold your abdominal muscles tight so that you don't arch your back.

Butterfly – legs
Leg press

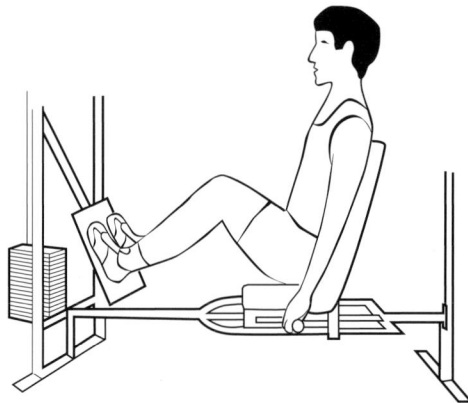

Starting position: sit on the apparatus with your knees bent as shown, grasping the side-bars.

Instructions: push forwards with your feet on the plate to straighten your legs (but do not lock your knees). Keep the movement smooth throughout, exhaling as you press with your legs, and inhaling as your knees bend and you return under control to the starting position. Contract your abdominal muscles so that you do not arch your back.

Diet and lifestyle

So much is written about diet and healthy living these days that the surfeit of information can be thoroughly confusing. This chapter sets out some straightforward guidelines for you if you are exercising regularly or if you perhaps want to take part in Masters swimming competitions from time to time.

The cornerstones of good body maintenance are regular meals, non-smoking and regular sleep. Food is your source of energy and once you start exercising regularly you will need more of it if you are to maintain your body weight and get the most out of your training sessions. In short, your daily calorific intake and output need to balance each other. Before you were exercising regularly, you probably needed between 2,000 and 3,000 calories a day (depending on your level of activity) in order to maintain your weight. Depending on how much swimming you are doing, the number of calories you need to remain at the same weight can be up to 25% greater.

Fuel for swimming

The components of food provide the fuel for all activity. Carbohydrate, fat, protein and alcohol are all capable of producing energy, the amounts per gram being as follows:

- carbohydrate – 4 kcal

- fat – 9 kcal

- protein – 4 kcal

- alcohol – 7 kcal.

Carbohydrate is stored as glycogen in the muscles and liver, fat is stored as body fat (or adipose tissue) all over the body – as is an excess of any food component not required by the body – and protein is what muscle and tissue are made from. All but alcohol can therefore be used to fuel your swimming as they can all be used directly by the muscles. However, protein is only really used as an energy source during very intense or prolonged training sessions when your glycogen stores begin to run out.

Energy systems

As discussed in Chapter 5, the intensity at which you swim determines the method by which your body provides you with energy (*see* pp. 52–3). If you are swimming at a very high intensity (i.e. working anaerobically, or without oxygen), carbohydrate will be your main source of energy. The glycogen stored in your muscles is broken down into glucose, which produces energy and lactic acid. As your stores of muscle glycogen are not endless, your reserves quickly become depleted, whilst the lactic acid gradually builds up. Thus, if swimming at top speed you quickly feel a heavy, burning sensation in your arms and legs and your pulling movements become weaker.

However, if you swim at a more moderate pace so that your body is working aerobically – i.e. with oxygen – energy can be generated from both glycogen and fat. Although it produces energy more slowly than when your body is working anaerobically, this kind of energy production can be sustained for much longer periods of time so it is the aerobic system that is used mainly when you are swimming for fitness.

Carbohydrate as a fuel

Carbohydrates therefore provide fuel for almost every type of activity and are particularly important to people taking part in exercise such as swimming. Most of the energy needed for muscular contraction comes from this source, with the remainder being supplied from your fat stores. If carbohydrate levels are not replenished after exercising, you may not be able to train as effectively as you would like at your next session. Allow this to happen over a period of time, and chronic fatigue can set in, resulting in a loss of interest in training and poor performance.

A real effort therefore needs to be made to increase carbohydrate intake on a daily basis, especially prior to and after hard training in order to maintain sufficient glyocogen stores. For most athletes, including swimmers, an intake of around 5–10 g of carbohydrate for every kg bodyweight will maximise daily muscle glycogen recovery. Alternatively, aim to get a minimum of 60% of your daily energy from carbohydrates.

Which are the best sources of carbohydrate?

The glycaemic index (GI) has been developed by scientists in order to identify the immediate effect of a particular source of carbohydrate on blood sugar levels.[1] It provides a scale which ranks foods from 0 to 100, with 100 working most quickly. All foods are compared to a base food such as glucose. This provides a useful reference for how your body will respond to various foods and will help determine the most suitable food to consume before, during and after exercise or competition. To find out more about GI, you will need to refer to a detailed sports nutrition book (*see* further reading suggestions on pp. 154–55).

The most important point to remember here is that the higher the GI rating, the more quickly the carbohydrate is absorbed from your small intestine into your blood stream, and the faster it can be utilised by the muscle cells. A low GI meal taken one to two hours before you go to the pool can help your swim by generating slow-release energy. This will help delay fatigue.

Low GI foods that can be eaten an hour before exercise include:

• dried apricots (1 small handful)

• pasta (1 medium bowl)

[1] *The Complete Guide to Sports Nutrition* by Anita Bean (London: A&C Black, 2000) p. 17.

- porridge (1 medium bowl)
- low-fat yoghurt (2 × 150 g cartons)
- muesli (1 medium bowl).

Note: Each portion will provide 50 g of carbohydrate.

Higher GI foods should be eaten after your swimming session. They will replenish the glycogen stores in your muscles immediately. Examples are as follows:

- breakfast cereals
- skimmed milk
- pancakes
- bread
- bagels
- isotonic sports drink (higher in sugar).

Note: Each portion will provide 75 g of carbohydrate.

Fats

If you have decided to go back to swimming in order to lose weight you may well ask the question: 'Why do I need fat? Isn't it something I should avoid in order to keep slim?' It is not quite this simple. The key is to ensure that you consume the correct *amount* and *type* of fat to ensure a healthy body and one that is better able to perform at its best.

Dietary fat

Many carbohydrate-based foods will also offer sufficient fat for the average diet, although the Department of Health (DoH) recommends that a maximum of 33–35% of your daily calorie intake comes from fat. There are three types.

Saturated fats are not considered good for you and have been linked to heart disease because they contribute to increased cholesterol levels. The DoH recommends a saturated fatty acid intake of no more than 10% of total calorie intake. Foods that contain saturated fats include:

- butter
- lard
- cheese
- meat fat
- and all foods processed using these fats, including biscuits, cakes and pastries.

Monounsaturated fats, on the other hand, have been shown to have the greatest health benefits, helping to reduce total cholesterol without affecting other cholesterol benefits. The DoH recommends a monounsaturated fatty acid intake of up to 12% of total calorie intake. Foods in which you will find this type of fat are:

- oils including olive, rapeseed, groundnut, hazelnut, almond

- avocado

- olives

- nuts and seeds.

Polyunsaturated fats can be found in vegetable oils and oily fish, and can help lower cholesterol levels. They are also important because they include the so-called 'essential' fatty acids, which cannot be made by the body so have to come from food (or supplements). Aim to eat about 10% of your total calorie intake as polyunsaturated fats.

In general, you should monitor your fat intake and eat the correct amounts of each type to ensure that you get the most out of your body. Try to use olive oil for cooking, remove the skin from some meats such as chicken and turkey and as a general rule, grill or boil rather then fry.

Body fat

There are two types of body fat: essential fat and storage fat.

- Essential fat is what your body actually requires to function properly, providing insulation, protection and cushioning against physical damage. In a healthy person it accounts for roughly 3% of body weight and can be found at specific sites such as around the heart, kidneys and liver. Women also have sex-specific fat that is essential to hormone (oestrogen and progesterone) production, and this is found in the breasts and around the hips. It accounts for a further 5–9% of body weight.

- Storage fat is an important energy reserve and can be found in the cells under the skin (subcutaneous) and around the organs. This fat is used almost all the time during any aerobic activity (including sleeping and walking around) and is relied on more heavily during exercise.

As a general rule, men should have between 13% and 18% body fat, and women between 18% and 25% body fat.

Proteins

Protein accounts for about 20% of your total body weight and is found in every cell and tissue in your body, including your muscles, tendons, internal organs, skin, hair and nails. It is primarily a building material – essential for growing and repairing muscular tissue after training, for instance – but has many other functions too, and can be used as a source of energy if you swim at a high level of intensity and for long periods of time.

If you have decided to invest in training for competitive swimming this will indeed involve regular, intense and prolonged exercise in the pool combined with a well-structured strength training programme. However, even if you are just starting out on a training programme it is very important to ensure that protein plays a part in your diet, and if you are vegetarian it is even more important to ensure that you are eating enough. The recommended daily intake for people who participate in regular exercise or sport is 0.75 g/kg bodyweight/day. If you are taking place in regular endurance training you will need to increased this intake to between 1.2–1.4 g/kg bodyweight/day. However, your exact protein needs depend on the type, intensity and duration of your training and you should refer to a more detailed text or a nutritionist to decide what is right for you.

The following foods are good sources of protein and should be incorporated into your daily meal plans:

- meat and fish (beef, chicken, turkey, cod, mackerel, tuna)

- dairy products and eggs (cheese, cottage cheese, skimmed milk, yoghurt, fromage frais, eggs)

- nuts and seeds (peanuts, peanut butter, cashew nuts, walnuts, sunflower seeds, sesame seeds)

- pulses (baked beans, red lentils, red kidney beans, chick peas)

- soya products (soya milk, soya mince, tofu)

- Quorn products

- grains and cereals (wholemeal and white bread, boiled pasta, brown and white rice).

Fluids

Despite the fact that while swimming you are surrounded by water you will still sweat! This is an important point to remember. It is also extremely important that you remember to replace lost fluid. The following few paragraphs are intended to help you understand and prevent dehydration during your swimming training.

How much will I sweat and how can I replace lost fluid?

The main function of sweating is to keep your body temperature down. When you exercise, your muscles will produce a lot of extra heat (75% of the energy you are using up is converted into heat and then lost). If you become too hot (over 38°C) your vital body functions are in danger of being damaged. So, it follows that the more you exercise, the more your body needs to sweat in order to cool down.

How much fluid you lose when exercising will also depend upon external factors such as the humidity of the environment you are exercising in and your own body chemistry. Swimming pools are often kept at a warm temperature and the general humidity is high so you may actually loose a substantial amount of fluid. You will know if you are suffering from dehydration if you notice any of the following symptoms:

- sluggishness

- a general sense of fatigue

- headaches

- loss of appetite

- feeling excessively hot

- light headedness

- nausea.

Another simple test is to examine your urine. If it is light or clear in colour, you are probably drinking enough; if it is dark in colour, you need to drink more.

A simple way to combat dehydration is by drinking water on a regular basis. If you are swimming regularly, you should look to take in 1.5–2 litres per day plus a further 500 ml about 2 hours before training and an additional 125–50 ml immediately before swimming. You should also drink 500 ml as soon as possible after exercise. It is too late when you feel thirsty: you should have already taken in the fluid by this point. A simple method of keeping your fluid levels topped up is to keep a bottle of water in your sports bag and place it at the side of the pool – reminding you to drink before and after your session.

Sports drinks are also useful if you are training at a high intensity or taking part in competition because they contain carbohydrates. To help improve endurance and performance you need to consume approximately 1 g carbohydrate/kg bodyweight prior to exercise. Taking in the equivalent amount through a sports drink is just as effective.

Vitamins and minerals

Our bodies are unable to make vitamins and minerals, so they must be supplied in our diets. They are required for growth, health and physical wellbeing and also contribute to our enzyme system – the system that enables all our metabolic functions – immune system, hormonal system and nervous system. Minerals are vital to regulatory and structural functions of the body.

If you eat a good balanced diet you should automatically achieve a high vitamin and mineral intake. However, regular, intense exercise increases your requirements for a number of essential vitamins and minerals, especially those involved in energy production, tissue growth and repair and blood levels. Those of particular importance are listed in Table 7.1. A balance of vitamins is important. A deficiency in vitamins B and C, the water-soluble vitamins, leads to a lower output of work; an excess means B and C being excreted in the urine. Vitamins A, D, E and K are more of a problem because they are fat-soluble and taken in excess can remain as toxins in the liver.

Iodine, calcium, zinc, phosphorus and iron, particularly for women, are minerals that the body needs to obtain in very small amounts and a regular intake can help to achieve this.

Table 7.1 Natural sources of vitamins and minerals

Vitamin or mineral	Food source
Vitamin A	Oily fish, meat, eggs, liver, cheese, butter and margarine
Vitamin B$_1$ (Thiamin)	Wholemeal bread and cereals, liver, kidneys, red meat, pulses (beans, lentils and peas)
Vitamin B$_2$ (Riboflavin)	Liver, kidneys, red meat, chicken, milk, yoghurt, cheese, eggs
Vitamin C	Fresh fruit (especially citrus), berries and currants, vegetables (especially dark green, leafy vegetables, tomatoes and peppers)
Vitamin D	Sunlight (UV light on the skin), fresh oils and oily fish, eggs, vitamin-D-fortified cereals, margarine and some yoghurts
Vitamin E	Wheatgerm, pure vegetable oils, egg yolk, sunflower seeds, nuts and avocado
Calcium	Milk, cheese, yoghurt, soft bones of small fish, seafood, green leafy vegetables, fortified wheat flour and bread, pulses
Sodium	Table salt, tinned vegetables, fish, meat, bread, cheese
Potassium	Vegetables, fruit juices, unprocessed cereals
Iron	Red meat, liver, offal, fortified breakfast cereals, shellfish, wholegrain bread, pasta and cereals, pulses, green leafy vegetables
Zinc	Meat, eggs, wholegrain cereals, milk and dairy products
Magnesium	Cereals, vegetables, fruit, potatoes, milk
Phosphorous	Cereals, meat, fish, milk and dairy products, green vegetables

Supplements

If you lead a hectic lifestyle and often do not eat a balanced diet you may benefit from vitamin and mineral supplements. This is particularly important if you are swimming regularly or taking part in competition, and will ensure that you are getting all the nutrients you need each day. Before taking supplements, it would be worth consulting a nutritionist or investing in a book that gives you all the information you need to decide what to take. This is recommended especially for female swimmers if you think you may be anaemic. There is no hard evidence to suggest that vitamins will improve your actual performance but they do form part of the total picture.

[2]*Handbook of Swimming*, David Wilkie and Kelvin Juba, Chapter 13, p. 177 'Associated Aspects of Swimming', (London: Pelham, 1986)

Snacks

If you need to squeeze in your training either early in the morning or at lunchtime, you should be aware of the advantage of quick snacks to replenish lost energy. Don't use snacks to replace meals. However, glycogen in the muscles needs replacing rapidly after exercise and this can be achieved by eating a snack with plenty of quick-release carbohydrate. This is particularly important if you have swum early in the morning and have to work for the rest of the day.

Snacks can be quite simple but may need a little preparation before you go swimming. The following are some suggestions that you might like to keep in your bag or arrange to keep at work so that you are able to snack as required:

• banana sandwich (2 slices of bread and 1 banana)

• 2 scotch pancakes

• 2 cereal bars and a carton of flavoured milk

• carton of low-fat rice pudding

• toast with honey (2 slices)

• peanut butter sandwich

• fresh fruit and low-fat yoghurt

Eating during competitions

If you are thinking about taking part in masters competitions you will need to give special thought to your nutrition. What and how you eat can mean the difference between winning and losing, or performing at your own personal best. The following offers some basic advice.

Generally speaking, in the week leading up to competition it is important to fill up your glycogen stores and to keep well hydrated. So, eat plenty of carbohydrate foods (*see* above) and drink plenty of water. It is vital to ensure that you replace muscle glycogen immediately after training in the week prior to competition. If you don't, you will enter the race with low energy stores and at a distinct disadvantage, and this will almost certainly lead to poor performance. Exact quantities will depend upon the type of event you are competing in (short-duration events such as sprints, or long- duration endurance events).

On the day of competition your main aims will be to top up glycogen stores in the liver, keep well hydrated, ensure that your blood sugar levels are maintained, and stave off hunger. You will need to eat at least one main meal (high in carbohydrates) before competition. This needs to be between 2–4 hours before your first race so that your stomach is empty and your blood sugar levels have normalised. Avoid heavy eating immediately before and between races. Remember to drink plenty of water. If you find a meal that works particularly well for you then stick to it and keep to your routine. This will most likely help your performance physically and mentally.

Stress can play a part on the day of competition and cause your digestive system to slow. A rise in stress levels leads to the movement of blood away from the stomach and small intestine toward the 'fight or flight' essential body systems such as the heart, liver and lungs. Stress also increases the amount of acid in the stomach. So, there is a balance to be struck. You should avoid competing on a full stomach but you need to have sufficient food to provide the instant energy you will need when you dive into the pool.

High or moderate GI carbohydrates that are more liquid and easily digestible are recommended prior to competition at the expense of protein and fats. Fatty foods take too much time to digest, while simple carbohydrates such as glucose and dextrose are not really suitable as they cause blood sugar levels to rise and fall very quickly leaving the body feeling weak. Tea and coffee contain caffeine, which is a stimulant and will increase your heart rate and interfere with focus and relaxation. They are also diuretics and will increase urine output and lead to dehydration. They should be avoided prior to competition.

Here are some useful foods to eat before, during and after you race:

The night before
- pasta or rice dishes with tomato-based sauces

- water.

Two–four hours before
- cereal and low-fat milk; bread, toast sandwiches, rolls, potatoes

- water.

One hour before
- sports drink

- energy or sports nutrition bar

- dried apricots

- water.

15–30 minutes before
- water

- sports drink.

Between heats
- sports drink

- meal replacement products

- bananas

- rice cakes, energy bars, rolls.

Post-competition

• sports drinks

• energy bars

• pasta/rice dishes

• pizza.

Gaining and losing weight

The gaining and losing of weight should happen reasonably naturally. Put simply, to lose weight, you need to be burning more calories than you consume. To gain weight you need to consume more calories than you are burning.

A regular diet supported by a steady programme of exercise should bring the body back to a suitable weight and body composition – basically how much body fat you have compared with muscle (*see* p. 88). However, you may feel that in taking up a swimming training programme, you actually need to gain weight and that you lack the musculature for the programme in mind. For some people, gaining weight can be difficult, requiring you to eat large meals on a regular basis. However, the best way to gain weight is to increase muscular mass through a programme of strength training on land. This will stimulate and enhance muscle growth – active tissue which will enhance your swimming rather than gaining additional body fat which may not. Either way, you should aim for gradual gain/loss; about 0.5 to 1 lb a week is a sensible target.

General body maintenance

Smoking is obviously not a healthy approach because it harms lung function and can contribute to various long-term conditions. Alcohol also needs consideration. In moderation it is something to be enjoyed and can be beneficial in terms of promoting relaxation and enjoyment. Research has shown that alcohol in moderation can help reduce the risk of heart disease.

Following consumption, about 20% of alcohol is absorbed into the blood stream via the stomach; the rest, through the small intestine. Most alcohol is then broken down in the liver. The result is that the liver has to work hard in order to dissipate the alcohol consumed. If you drink more than your liver can process over a specific period of time then you are in danger of causing damage to your liver and other vital organs. Also, alcohol has a high calorie content (*see* p. 85), increasing the possibility of fat gain.

Sleep is also a key factor in your programme, and in an ideal world regular, quality sleep would be ideal. For many people however, sleep is governed by external factors like young children or work patterns. If you work long shifts, for instance it may be difficult to get good quality sleep at the times you are forced to sleep. Try to make matters easier by attempting regular sleep and sticking to a routine if you can. Every person differs but eight hours of good quality sleep every night will be a great help to you – both physically and mentally.

Dehydration is something we have already discussed (*see* pp. 89–90). The importance of regular fluid intake in order to avoid dehydration in training cannot be overstressed. How can you keep a check on whether you are taking enough fluid when training? There is a simple way. Weigh yourself before and after training. If you find you have lost one kilogram in body weight, you will need to replace it with 1.5 litres of fluid drunk over a period of time. Do not drink the whole amount immediately after exercise! You can always weigh yourself again an hour later when you get to work or at home. If you find that you are still down on weight, take in further fluids until you have recovered the loss.

Regular swimmers also lose water through conduction into the water while training. If you swim outdoors in the heat, you will lose more fluid than swimming indoors in the winter, although even then, you can still become dehydrated. Try to take in more water in order to compensate for these losses and make sure that at least some of this is around the time of your swimming session.

Summary

Diet and lifestyle are vital aspects of your fitness programme. You should be careful that you eat a regular balanced diet and drink plenty of water. If you are competing regularly then you will need to be a little more scientific in your approach so that you always have enough stored up energy to ensure maximal performance. If you would like to learn more about nutrition there are a number of more specialist books available, some of which are listed in the further reading section of this book on p. 151–5. You may also wish to refer to this section for further information on swimming associations and web resources.

8 Health and safety

Although a number of people drown each year as a result of accidents, swimming is one of the safest of sports for those people undergoing a fitness programme. Body weight is carried by the water during swimming, making the sport less taxing on joints and placing less stress on the skeletal structure during exercise. Many of the injuries that occur in other activities, particularly contact sports, very rarely occur in swimming. This makes it a great sport for those who either do not have the time to train regularly, or who are not very sporty in general. Swimming should, however, be treated with respect, and care needs to be taken to avoid some of the common pitfalls.

This chapter looks at some of the common illnesses and injuries that can occur as a direct or indirect result of swimming, and at ways in which they may be avoided. If you have any doubts with regard to illnesses or any form of injury, please consult your GP for advice.

Swimming-related injuries and illnesses can be split into three types.

- Injuries that occur as a result of accidents on the pool side – e.g. slipping – or as a result of someone else swimming into you. Use your common sense to prevent these: take care when walking to and from the pool; avoid pools and swimmers with poor lane discipline. Do not dive into shallow water. Take a look before pushing off from the wall.

- Injuries that occur as a result of the swimming action itself – i.e. repetitive strain injuries. Be mindful of niggling pains. A small amount of pain while training is often something to be overcome, but regular and persistent pain in one area, inflammation or continuous soreness will tell you that this is something you cannot just swim off and needs rest – or even treatment by a physiotherapist.

- Illnesses and infections that are directly attributable to being in swimming pools or taking part in swimming as an exercise. Follow the basic hygiene and common sense guidelines given below. If you are unwell, consult your GP – there are clearly certain occasions when persisting with your training programme will do you more harm than good. Swimming with a cold or flu is to be avoided, since you may make things worse and are likely to pass on your illness to others.

Basic swimming hygiene and good practice

Swimming pools with their warm, damp atmospheres are opportunities for germs and viruses to spread. In order to care for yourself and in consideration of other bathers, follow the basic hygiene rules recommended by your pool. It's always best to try to avoid injury and illness in the first place. Take the following precautions:

- Have a warm shower before going into and after coming out of the pool, and walk through the footbath.

- Wash your hair if you have sufficient time on exiting, in order to rinse out pool chemicals. If left in, these can damage your hair and cause minor skin irritation.

- Dry yourself thoroughly before leaving the pool (and avoid using someone else's towel). The temptation is to skimp on this when you are in a hurry, but dampness can encourage the development of fungal infections and skin irritations (*see* also below). In particular, dry inside your ears, your feet and between your toes after every session.

- Wrap up warm on cold days when leaving the pool.

- If you have long hair or find that your hair gets in the way when you are swimming, wear a swim cap. This will prevent it from getting tangled in pool equipment (etc.).

- If you find that your eyes become sore during swimming, then lightweight goggles will make life easier.

These are all simple things to do, but also simple things to forget. Below are listed some of the more common swimming-related ailments, with some advice on how to recognise them – and how to prevent or alleviate them.

Some common swimming-related ailments

Breaststroker's knee and chondromalacia patellae

Breaststrokers knee is one of the most common swimming ailments. If you consider breaststroke to be your best stroke, and swim it regularly, you are likely to have suffered some soreness from time to time. Pain is felt around the inside area of the knee due to excess strain of the medial ligament. Repeated bending of the knee and load-bearing while rotating the knee joint are the main causes of the soreness. This condition can be improved by narrowing the leg kick so that rotational strain on the medial ligament is reduced. Also strengthening the quadricep muscles can help. Sometimes breaststroker's knee develops as a result not just of swimming breaststroke, but also of overloading the knee during land conditioning.

Chondromalacia patellae[1] refers to damage to the under surface of the patella or softening of the knee cartilage. Pain can also be felt when the patella is pressed against the lower part of the femur upon extension of the knee and especially when climbing. This tends to cause creaking, grinding or crepitus[2]. The collateral ligaments that lie around the knee inflame. Often, this condition – in which the pain is centred on the patella – occurs in tandem with a weak quadriceps muscle. If you do feel the onset of pain, you need to rest the knee. When pain has reduced, quadricep and hamstring exercises should be performed.

[1] Dr P. Penny, Occupational Physician, 'Patella Pain Syndrome', *Swimming Times*, May 2000.
[2] Ibid.

Eye irritation

The human eye easily becomes inflamed when it is subjected to pool water. The main cause of inflammation is the mix of human urea with that of water disinfectants. When the pH (acid-alkaline relationship) of water is significantly greater or smaller than 7.4, pool water is more likely to cause eye irritation. Modern disinfectants tend to be less painful for the eyes.

Eye irritation becomes further exacerbated when the water is very warm and strong sunlight shines through so that the conjunctiva is also irritated. The eye really does become inflamed, with the cornea filling with water and resultant swelling. The tendency is then to rub the cornea and cause pink or red eye. Although a number of people still prefer to swim without goggles, these can all but eliminate eye irritation. You can even obtain goggles that are tinted to counteract strong sunlight when swimming. However, *always* use your own goggles, to avoid contracting an infection from another swimmer.

Conjunctivitis can be highly contagious but is rarely serious and normally clears up after a few days. It is often an allergic reaction that produces tears, itching and a runny nose. If you simply cannot swim with goggles, eye-drops will help to relieve the condition; alternatively, try using a cold compress on your closed eye. If symptoms persist please consult your GP.

Ear and sinus infections

The ears are in close contact with the water throughout training. Repeated movements in and out of the water can make it difficult to balance the air pressure inside the nose and ears with the water pressure outside. This can cause irritation in the sinuses and ears. Some people use nose-clips to help prevent this; others wear moulded earplugs (*see* also p. 8).

The most common ear infection amongst swimmers is known as *otitis externa*. If you don't dry your ears properly after training, water remains inside the ear canal and the moist warm conditions are perfect for bacterial growth. Further swimming, with its repeated movements in and out of the water, usually makes matters worse, and you may have to rest completely to rid yourself of the problem. So, if you suffer regularly from ear infections or inflammations it is particularly important that you dry inside your ears thoroughly at the end of each session. If you get an infection which persists, consult your doctor.

Ear infections are often related to nose and throat conditions. If you have a sinus infection, you may contract a middle ear infection because blowing your nose forces catarrh and pus up the Eustachian tube into the middle ear. Fluid then builds up behind the eardrum, causing a condition known as *serous otis media*. Antibiotics are usually needed in such cases. For this reason, it's best to avoid swimming until your condition has eased.

Infections of the feet

Athletes' foot (*tinca pedis*) occurs commonly amongst regular swimmers. If you don't dry the skin of your feet and between your toes properly, a fungal condition can develop which manifests itself as itchy blisters especially between the toes. If the condition goes untreated it develops into cracked and blistered skin that can become infected. The fungi that cause it are part of a group called *dermatophytes*; they particularly like hot and damp atmospheres and feed on keratin, a protein found in nails and skin.

So how can you prevent and treat this irritant? These days, it is easy to purchase over-the-counter anti-fungal ointments. Change your socks daily and ensure that your feet are dry at the end of swimming. Another way of reducing the infection is to soak your feet at home in warm, soapy water and then dry thoroughly. Also, avoid breaking off flaking skin; this can tear the healthy skin that is adjacent, thereby increasing the risk of spreading the infection.

Verruccas are another common and equally painful condition affecting the soles of the feet. They are caused by a virus similar to the one that causes warts on the hands. No treatment is required unless they become painful, as the body develops antibodies to the virus so that it can disappear on its own. However, if the varrucas do become painful, your doctor can treat the condition.

Problems with your hair

Unless you are careful, regular training can lead to a deterioration in the condition of your hair, causing split ends and bleaching (from strong sunlight reflected by the water). The use of a swim cap can help, but the best approach is to wash your hair immediately after swimming in order to get rid of any pool chemicals. Try not to get the shower water and shampoo into your ears while doing so! Use a conditioner on a regular basis if your hair needs it.

Anaemia

Iron-deficiency anaemia affects both men and women but tends to affect women more. Anaemia occurs when there is a reduced haemoglobin content in the red blood cells. Since these cells are responsible for transporting oxygen around the body to the exercising muscles in the form of oxyhaemaglobin, anaemia can adversely affect your ability to train as well as your general state of health – causing pallor, lethargy and excessive fatigue.

The recommended daily intake of iron is 12 mg for men and 14.8 mg for women. A normal diet contains 6 mg for every 1000 calories,[3] so it follows that if you are consuming 3000–4000 calories each day, you should be meeting your iron needs. Always try to include foods that are rich in iron in your diet, such as dark green, leafy vegetables – spinach and watercress are especially good – pulses, red meat and eggs. This is particularly important for women who are training heavily, are pregnant, or who menstruate heavily. If you suspect that you are at risk of anaemia – or if you are experiencing unusual tiredness, breathlessness or light-headedness – consult your doctor. He or she will advise you whether or not you should be supplementing your iron intake.

Tendonitis

One of the biggest single problems for swimmers is tendonitis, especially in the shoulder region (*supraspinatus tendinitis*), caused by the repeated arm movements of the swimming stroke. While tendonitis normally occurs in freestyle and butterfly, it also can be seen in backstroke where it takes the form of backstroker's shoulder.

[3]Ernest Maglischo, *Swimming Faster*, p. 433 (Mayfield Publishing, CA; 1982)

Here, the adduction and rotation movements of the arm when the hand is driven down into the water prior to the pull, cause acute pain.

Tendonitis first of all affects the top of the shoulders. It becomes painful to lift the arms in any direction, but is more marked when lifting the arms laterally from the side of the body when in the standing position. This condition, which is sometimes known as frozen shoulder, makes it increasingly difficult to lift the arm above the head. If you are unfortunate enough to suffer from tendonitis, you may find that you get it when swimming one particular stroke. A change of stroke for a week can keep you in the swim but reduce the pain considerably. Ice packs applied to the area for a period of up to 20 minutes after a training session can further help to lessen the pain, although you will need a helpful pool staff to store the ice in a fridge for you while you swim. In general, strength and flexibility work can help to make you less susceptible to this condition (*see* Chapter 6 on land conditioning). You may also wish to check your stroke technique and correct any irregularities that may be causing the pain.

For some swimmers, the pain becomes acute and persistent. In such cases stop training and consult a medical practitioner.

Over training

As discussed in Chapter 2, overtraining can occur in swimmers who are undertaking hard prolonged training. They will find that times do not improve and the harder they train the more their times fall off. They will often feel depressed and may also suffer from recurrent infections due to a suppression of their immune system. They may also become irritable and complain of feeling tired. Recovery times will also increase. The most effective solution is to stop training for 3–4 weeks and then gradually build up training levels and intensities again.

Part III

Planning your swimming year

9 Planning principles

Planning an annual training programme is really a decision-making process. After your initial couple of weeks of swimming you are faced with the first real decision – basically, whether to build your swims into an annual programme, or just to swim occasionally. On the assumption that you do decide to swim regularly throughout the year, you then need to decide on the following parameters before developing your programme.

- Are you going to train regularly but keep the training fairly light, or are you going to work towards a specific goal, perhaps a race or competition?

- Taking this decision into account, how many sessions do you plan to do each week?

- Then, how much time can you afford to give to each training session?

- And finally, what time of the day can you swim at? This question is important, as you will have to marry up the time that you can actually swim with work, social and family pressures – as well as with the times at which your local pool is available. Pools are often clearer during early-morning sessions, and some people prefer to swim at that time to start off the day in the right way. The disadvantages of this are having to get changed for work and possible fatigue – making it hard to work afterwards.

Bear in mind that you do need to undertake a minimum amount of training in order to see fitness gains. As noted in Chapter 2, the recommended training requirements for improving cardiovascular fitness are as follows:

frequency: 3–5 times a week, ideally varying the activities performed and altering the impact (and similarity of movement) in order to avoid repetitive strain or injury to joints and muscles

intensity: working hard enough to causes the heart rate to increase to between 55% and 90% of its maximum. Lower levels of intensity are appropriate for less active people

duration: between 15 and 60 minutes is an optimal length of time, with approximately 20 minutes being sufficient to maintain any given fitness level. Less fit individuals need to progress gradually to this duration.

Activities that use the large muscle groups, require oxygen and are rhythmic in cadence are most effective.

Most people, unless they are retired, can only afford to give up about an hour per session two or three times a week. Given today's busy lifestyles, few of us can swim every day – however much we would like to. This obviously limits the distance you will be able to cover in a week.

As a guide, world-class 1500 m swimmers are capable of swimming at the rate of about 5000 m an hour – given that a world-class 1500 m time is approximately 15 minutes. If you are capable of working at 4000 m per hour, you will be working at a really hard rate with little rest and probably little variety in your training. On the other hand, the average swimmer, looking for plenty of variety in their training, should aim to cover 2500–3000 m per session. In a 25-m pool, this amounts to around 100 lengths. You need to allow some three months to build up to this level (see also Chapters 10–12, on planning your swimming year).

Finally, you need to decide what your goal is for the year. Most people embark on a programme to get fit, but beyond that objective there is often a further goal. This could just be a matter of getting your body in shape and looking good. It could be that you want to use swimming to overcome illness (for example, to improve your asthma) or an injury. Alternatively, you may wish to make new friends and meet different people. The important thing is to keep that goal in the back of your mind throughout your training, so that you can maintain your motivation and answer the question 'why am I doing this?' Sometimes, when you are tired and you know that getting fitter is going to involve some discomfort as well as pleasure, it is hard to stay motivated.

The more serious Masters swimmer will need a specific target, such as a race or competition, to aim for. Your training programme will need to be directed towards the race you have in mind: for example, if you are going to compete in a 400 metre race at the end of the year, your training needs to be tailored to this rather than focusing on, say, sprint training (*see* also pp. 53–7 on different training methods). Therefore, start with your objective and work backwards in planning your programme.

Schedules to kick-start your programme

The first month is the hardest part: try not to be over-ambitious. At first, it is better to concentrate on technique and breathing, and easing your way back into regular swimming. Work out a basic structure for your first few weeks' training, such as that suggested in Table 9.1

Table 9.1 Suggested framework for the first three months

Month	Week	No. of sessions	No. of hours	Distance per session*
1	1	1	30 min	300 m
	2	1	30 min	400 m
	3	2	45 min	600 m
	4	2	45 min	750 m
2	1	2	45 min	800 m
	2	2	45 min	800 m
	3	2	1 hr	1200 m
	4	2	1 hr	1200 m
3	1	2	1 hr	1500 m
	2	2	1 hr	1500 m
	3	2	1 hr	2000 m
	4	2	1 hr	2500 m

*Not including warm-up/swim-down.

The tables below give some suggestions for the content of your training sessions for month 1.

Table 9.2 Sample training session – month 1, week 2, session 1

Distance (m)	Stroke	Rest between repetitions (sec)	Concentrate on
50	freestyle		Very loose, easy warm-up
4 × 50	freestyle	1 min	Breathing out fully before inhaling
2 × 50	backstroke legs	1 min	Straightening the legs on the upkick
50	backstroke		Loosen-off

Total distance: 400 m

Table 9.3 Sample training session – month 1, week 3, session 2

Distance (m)	Stroke	Rest between repetitions (sec)	Concentrate on
100	backstroke		Very loose, easy warm-up
3 × 100	freestyle	1 min	Stroke counting, trying to complete the pull right back to the hips
4 × 25	breaststroke	30 sec	Pausing slightly with the arms stretched out in front at the end of each kick
100	freestyle		Loosen-off – work on breathing out

Total distance: 600 m

Table 9.4 Sample training session – month 1, week 4, session 1

Distance (m)	Stroke	Rest between repetitions (sec)	Concentrate on
100	freestyle		Finishing off the pull at the hips
6 × 50	freestyle-progressive	1 min	Timing yourself, aiming to swim faster each time. Start very slowly and make the last swim as fast as you can
10 × 25	Alternating freestyle and backstroke legs	30 sec	Working with your hands in front of you on the freestyle, concentrating on getting the lower legs high; do the backstroke with your hands on your thighs
100	backstroke		Loosen-off

Total distance: 750 m

Table 9.5 Sample training session – month 2, week 2, session 1

Distance (m)	Stroke	Rest between repetitions (sec)	Concentrate on
200	freestyle – breathe every 4 strokes		Centring the head once in every arm-cycle
4 × 50	freestyle legs with kick board	45 sec	Small kicks, emphasising the shaking of the ankles
4 × 50	freestyle arms with pull buoy	45 sec	Keeping the elbows high and the fingers relaxed on recovery
200	alternate backstroke and breaststroke		Loosen-off

Total distance: 800 m

Table 9.6 Sample training session – month 3, week 1, session 1

Distance (m)	Stroke	Rest between repetitions (sec)	Concentrate on
200	backstroke		Warm-up
6 × 75	freestyle – 25 kick, 25 pull, 25 stroke	45 sec	Working on stroke lengthening by building through the arms only to the full stroke each time
4 × 100	freestyle – bilateral	45 sec	Concentrating on breath control
3 × 100	breaststroke	1 min	Trying to lift the heels high in the recovery phase
100	freestyle		Relaxing the fingers during the arm recovery

Total distance: 1500 m

Table 9.7 Sample training session – month 3, week 4, session 1

Distance (m)	Stroke	Rest between repetitions (sec)	Concentrate on
400	freestyle		Warming up with a focus on exaggerated pull back
10 × 100	freestyle	45 sec	Swimming the second half of the swim faster than the first
10 × 25	backstroke arms with pull buoy	30 sec	Pushing towards feet at the end of the arm stroke
10 × 25	backstroke legs	30 sec	Tucking the chin in and trying to prevent the water coming over your face
8 × 25	backstroke	30 sec	Leading the arm recovery with the little fingers
400	breaststroke		Warming down with a focus on stretching through the front part of the stroke

Total distance: 2500 m

You will have noted that most of the swimming in the above sessions takes the form of freestyle. As discussed in Chapter 4, freestyle is a good stroke for conditioning and getting fit: being the fastest stroke, it lends itself to 'getting more lengths under your belt', thus improving the efficiency of the cardiovascular system. Initially you should adapt your rests to suit your fitness level, but after 3–4 weeks you will be able to take a systematic and consistent break.

No matter what strokes you are swimming, it is important to have a technical point to concentrate on during a session. This gives you greater focus and leads to continuous improvement. After a short period of time, you will be able to plan your own sessions with both fitness and technical goals in mind.

Target distances for an annual programme

Table 9.8 suggests target distances for an annual programme, for fitness and Masters swimmers respectively. It indicates both the number of sessions to be swum, and the number of hours to be devoted to each. (Breaststroke swimmers may find this harder to maintain, due to breaststroke being a slower stroke than the other three.)

The Master's plan is geared to two 'peaks' in the year – one in October and one in June, when the competitive short-course (pools of 25 m or less) and long-course (in 50 m pools) seasons normally have their major competitions in Britain. The programme tapers down in order to allow for the swimmer to peak before two main annual swimming races. This is discussed in more detail in Chapter 13.

The fitness and over 40s' programmes are designed to allow for smaller numbers of training sessions in the summer and in the period leading up to Christmas.

Anyone who is starting or returning to training should allow at least a three-month period of fitness development before attempting any of the weekly targets listed below.

Table 9.8 Target distances for an annual programme

	Fitness			Over 40s			Masters		
	Distance	Ses	Hours	Distance	Ses	Hours	Distance	Ses	Hours
Jan:	44,000			32,000			56,000		
Week 1	11,000	4	4	8000	3	3	14,000	4	4
Week 2	11,000	4	4	8000	3	3	14,000	4	4
Week 3	11,000	4	4	8000	3	3	14,000	4	4
Week 4	11,000	4	4	8000	3	3	14,000	4	4
Feb:	50,000			36,000			60,000		
Week 1	12,500	5	5	9000	3/4	4	15,000	5	5
Week 2	12,500	5	5	9000	3/4	4	15,000	5	5
Week 3	12,500	5	5	9000	3/4	4	15,000	5	5
Week 4	12,500	5	5	9000	3/4	4	15,000	5	5
Mar:	52,000			40,000			60,000		
Week 1	13,000	5	5	10,000	4	4	15,000	5	5
Week 2	13,000	5	5	10,000	4	4	15,000	5	5
Week 3	13,000	5	5	10,000	4	4	15,000	5	5
Week 4	13,000	5	5	10,000	4	4	15,000	5	5
Apr:	44,000			40,000			64,000		
Week 1	11,000	4	4	10,000	4	4	16,000	5	5
Week 2	11,000	4	4	10,000	4	4	16,000	5	5
Week 3	11,000	4	4	10,000	4	4	16,000	5	5
Week 4	11,000	4	4	10,000	4	4	16,000	5	5
May:	52,000			40,000			42,000		
Week 1	13,000	4/5	4/5	10,000	3	3	14,000	5	5
Week 2	13,000	4/5	4/5	10,000	3	3	12,000	5	5
Week 3	13,000	4/5	4/5	10,000	3	3	10,000	4	4
Week 4	13,000	4/5	4/5	10,000	3	3	6,000	3	3
Jun:	52,000			40,000			28,000		
Week 1	13,000	4	4	10,000	3	3	6,000R	3	3
Week 2	13,000	4	4	10,000	3	3	Rest		
Week 3	13,000	4	4	10,000	3	3	10,000	4	4
Week 4	13,000	4	4	10,000	3	3	12,000	4	4
July:	48,000			40,000			60,000		
Week 1	12,000	3/4	3/4	10,000	3	3	15,000	5	5
Week 2	12,000	3/4	3/4	10,000	3	3	15,000	5	5
Week 3	12,000	3/4	3/4	10,000	3	3	15,000	5	5
Week 4	12,000	3/4	3/4	10,000	3	3	15,000	5	5
Aug:	48,000			40,000			64,000		
Week 1	12,000	3/4	3/4	10,000	3	3	16,000	5	5
Week 2	12,000	3/4	3/4	10,000	3	3	16,000	5	5
Week 3	12,000	3/4	3/4	10,000	3	3	16,000	5	5
Week 4	12,000	3/4	3/4	10,000	3	3	16,000	5	5

Table 9.8 continued

	Fitness			Over 40s			Masters		
	Distance	Ses	Hours	Distance	Ses	Hours	Distance	Ses	Hours
Sept:	**52,000**			**40,000**			**68,000**		
Week 1	13,000	4	4	10,000	3	3	17,000	5	5
Week 2	13,000	4	4	10,000	3	3	17,000	5	5
Week 3	13,000	4	4	10,000	3	3	17,000	5	5
Week 4	13,000	4	4	10,000	3	3	17,000	5	5
Oct:	**52,000**			**44,000**			**28,000**		
Week 1	13,000	4	4	11,000	3/4	4	14,000	4	4
Week 2	13,000	4	4	11,000	3/4	4	8,000	3	3
Week 3	13,000	4	4	11,000	3/4	4	6,000R	2	2
Week 4	13,000	4	4	11,000	3/4	4	15,000R		5
Nov:	**52,000**			**44,000**			**48,000**		
Week 1	13,000	4	4	11,000	3/4	4	12,000	4	4
Week 2	13,000	4	4	11,000	3/4	4	12,000	4	4
Week 3	13,000	4	4	11,000	3/4	4	12,000	4	4
Week 4	13,000	4	4	11,000	3/4	4	12,000	4	4
Dec:	**40,000**			**40,000**			**52,000**		
Week 1	10,000	3	3	10,000	3	3	13,000	4	4
Week 2	10,000	3	3	10,000	3	3	13,000	4	4
Week 3	10,000	3	3	10,000	3	3	13,000	4	4
Week 4	10,000	3	3	10,000	3	3	13,000	4	4

Key:
Distance = Distance to be attempted, Ses = Sessions per week,
Hours = hours per week, R = race

Chapters 10–12 contain advice and guidance about how to break this down into a structured monthly programme, and how to devise each individual session content.

Keeping a training diary

As noted at the start of this book, a training diary can be a very useful tool for the fitness and Masters swimmer. It can help you monitor your progress year on year, and also help you to plan and focus on what you are trying to achieve. And it takes literally five minutes each evening to write down what you did in your swimming session that day.

What, then, are the things that you need to record in your training diary?

(1) Your 'medical' details:
  • your resting heart rate (*see* p. 19)
  • percentage body fat – a measurement you can find out from a physio or at a gym (*see* p. 88)
  • flexibility levels (see pp. 66–76)

Update all of these every six months

(2) Your personal details: height and weight – bearing in mind that your body composition is more important than your weight *per se.*

(3) Details of all training sessions: date, time of day, venue, the swims you have made, amount of rest between each rep (if any).

(4) Targets and general records for each month (*see* also below, on setting target times):
  • any target times set at the start of the month in training and then achieved
  • any target times set at the start of the month for races and then achieved
  • the distance you plan to swim
  • how much time you plan to devote to your swimming
  • an overall framework of sessions for the month.

(5) Mechanical details such as:
  • number of strokes achieved by stroke counting at medium speed
  • number of strokes achieved by stroke counting at maximum speed.

Swimmer's shorthand

Always try to write your swims in shorthand to make life easier, e.g. '4 × 100 back + 30 sec' rather than 4 × 100 metres backstroke with 30 seconds rest between each swim'.

Eventually you may prefer to plan and write your own schedules before you train, rather than to plan the session in your mind, do it and write it up afterwards. It is a good idea to do this for all your monthly schedules, about two weeks beforehand. The difficulty, of course, is in sticking to them!

Setting your target times

Target times for both training and racing are not something that the majority of fitness swimmers are concerned about. However, if you are training more seriously these are often set by an experienced swimming coach. If you do not have the benefit of a coach, one way of looking at target times for the year is to set yourself a realistic margin of improvement based on what you achieved in the previous year. This is very much a matter of personal judgement rather than scientific approach. For example, if you improved your best time for 100 m by 10% in the previous year, you will need to determine at the start of the year whether you think you can repeat this kind of improvement.

If, as an illustration, you decide that 5% is more realistic, then you should aim to be hitting your previous best time less 5% in June at the height of the season. You can then work backwards. Based on trying to reach a peak in October at the end of the short-course season, and a peak in June (or even later in the case of British Masters swimmers) for the long-course season, then here is a rough guide:

November–March	previous year's best plus 5–10%
April	previous year's best plus 3–5%
May	previous year's best less 1%
June	previous year's best less 5%
July	previous year's best less 1%
August–September	previous year's best less 1.5%
October	previous year's best less 3–4%

The same principle can be applied whatever time goal you decide to set for yourself.

Recording and benchmarking performance

Do not expect to progress continuously. Continuous improvement would be great but it never happens, even in the best swimmers. One reason is that during training, you make demands on your body by overloading it. This causes the body to adapt so that it is better able to cope with the work imposed on it in the future. Eventually, though, as your training increases, this rate of progression will slow; the body can no longer adapt and you will need to ease back in order to allow for the process of recovery. You will then be in a position to progress again.

A certain amount of progression accompanied by slight regression and 'plateauing' is all part of the overall upward trend. Benchmarking does, however, play a significant role. At the end of each month, your original targets need to be compared to what you actually achieved. Weight, stroke counting and pulse rates are things that you can regularly monitor – partly as a way of ensuring that you are not overdoing things (*see* also p. 21 and 100).

Another good way of benchmarking is to use the Amateur Swimming Association Adult SwimFit Award Scheme (for contact details, *see* Further information on p. 151). Under this scheme, you can log and record the metres you clock each month.

It is organised with adult fitness in mind and used by thousands of people. The awards are built around distances completed, not swimming technique and are as follows (in miles):

1, 5, 10, 15, 20, 25, 30, 40, 50, 60, 70, 80, 90, 100, 150, 200, 250, 300, 350, 400, 450, 500, 750, 1000, 1500, 2000, 3000, 4000 and 5000.

Determining your goals for the year

As discussed in Chapter 9, your swimming year will hinge on your objectives. Start by determining your goals. Then, you can decide which of the two programme structures given in the following pages is most appropriate to what you want to achieve. These are based on whether you want to improve your fitness base or swim in competitions.

Programme 1

If you decide that Programme 1 is the most suitable, then you will not be competing against other swimmers. You will probably want to be both looking and swimming at your best for two holiday periods: in April/May around the Easter holiday period; and in July/August, around the summer holiday period. On both occasions you may be swimming outdoors, either abroad or in the UK, and you will want to look and feel trimmer and fitter.

Programme 2

Programme 2 is for competitive swimmers – in other words, Masters swimmers. As a rule, there are two peaks to the competitive year. One peak is the short-course season in October, and the other is the long-course season in June. Chapter 12 looks at these in more detail. Those looking to compete should aim to peak twice a season, probably for a period of two to three days at the most. During the rest of the season you will not be able to record times close to those peaks. The younger you are, the more likely you are to be able to compete close to your target or best times. As you get a little older, it becomes increasingly difficult to compete at your best level every week.

Table 10.1 below gives some examples of what your annual goal(s) might be, matching these to the programme that will best help you to achieve them.

Your programme on a monthly basis

A goal-orientated approach to your planning will help you think ahead about your programme. You should know exactly what sort of training you should be undertaking during any month of the year in order to target accordingly. This does not necessarily mean that you will know in advance what you plan to achieve in any one swimming session – or, for that matter, in any one week – but you should have an outline plan in your head. In other words, you start with your goal and work backwards.

Table 10.1 Matching your objectives to the right programme

Objective	Programme
To become generally fitter	1
To improve or recover my health	1
To improve my swimming for other water sports	1
To improve the technique of all my strokes	1
To swim a certain distance each week throughout the year	1
To socialise and take part	1 or 2
To become faster	1 or 2
To turn over a new leaf	1 or 2
To improve my swimming to help my triathlon, biathlon or pentathlon	1 or 2
To beat a specific time target during the year	1 and 2
To be the best for my age	2
To repeat the times achieved when previously a competitor	2
To race against friends or others	2
To complete an open water swim of a certain distance	2

There are considerable differences between what the Masters swimmer and the fitness swimmer need to achieve in their training programmes in order to reach their peaks. These are outlined in the month-by-month chart given below.

Table 10.2 Differences in emphasis between the fitness programme (1) and Masters programme (2)

Month	Programme 1 emphasis	Programme 2 emphasis
September	Easy: peak condition first 2 weeks, then move back to medium swimming at end of month	Hard swimming
October	Medium swimming	Taper and race
November	Hard swimming	Hard swimming
December	Hard swimming	Hard swimming
January	Hard swimming	Hard swimming
Febraury	Hard swimming	Hard swimming
March	Starting to ease up	Hard swimming
April	Easy swimming: concentrate on peak condition	Hard swimming
May	Easy swimming	Taper
June	Hard swimming	Taper and race
July	Hard swimming	Stay in race condition with medium swimming
August	Ease back: concentrate on peak condition	Begin to return to hard swimming

This can then be broken down into a general month-by-month analysis of your training content, as shown in Tables 10.3 and 10.4 below.

Table 10.3 Programme 1: fitness swimmers

Period and month	Training in pool	Land conditioning and planning
Preparation period Sept–Oct	• Break into training steadily and build up to hard swimming in October • Work on swims of 200 m and 400 m with short rest • Work on kicking and pulling sets • If possible, video technique and playback • Monitor heart rates and record times swum as well as stroke-counting • Develop range of strokes • Get partner to help you with your technique	• Start with a little distance running for general conditioning • Introduce endurance weights, i.e. high number of repetitions, low weight • Measure pulse rates when resting and exercising on land • Compare to rates in water • Lay down personal target training distances/times for season • Work hard on flexibility exercises or try yoga
Conditioning period Nov–Mar	• Introduce starts and turns training (*see* Chapter 14, pp. 140–151). Work on your own initially • Increase quality of swims by going for faster times: work on pace • Maintain endurance base, i.e. aerobic work, but increase distances to 400 m and 800 m • Introduce more stroke drills • Continue to work on stroke technique with partner • Try kicking with fins and using hand paddles to increase resistance	• Increase flexibility levels. Work with partner on flexibility • Test levels of flexibility to look for gains • Introduce heavier weights. Supplement free weights with use of fixed weights system • Keep regular check on weight and diet
Holiday period – peak fitness phase April	• Swim much less. Work on high quality and reducing/descending swims (*see* also p. 55) • Bring in more swims of 50 m and 100 m with longer rests • Kick 50's to sharpen legs • Concentrate on quality of starts and turns	• Decrease weights but maintain power work on legs • Increase flexibility work to reduce any stiffness emanating from weight programme • Be positive in your approach. Review achievements so far. Compare performances to goals. Reset goals

Table 10.3 continued.

Period and month	Training in pool	Land conditioning
Return to conditioning phase May–July	• Replenish lost endurance. Work on fartlek and over-distance training. 400–800 m swims, add freestyle breathing exercises • Increase variety by adding strokes, CIS, etc • Work on reducing sets but over longer distances; decrease rests	• Keep strength training at similar levels while you increase distance training loads in water • Get partner to help refine weight technique • Maintain flexiblity
Holiday period – second peak phase Aug	As per April	As per April

Table 10.4 Programme 2: Masters swimmers

Period and month	Training in pool	Land conditioning
Conditioning/ preparation period Nov–Feb	• Break into training steadily and build up to hard swimming • Work on swims of 400 m and 800 m with short rest • Get partner to help you with your technique • Work on kicking and pulling sets • If possible, video technique and playback • Monitor heart rates and record times swum as well as stroke-counting • Develop range of strokes	• Start with a little distance running for general conditioning • At the beginning, start with endurance weights, i.e. high number of repetitions, low weight • After a month, introduce heavier weights, going for power with less repetitions • Measure pulse rates when resting and exercising on land. Compare to rates in water • Lay down target times for season • Work hard on flexibility exercises or try yoga
Pre-competitive/ step-up period Mar–May	• Introduce starts and turns training (see pp. 140–151) • Increase quality of swims by going for faster times: train and work on pace • Maintain endurance base, i.e. aerobic work over 400 m and 800 m while increasing quality and introducing swims of 150–200 m	• Increase both flexibility and strength training levels. Work with partner on flexibility • Test levels of flexibility to look for gains • Supplement free weights with use of fixed weights system • Keep regular check on

Table 10.4 continued

Period and month	Training in pool	Land conditioning
	• Introduce more stroke drills • Continue to work on stroke technique with partner • Try kicking with fins or pumps, swimming in a T–shirt and using hand paddles to increase resistance	weight and diet. Sleep regular and consistent hours
Long-course competitive phase June	• Work on high quality and reducing/descending swims (*see* p. 55) • Bring in more 50s and 100s with longer rests • Kick 50s to sharpen legs • Retain some endurance with some longer aerobic swims over 400 m without too much overload • Concentrate on quality of starts and turns • Work on broken swims over competition distance	• Decrease weights but maintain power work on legs • Increase flexibility work to reduce any stiffness emanating from weight programme • Prepare mind for competition by race planning • Be positive in your approach. Review achievements so far. Compare performances to goals. Reset goals
Mid-season July–Sept	• Replenish lost endurance. Work on fartlek and over-distance training. 400–800 m swims, add freestyle breathing exercises. • Increase variety by adding strokes, CIS, etc. • Work on reducing sets but over longer distance; decrease rests	• Keep strength training at similar levels while you increase distance training loads in water • Get partner to help refine weight technique • Maintain flexibility
Short course competitive phase October	As per June	As per June

The next stage is to work out what you are actually doing in your individual training sessions. This is covered in detail in the following chapter.

Constructing your training sessions

Most people do not have the advantage of their own personal fitness or swimming coach throughout the year. Therefore, you need to know how to set the majority of your training sessions yourself. There are a few things to bear in mind when designing your own session. The first is to remember what you are capable of, and to set reasonable sessions and weekly targets. You need to take into account not only your current level of fitness, but also your state of health and your physical condition, such as your weight. Be realistic about the amount of time you are able to dedicate to your session. If you know that you only have about half an hour to take a lunchtime swim while at work, then schedule accordingly.

Olbrecht[1] refers to the principle of *declining training investment*: the swimmer should look for the smallest increment of training load to produce the greatest possible training effect. Each training load is brought about gradually over time. He further refers to the fact that eventually, stagnation sets in and the swimmer stops training or becomes discouraged by lack of progress. In setting your swimming sessions you need to bear in mind that you will not always progress (*see* also p. 112), so that your scheduling needs to cater for dips in your form. More importantly, Olbrecht refers to the Wave Principle in the training process, which dictates that training load should be changed every six weeks. In general, he is referring to high-performance swimmers – but the principle applies to everyone. The inference is that swimming training schedules should be a mix of high-intensity training with periods of reduced training. He calls this 'regeneration training'.

Olbrecht also refers to training having two objectives. The first is capacity training, which aims to improve efficiency with which your body utilises oxygen (i.e. VO$_2$max), carbohydrate breakdown (glycolysis) and power. These elements are seen as the conditioning elements necessary for swimming. The second objective is associated with fine-tuning; such training is referred to as *power training* and follows on from capacity training.

You need to plan your training systematically and build up steadily. For Masters swimmers, your early-season (November/December) training speeds will probably reach 70–80% of your race speeds; but as the season progresses this will improve to about 75–85%.

What, then, should you do in each individual swimming session? To begin with, it is helpful to include at least one part of the training that tests each energy system – whether that be aerobic or anaerobic (*see* pp. 52–3). You also need to think about provision for monitoring your own heart rate, stroke-counting to control economy

[1] Olbrecht, J. (2000), '*The Science of Winning: Planning, Periodizing and Optimizing Swim Training*' (Olbrecht and Swim Shop), p. 10.

of stroke and a regularity of training sets so that you can compare the results of one set with that of a previous set over the same distance.

If we work on the basis that your available training time is limited to 45 minutes, then your main set – i.e. the set of repetitions that make up the main part of your training programme on that day – should take up about 20 minutes. Your warm-up should be at least 5 minutes. You also need to include recovery sets that link one training set to another while allowing the body to adapt and recover. Recovery sets include long, easier swims or swims that concentrate on breathing.

Table 11. 1 gives the framework of a typical session (appropriate for both fitness and Masters swimmers).

Table 11.1 A typical training session

Description	Typical distance	Objective
Warm-up	400 m alternating freestyle and backstroke	To get the body used to the feel of the water; to acquaint the swimmer with the pool; to get the body used to the pool and air temperature
Main set	6 × 200 m + 10 sec rest: preferred stroke	To work on VO$_2$max (also known as aerobic capacity)
Kick	6 × 50 m + 20 sec rest: second-choice stroke	To overload muscles in the legs while resting the arms for the next main set
Sub-set	6 × 100 m + 15 sec rest: alternating second- and 3rd-choice strokes	Again, aerobic work using as many muscle groups as possible in one session
Sprints	10 × 25 m + 30 sec: freestyle	Aerobic moving towards anaerobic work: encouraging the body to resist heavy lactate build-up while training
Loosen-down	200 m easy dive breaststroke drill	To clear lactate build-up and loosen down slowly

However, there is no set pattern that you must follow. Variety is the key, and provided that you stick to the main variables in your training as given in Table 11.2 below, you should be able to design any number of individual sessions.

Table 11.2 Key variables on a monthly basis for fitness (1) and Masters (2) swimmers

Month	Programe 1 emphasis	Variables	Programme 2 emphasis	Variables
Sept	Easy: peak condition	Very long rests, few repetitions, add in occasional long swim	Hard swimming	Short rests, long swims, low–high repetitions, multiple strokes
Oct	Medium swimming	Short rests, long swims, medium–distance repetitions	Taper and race	Very long rests, fewer repetitions, add in occasional long swims. Swims are made at high intensity and focus on technique, starts and turns.
Nov	Hard swimming	Short rests, long swims, low–high repetitions, multiple strokes	Hard swimming	Short rests, long swims, low–high repetitions, multiple strokes
Dec	Hard swimming	Short rests, long swims, low–high repetitions, multiple strokes	Hard swimming	Short rests, long swims, low–high repetitions, multiple strokes
Jan	Hard swimming	Short rest, long swims, low–high repetitions, multiple strokes	Hard swimming	Short rest, long swims, low–high repetitions, multiple strokes
Feb	Hard swimming	Short rest, long swims, low–high repetitions, multiple strokes	Hard swimming	Short rest, long swims, low–high repetitions, multiple strokes
March	Starting to ease up	Longer rest, fewer repetitions, shorter distance	Even harder swimming	Short rest, long swims, low–high repetitions, increased pace, multiple strokes
April	Easy swimming: concentrate on peak condition	Very long rests, fewer repetitions, add in the occasional long swim	Even harder swimming	Short rest, long swims, low–high repetitions, increased pace, multiple strokes

Table 11.2 continued

Month	Programe 1 emphasis	Variables	Programme 2 emphasis	Variables
May	Harder swimming	Short rests, long swims, low–high repetitions, multiple strokes	Taper	Very long rests, fewer repetitions, add occasional long swims. Swims are made at high intensity and focus on technique, starts and turns
June	Hard swimming	Short rests, long swims, low–high repetitions, multiple strokes	Taper and race	As in May
July	Hard swimming	Short rest, long swims, low–high repetitions, multiple strokes	Ease back, concentrate on peak condition	As in May
Aug	Ease back: concentrate on peak condition	Very long rests, fewer repetitions, add in occasional long swim	Begin to return to hard swimming	Short rests, long swims, low–high repetitions, multiple strokes

Below are some swimming schedules to get you started. The following tables are based on a sample workout for each month of the year, for both fitness and Masters swimmers. These can then be used alongside the programmes detailed in Chapter 10, to compile your full annual training schedule.

Table 12.1 Sample workout for each month of the year by content and distance

Fitness swimmer		Masters swimmer	
Content	Distance (m)	Content	Distance (m)
September			
200 easy backstroke warm-up	200	400 backstroke warm-up: concentrate on deep arm position on hand entry	400
10 × 100 @ 2 min 1st choice	1000		
6 × 50 kick + 10 sec backstroke legs	300		
400 freestyle stroke-counting	400	8 × 200 @ 4 min – 1st choice: broken @ 100 by 10 sec – negative splits	1600
6 × 50 arms + 10 sec: 1st choice with pull buoy	300	12 × 50 + 30 freestyle legs	600
100 ease down	100	10 × 50 reducing, sprints @ 2 min 30, 2nd choice	500
		200 very floppy warm-down	200
Total	2200	Total	3300
October			
300 alternating backstroke/ freestyle warm-up	300	600 freestyle – stroke-counting	600
4 × 200 freestyle @ 3 min 30 sec	800	8 × 100 1st choice @ 4 min – high quality	800
6 × 75 + 15 sec alternating 1st/2nd choice	450	200 easy freestyle	200
		6 × (4 × 25) CIS + 30 sec	600
8 × 50 + 10 sec breaststroke legs with hands by side	400	8 × 50 @ 2 min 30 sec, reducing freestyle	400
400: 1st choice fartlek with loosen-down	400	300 ease-off concentrating on breathing	300
Total	2350	Total	2900

Key:
Individual medly – consists of butterfly, backstroke, breaststroke and one stroke not of the first three, in that order
@/off – the time taken for the swim + rest
+ (a time) – the amount of time to be taken for the rest
1st/2nd choice – your preferred or second-choice stroke

Table 12.1 continued

Fitness swimmer		Masters swimmer	
Content	Distance (m)	Content	Distance (m)
November			
8 × 50 + 5 sec 2nd choice warm-up	400	400 alternating backstroke/ freestyle warm-up	400
4 × 300 freestyle + 20 sec, reducing	1200	6 × 200 freestyle @ 3 min 30 sec	1200
		8 × 75 + 5 sec alternating 1st/2nd choice	600
5 × 100 + 10 sec alternating pull/kick on 3rd choice	500	10 × 50 + 10 sec breaststroke legs with hands by sides	500
300 glide breaststroke, concentrating on getting the best out of the kick	300	400: 1st choice fartlek with loosen-down	400
200 warm-down on freestyle	200		
Total	2600	Total	3100
December			
200 bilateral freestyle	200	10 × 50 + 5 sec 2nd choice warm-up	500
4 × 200 alt. with 4 × 100 1st choice @ 3 min 30 and 2 min – testing heart rate	1200	6 × 300 freestyle + 20 sec, reducing	1800
6 × 50 + 10 breaststroke pull	300	5 × 100 + 10 sec alternating pull/kick on 3rd choice	500
600 backstroke alt. stroke/ legs only	600	300 glide breaststroke, concentrating on getting the best out of the kick	300
6 × 50 + 10 breaststroke legs	300	200 warm-down on freestyle	200
200 freestyle loosen-down	200		
Total	2800	Total	3300
January			
400 freestyle – normal breathing 1st length, breathe every 3 strokes on 2nd, every 4 strokes on 3rd and so on	400	400 freestyle – normal breathing 1st length, breathe every 3 strokes on 2nd, every 4 strokes on 3rd and so on	400
4 × 400 + 15 freestyle: descending – final target times 20 sec slower than personal best	1600	5 × 400 + 15 freestyle: descending – final target times 20 sec slower than personal best	2000
4 × 100 + 10 alt. 2nd/3rd choice legs	400	6 × 100 + 10 alt. 2nd/3rd choice legs	600
300 dive breaststroke – stroke drill	300	300 dive breaststroke – stroke drill	300
4 × 50 @ 1 min: 1st choice sprints	200	4 × 50 @ 1 min: 1st choice sprints	200
Total	2900	Total	3500

Table 12.1 continued

Fitness swimmer		Masters swimmer	
Content	Distance (m)	Content	Distance (m)
February			
16 × 25 + 5: 2nd choice, warm-up concentrating on strong push-off	400	200 easy backstroke warm-up	200
		10 × 150 @ 2 min 30 sec 1st choice	1500
3 × 600 + 15 freestyle – alt. steady and fast lengths	1800	8 × 50 kick + 10 sec backstroke legs	400
8 × 25 + 5: backstroke legs	200	600 freestyle stroke-counting	600
300 freestyle catch-up – stroke drill	300	8 × 100 arms + 10 sec: 1st choice with pull buoy	800
6 × 25 + 15 butterfly fast	150	100 ease down	100
Total	2850	Total	3600
March			
300 backstroke warm-up: concentrate on deep arm position on hand entry	300	400 bilateral freestyle	400
		6 × 200 alt. with 6 × 100 1st choice @ 3 min 30 and 2 min – testing heart rate	1800
6 × 200 @ 4 min – 1st choice: broken @ 100 by 10 sec – negative splits	1200	6 × 50 + 10 breaststroke pull	300
8 × 50 + 30 freestyle legs	400	800 backstroke alt. stroke/ legs only	800
8 × 50 reducing, sprints @ 2 min 30, 2nd choice	400	6 × 50 + 10 breaststroke legs	300
200 very floppy warm-down	200	200 freestyle loosen-down	200
Total	2500	Total	3800
April			
400 freestyle – stroke-counting	400	16 × 25 + 5: 2nd choice, warm-up, concentrating on strong push-off	400
4 × 100 1st choice @ 4 min – high quality	400		
200 easy freestyle	200	4 × 600 + 15 freestyle – alt. steady and fast lengths	2400
4 × (4 × 25) CIS + 30 sec	400	12 × 25 + 5: backstroke legs	300
8 × 50 @ 2 min 30 sec, reducing – freestyle	400	400 freestyle catch-up – stroke drill	400
300 ease-off concentrating on breathing	300	6 × 50 + 15 butterfly fast	300
Total	2100	Total	3800

Table 12.1 continued

Fitness swimmer		Masters swimmer	
Content	Distance (m)	Content	Distance (m)
May			
4 × 100 individual medley	400	2 × (4 × 100) individual medley	800
4 × 300 + 10 freestyle: breathe every 4 strokes – negative splits	1200	4 × 300 + 10 freestyle: breathe every 4 strokes – negative splits	1200
4 × 200 + 15, 2nd choice arms alt. with 4 x 100 1st choice legs	1200	6 × 200 + 15, 2nd choice arms alt. with 6 × 100 1st choice legs	1800
4 × 50 + 10 breaststroke	200	4 × 50 + 10 breaststroke	200
Total	3000	Total	4000
June			
200 alt. backstroke and freestyle	200	400 freestyle–stroke-counting	400
2 × 800 + 15 – each 800 broken into 200's: 1st full stroke, 2nd arms only, 3rd legs only, 4th full stroke hard	1600	4 × 150 + 1 min 30 – reducing, broken by 10 sec @ 75	600
4 × 50 + 5 butterfly legs	200	400 pull, kick, swim alt. length on freestyle	400
4 × 50 + 5 butterfly legs swum with lateral kick	200	4 × 75 + 2 min high quality – concentrate on explosive dive	300
4 × 50 + 5 butterfly	200	Starts and turns practice: 10/15 min	
4 × 50 + 5 backstroke legs	200	4 × 25 + 1 min – 1st choice	100
4 × 50 + 5 backstroke legs with hands locked above head	200	200 loosen-off	200
4 × 50 + 5 backstroke	200		
Total	3000	Total	2000
July			
(4 × 100) reverse individual medley	400	(4 × 100) reverse individual medley	400
16 × 25 + 5: 2nd choice, hard kick	400	8 × 25 + 45: 2nd choice, hard kick	200
4 × 400 + 10: 1st choice alt. steady/hard 100's within each 400	1600	6 × 100 freestyle @ 3 min 30 sec: high quality	600
4 × 100 individual medley legs only – broken by 5 sec at 100's	400	200 glide breaststroke – fairly easy	200
4 × 100 individual medly arms only – broken by 5 sec at 100's	400	6 × 75 @ 2 min 30 sec: 1st choice – reducing	450
2 × (4 × 25) individual medley	200	200 loose backstroke	200
		6 × 25 @ 1 min 30 sec – 1st choice hard	150
Total	3400	Total	2200

Part IV
Training for competition

As discussed earlier in this book, you may decide to swim purely for the enjoyment and health benefits that it offers. On the other hand, you may decide to train in order to compete. You should not be daunted by this prospect: many slower swimmers take part in competitions in order to stretch themselves, and for the social opportunity that they offer. There is a huge amount of interest in Masters swimming across the UK; the Amateur Swimming Association has a list of about 400 clubs that are involved – both existing swimming clubs with a Masters section, and dedicated Masters swimming clubs (in all, numbering some 5000 members). An ASA National Masters Committee advises on grass roots development as well as promoting competitive opportunities, and each of the five ASA Districts – West, South, Midlands, North and North East – has a District Secretary with responsibility for Masters swimming in their area.

Masters swimming is designed to offer opportunities for competition at all levels on all strokes. According to the rules of FINA (the world governing body): 'The Masters programme shall promote fitness, friendships and understanding through swimming, diving, synchronised swimming, water polo and open-water swimming among those competitors with a minimum age limit of 25 years.' The movement is now worldwide, making it possible for adult swimmers to compete all the year round in different parts of the world against people of similar age. Age groups are split into the following years: 25–29, 30–34, 35–39, 40–44, 45–49, 50–54, 55–59, 60–64, 65–69, 70–74, 75–79, 80–84, and 85 and over. For record purposes, the age groups extend to 85–89, 90–94, 95–100, and – amazingly – 100–104. Normally, heats of competitions are seeded from slowest to fastest, making it possible for people of the same standard to compete against one another. There are generally no qualifying times to enter. Anyone can take part, however slow.

In relay races, FINA lays down rules requiring the team entry to be based on the total age of the team (based on whole years): 100–119, 120–159, 160–199, 200–239, 240–279, 280–319, 320–359 years and then in 40-year increments going up as high as necessary. They also allow for age groups to be combined, whether swimmers are competing individually or as a team. This means that no one need compete in their age group on their own if they are the only entry for an event.

The first Masters swimming competition with ASA approval was held at the City University Swimming Pool in London in 1971, when the author and a group of enthusiasts from Otter Swimming Club got together to organise a competition for British swimmers. We copied the US format of age groups, although the oldest group only went up to 65 years! Nearly 200 people took part and the Masters movement in

Britain was born. The first ASA National Masters Competition was introduced in 1981 and the first European Masters at Blackpool in 1987. In recent years, the World Masters has been held in places as far apart as Brisbane, Rio de Janeiro, Indianapolis and Montreal.

There are two types of Masters competition: short-course and long-course. The short-course competitions are held in pools of 25 metres or smaller, and the long-course ones in 50-metre pools. The long-course events are much more tiring, for obvious reasons!

How to begin?

Let's imagine that so far, you have been swimming for fun – but now you would like to try for one or two competitions. How do you go about it? Probably the best approach would be to contact the ASA (*see* p. 152, Further information, for contact details) and ask to speak to the Customer Services Department. The ASA keeps a comprehensive list of clubs and county secretaries and will probably put you in touch with your local representative. They will be able to advise you on the clubs available, where they train and the days on which they meet. There are also some handy ASA leaflets on Masters swimming that include useful tips for when you enter your first competitions.

Trying something new raises lots of questions, and in this case some of them might be:

'How fast do I need to be to take part?'

The answer is that you generally don't need to be very fast – Masters swimming sees itself as the epitome of the Corinthian swimming spirit. Fast swimmers do take part, but they tend not to intimidate the less speedy performers. As a guide, a current set of records – British, European and World – are listed at the back of this book. Inevitably, by the time you read this book a number of these records will have been improved – but they do give you an idea of the sort of standards that people are achieving.

'How often do I need to train to attain a reasonable level for Masters competitions?'

There is no set distance but as a guide, four sessions a week of about one hour, aiming to complete 2500–3000 m per session, would be a realistic target. If possible, swim and enter competitions with a partner.

'What type of structure exists for competitions?'

There is a progression to the structure that makes it easier for a swimmer to build into the system. You can start in county events then move to open competitions (i.e. ones in which anyone can take part), then on to national and finally international open events.

'Do I need to have competed before as a young swimmer?'

The answer to this one is a clear no. You do not have to be a very experienced swimmer to take part. In fact, many Masters swimmers comment that they are faster in their later years than when they were at school.

One interesting point to be aware of is that many former world record holders and Olympic champions do take part in Masters competitions – particularly in the USA, where they have more such champions anyway. As a result, it is easy to rub shoulders with and meet stars of the past, even if they are competing in much faster heats of the same event than yours. By comparison, this happens to a much smaller extent in veteran's athletics. One of the endearing features of Masters swimming is that top swimmers can and do mix with average ones.

What masters swimming can mean to you

Why, then, would you take part in Masters swimming? There are a number of reasons:

- as a competitive outlet

- as a form of enjoyment

- to create friendships and socialise

- as an opportunity to travel and meet people

- if you have previously been a competitive swimmer, as an opportunity to re-acquaint with friends

- to experience once again the excitement of competing that you felt in younger years.

Many pools that have fitness sessions claim that the friendships made there last for years. For example, at the ASA Swim Scheme at Crystal Palace National Sports Centre, an adult fitness session takes place in the 25 m pool each week. The organisers maintain that some of the swimmers have been both attending and friends for years. About 40 swimmers are split into two lanes according to speed. They start with stretching exercises on the pool side before entering the water. Some of the swimmers use these sessions to build up their water work as triathletes.

Families can also take part together. There are many examples of husband and wife, mother and daughter and father and son combinations taking part in the same competition or training session. For instance, Sue Shrimpton, who swam for Britain at the 1968 Mexico Olympics, holds British Masters Records over 50 and 100 m freestyle in the 45–9 years age group – with times not much slower than when she was competing for Britain. Her mother, Doreen Cope, often competed in the same Masters competitions and holds British Masters Records in the 70–4 year group.

The competitive programme

In terms of events and distances, there is plenty of scope. The full international competitive programme includes the following:

Table 13.1 Events featured in the full international Masters programme

Individual				
Freestyle (m)	Backstroke (m)	Breaststroke (m)	Butterfly (m)	Individual medley (m)
50	50	50	50	
100	100	100	100	100
200	200	200	200	200
400				400
800				
1500				
Relays				
Freestyle (m)	Backstroke (m)	Breaststroke (m)	Butterfly (m)	Individual medley (m)
200				200
200 (mixed)				200 (mixed)

Masters swimming in the UK and abroad

There are a number of major competitions that are held each year in both the UK and aboard. FINA provides a full list of competitions listing the month in which the event is normally held, the length of pool (in yards or metres) and the venue of the 2000 event as a guide. Some of the events will be fixed; others will move from place to place each year. A full list of these events can be obtained from www.fina.org.

Whatever event you are aiming for, remember that if you are competing abroad as an individual, you need to inform the ASA. It is also important to keep all of your competition performances as well as details about the venue in your training diary. In the UK, the ASA Masters Championships rotate annually within the five districts, but due to the rising number of competitors (over 1000), the competition has been held recently in Sheffield.

Masters swimming has continued to expand throughout the world. In Europe alone, 29 countries now hold competitions.[1] More than 20,440 competitors took part in the 1999 national championships of each of these countries. At the Vll World Masters Championships in Munich in 2000, more than 7000 swimmers took part.

[1]FINA Masters Swimming, December 2000.

The British contingent won 48 gold medals and broke four World Records. Germany was the overall winner with 3941 points, the USA was second with 2073 points, and Britain was third with 1539 points.[2]

In April 2000, the first ever National Masters Conference was held in Britain as part of an effort to improve communications. Recent introductions into the programme include a half-hour national Masters postal swim, the compilation of top-ten ranking lists as an incentive for people to improve, and a national Masters survey. Also in 2000, for the first time ever, a 19–24 age group was added to the National Masters Championships.

The ASA Masters Swimming Committee now holds a long-course training day open to everyone in April, and a warm weather training camp in February and March.

Progression through Masters swimming

The ASA identifies the progression through Masters swimming as follows:

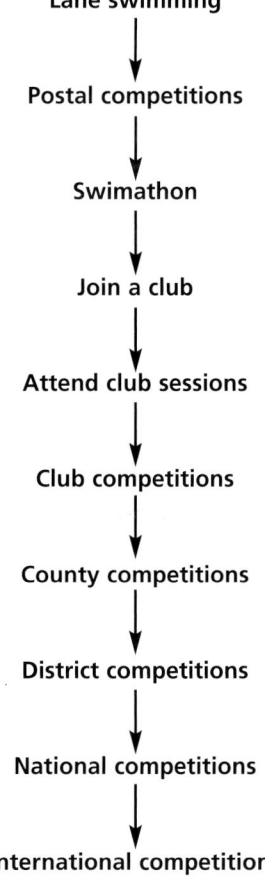

Lane swimming

↓

Postal competitions

↓

Swimathon

↓

Join a club

↓

Attend club sessions

↓

Club competitions

↓

County competitions

↓

District competitions

↓

National competitions

↓

International competitions

[2]Unofficial points list published in ASA Annual Report, 2000.

In order to progress according to your own goals, you need to create a swimming strategy – this is important for both your training and your racing. The first thing is to take a long-term view: given that strategy is all about where you are now, where you want to be in the future and how you are going to get there, a long-term perspective is important. Remind yourself of your overall goals, and of the objectives of your swimming programme. Are you training to compete in Masters swimming at the very highest level? Do you just want to maintain a certain level of fitness – or to compete in order to maintain similar times to those you held previously, despite the passing of the years? These are all perfectly valid reasons for taking part, but different goals will determine the way in which you proceed. Ask your club for advice on setting your targets, and remember to build up to these gradually, breaking your season into phases.

As discussed in Chapter 10, you should be looking to come to two peaks in the year – for the short-course season in October, and for the long-course season in June. Your peaks should last for a period of two or three days at most, and during the rest of the season you will not be able to record times close to these peaks.

Below are some examples of how you might slowly reduce your training times over the year, in order to reach your target in a progressive way. Note the peaks in October and June. There is obviously no formula for this, so use the figures as a guideline only for planning your season – and refer to Chapters 10–12 for advice on planning and devising your schedules.

Table 13.2 Sample progressions – 100 m freestyle

Month	Target time 1:30	Target time 1:20	Target time 1:10	Target time 1:00
January	1:50	1:40	1:30	1:15
February	1:50	1:40	1:30	1:15
March	1:45	1:35	1:25	1:09
April	1:45	1:35	1:25	1:09
May	1:35	1:26	1:15	1:05
June	1:30	1:20	1:10	1:00
July	1:33	1:21	1:11	1:01
August	1:36	1:24	1:14	1:04
September	1:36	1:24	1:14	1:04
October	1:33	1:21	1:11	1:01
November	1:45	1:35	1:25	1:10
December	1:45	1:35	1:25	1:10

Table 13.3 Sample progressions – 100 m backstroke

Month	Target time 1:40	Target time 1:25	Target time 1:15	Target time 1:10
January	2:00	1:45	1:35	1:25
February	2:00	1:45	1:35	1:25
March	1:50	1:35	1:25	1:20
April	1:46	1:30	1:20	1:15
May	1:45	1:29	1:19	1:14
June	1:40	1:25	1:15	1:10
July	1:41	1:26	1:16	1:11
August	1:43	1:28	1:18	1:13
September	1:45	1:29	1:19	1:14
October	1:41	1:26	1:14	1:11
November	1:50	1:40	1:30	1:22
December	1:50	1:40	1:30	1:22

Table 13.4 Sample progressions – 100 m butterfly

Month	Target time 1:40	Target time 1:25	Target time 1:15	Target time 1:10
January	2:00	1:45	1:35	1:25
February	2:00	1:45	1:35	1:25
March	1:50	1:35	1:25	1:20
April	1:46	1:30	1:20	1:15
May	1:47	1:31	1:19	1:14
June	1:40	1:25	1:15	1:10
July	1:41	1:26	1:16	1:11
August	1:43	1:28	1:18	1:13
September	1:45	1:30	1:20	1:15
October	1:41	1:26	1:16	1:11
November	1:50	1:40	1:30	1:22
December	1:50	1:40	1:30	1:22

Table 13.5 Sample progressions – 100 m breaststroke

Month	Target time 1:45	Target time 1:30	Target time 1:20	Target time 1:15
January	2:05	1:50	1:40	1:30
February	2:00	1:50	1:40	1:30
March	1:55	1:45	1:30	1:25
April	1:50	1:37	1:25	1:20
May	1:49	1:38	1:26	1:21
June	1:45	1:38	1:20	1:15
July	1:46	1:39	1:21	1:16
August	1:48	1:41	1:23	1:18
September	1:47	1:42	1:24	1:16
October	1:46	1:39	1:21	1:16
November	2:00	1:45	1:35	1:25
December	2:00	1:45	1:35	1:25

Training before a competition

The period before a competition always requires a different form of training, as you prepare for the mental as well as physical battle ahead. Here are some of the things you need to do:

- decrease distances swum

- increase pace of swims

- decrease number of repetitions swum

- rest as much as possible between training sessions in order to let the body recover from a build-up of training effects

- ease back on strength training

- maintain high levels of flexibility training

- focus mental approach on performing at a high level in the forthcoming event

- sleep as much as possible

- sharpen up on starts and turns (*see* Chapter 14)

- visualise a race situation and mentally prepare for it.

Preparing for a race – the taper period

During the taper period, the swimmer eases off in preparation for competition. The aim is to achieve both physical relaxation and mental alertness. The tapering process can vary from swimmer to swimmer: generally, it calls for longer rests between repetitions, fewer training sessions, slightly shorter distances in order to sharpen up, and more sleep. These factors combine to bring a swimmer to their peak.

Knowing how much tapering you need requires considerable practice, especially since this varies widely from individual to individual. The only way you can determine what suits you is to try out different variations. Sometimes swimmers rest up too much and find that they have lost some of the crucial endurance-based fitness that they had built up during training. This might manifest itself in poor performance over, say, the last 30 m of a 100 m race. On the other hand, there are swimmers who do not rest enough, and find that they are too tired and insufficiently sharp when they compete.

Some swimmers like a long taper that lasts for a number of weeks; others prefer just two or three days. Yet another approach is to go the other way. In the month before competition, the swimmer 'overdoes' their training, increasing the workload by 30–40%. They then taper from this increased workload.

There is a fine dividing line between what works for you and what doesn't, and trial and error is often the only way to find out. As a general guide, swimmers taking part in longer races do not need as much taper time as sprinters. Sprinting, being an explosive event, requires more rest. In addition, you will need to make a judgement based on the number of races you are taking part in during a competition. If you have a long taper, your performances are likely to drop more quickly in a competition where you have a whole number of races on different days. In such cases, you may need a much shorter taper. Chapters 10–12 give more specific advice about tailoring your training programme towards your peaks.

Race day

You have been looking forward to this day for many months. Avoid ruining it with poor application and an unplanned approach. Here is some general advice for race-day preparation.

- Rise reasonably early in order to get your body's metabolism working. Ensure that you get a good night's sleep the night before.

- Ensure that your breakfast contains plenty of carbohydrate, some proteins but little fat, as fats take time to digest. If you are racing in the afternoon, ensure that you eat a main meal (high in carbohydrates) at least 2 hours prior to the start of the race.

- Take a short walk before your race, to work any stiffness out of your system.

- When you arrive at the swimming meeting, make sure you have a good warm-up. This should consist of anything between half an hour to an hour's swimming in which you also practise starts and turns.

- Remember to take water every hour to prevent dehydration.

- Wrap up warm – and that particularly includes wearing training shoes to prevent loss of body temperature through the soles of the feet.

- Carry out your due diligence in terms of knowing where everything is, including the warm-up pool, reporting area, etc. Make sure you know your reporting time and your event number

- There is one further useful tip before you race. When awaiting their event, swimmers usually sit in a row of seats behind the start. At this point in time, swim the race through in your mind, remembering all the key points about starting and turning and finishing the race with the arms at long reach. This thought process should help to build the adrenalin at the right time – just before you go into your race. Swim the race through earlier, and the adrenalin necessary for the race will have come and gone.

Open-water swimming

Nowadays, there are only a few Channel swims made each year. Hazardous and overcrowded shipping conditions have made it difficult for the Captain Webbs of today! Long-distance or open-water swimming is, however, something that you can do into later life. James Counsilman, who was Mark Spitz's coach at Indiana University, swam the English Channel when he was 58 years old.

You don't have to swim the Channel to take part in long-distance swimming, though: there are many shorter swims, and the steady pace of the races combined with the fresh air make this an attractive alternative to pool swimming.

Open-water swimming is a discipline involving competitions of up to 25 km in any outdoor body of water – lakes, rowing courses, seas and reservoirs. The first Open Water World Championships were held in Hawaii in October 2000; and as a recent development, a Great Britain Open Water Grand Prix has been introduced, with events ranging from 4–10 km in length. These take place between May and October.

Tips and training

Training consists of a structured pool schedule with an emphasis on over-distance swims. This is mainly in the form of long aerobic swims, although a strong speed base is also essential. As far as preparation is concerned, it is sometimes better to make short, frequent training swims or shorter open-water races early in the year in order to build up to the longer races later.

The most essential skill specific to this kind of swimming is the ability to go in a straight line without any guide to follow. This can be learned by practising lifting your head every so often – to breathe and to look where you are going. The ability to swim in opposing conditions – i.e. wind and waves, can only be developed with experience. This can be conquered to some extent by learning to breathe on both sides, which enables you to breathe away from the approaching waves or wind.

Safety considerations

Safety factors have to be considered in this kind of swimming. Some homework in order to build a fuller knowledge of the area of water, regulations, weather and tidal reports will help to avoid dangers. Swimmers should avoid training in waters where fast craft are present. Most important of all, swimmers should never train alone without an observer. The use of a brightly coloured hat will help an observer spot you. And finally, you should always be aware of the risk of hypothermia – this dangerous condition occurs when too much heat is lost through the body. Low skin-surface temperatures can cause discomfort, but it is only when core temperatures drop that danger arises. Take the appropriate precautions: when in doubt, consult your club or your local ASA representative.

In order to be able to compete, you will need to sharpen up on your starts and turns. We will therefore quickly review the key points involved ready for competition.

Starts

There are four different types of start that can be used for freestyle, butterfly and breaststroke.

The standard start

Most of you will already be able to perform this dive, but it is worth recapping on the basic technique (*see* fig. 14.1).

The basic dive is made with the toes wrapped over the edge of the pool and the feet in line with the hips. Your knees face forwards and are bent to approximately 140 degrees. Fix your eyes on the surface of the water immediately beneath your face, and lean your body slightly forwards so that your centre of gravity is positioned perpendicularly above your feet. The shoulders should be curled and the arms held diagonally, in line with them – your hands being in front of your head.

On the starting signal, swing your arms back behind your body, more or less in line with your shoulders. As your centre of gravity is transferred slightly forwards above the hips, swing your arms forwards. Push your feet away from the poolside and straighten your knees. Now, keeping your head down, straighten your arms at the elbows so that the hands are swung in front of your head. Your body should now be projected forwards in a straight line, with the head between the arms and the fingers stretched out in front. The ears should be protected by the inside of the upper arms. The fingers now come together.

Try to make a 'hole' for your head as your body starts to enter the water. Your fingers cut through the water, and your straightened body does the same in parallel with the surface – about 1 m beneath the surface. As the dive slows down to swimming speed, either begin your kick first and your arm movements immediately afterwards, or start both arms and legs at the same time.

The initial start position can be made either with the hands in front or the hands behind the back. This can only be determined based on the comfort and ease of use for each individual.

> **Caution**
>
> Do not dive into water of a depth less than 1 m – and even if the water you are diving into is deeper, still take care.

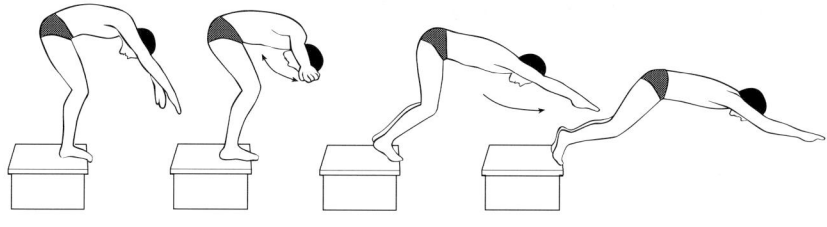

Figure 14.1 The standard start

The grab start

The grab start became popular in the 1970s (*see* fig. 14.2). It is used less frequently these days, but is still fairly common. Since it lacks the power of the conventional start, the swimmer aims to compensate by making maximum use of speed.

Prior to the start signal, bend forwards with your toes curled over the starting block or poolside. Bend your knees once again so that you can wrap your fingers over the block; the angle of knee-bend is about 120 degrees. Your body weight should be balanced on the balls of your feet.

On the starting signal, flex your elbows initially and then extend the shoulders by straightening the elbows. Breathe in ready to explode air out on the first movement. At the same time, by pulling with your arms and leaning forwards, move your weight forwards over the original starting position. This all happens more or less instantaneously, as you are seeking to enter the water as quickly as possible. This is achieved by entering the water earlier than in the conventional start. The short radius of rotation and the lower centre of gravity mean that an earlier entrance is inevitable.

The next phase is for the arms to be lifted in front of the head and the spine to be straightened. The whole body moves in an upward curve until the legs are in line with the upper body. The body is therefore extended forwards powerfully as a result of momentum being transferred, with the fingertips entering the surface first. The angle of entry to the water is 10–15 degrees.

Figure 14.2 The grab start

Like the basic start, this is fairly easy to practise and can be worked on during your normal swimming sessions, as you do not need starting blocks. The pool deck will suffice for day-to-day practice.

The track start

The track start (*see* fig. 14.3) is currently the most widely used technique, since most competitive swimmers want to enter the water as early as possible. It was first used in athletics and has now been adopted in the swimming pool – a combination of the grab start and a track racing start.

Place your hands over the starting block or poolside in a similar way as for the grab start (*see* below). The arms are positioned in line with the shoulders. Crouch with your knees bent and the toes of one foot over the poolside. The leg of the other foot is positioned one pace behind (approximately 10 cm) and is bent at the knee for stability and future projection. The eyes look down towards the water immediately in front of the poolside and, at this point, there should be no tension in the neck and shoulders.

When the 'Take your marks' command is made, lift your hips forwards and up – higher than your shoulders (the front leg is now at an angle of approximately 140 degrees). This movement has the effect of transferring the centre of gravity forwards and moving the weight from the back to the front foot. You should aim to keep your centre of gravity low by not straightening your front leg too much.

On the starting signal, drive yourself forwards and out at an angle of 45 degrees to the poolside. This is done by bending your elbows and levering down on the starting block with your hands. Immediately following this move, throw your arms laterally until they come together in front with the head between the arms. The trunk is bent

Figure 14.3 The track start

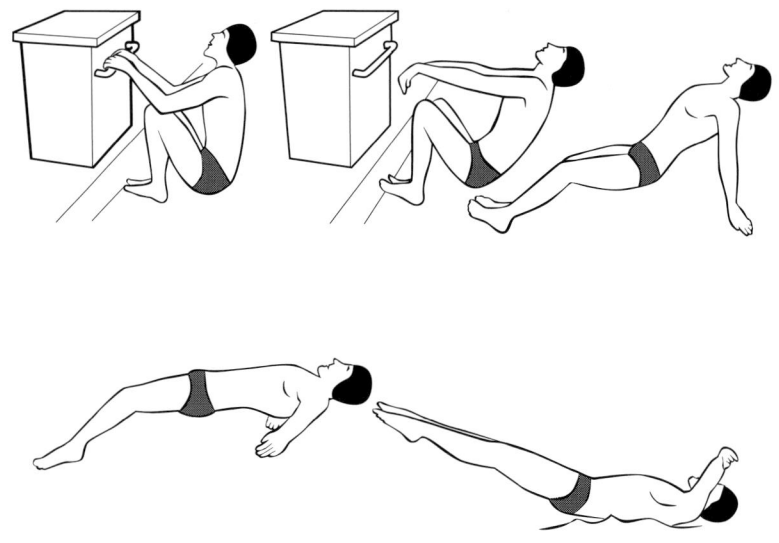

Figure 14.4 The backstroke start

at first but extends at the hips as the hands are thrown forwards. As the trunk straightens out, the knees extend and straighten.

Swimmers who are able to bend their knees more fully without losing balance will be able to achieve a more powerful thrust of the legs prior to entry. The last part of the actual diving movement is completed when the rear leg pushes back and is brought side-by-side with the lead leg. The total movement is one in which the start first of all rocks back but then rocks forwards on the feet prior to extension.

The backstroke start

The rules of the backstroke start require that the swimmer's head break the surface after 10 m. This affords the opportunity to extend the start and glide with several powerful, underwater butterfly leg-kicks.

Again, a backstroke start is a technique that can be practised on your own without a starting block – although the use of a block would be more satisfactory. Start by holding the starting block handle. Face the poolside and wrap your arms over the top on either side of the handle, the arms being in line with the shoulders. Your shoulders should remain under the surface; your legs are bent at the knees in order that your curled feet can rest on the pool wall with the balls of the feet and the toes in full contact with it. The feet are about 10 cm apart.

Breathe in, ready to explode air out. On the command 'Take your marks', bend your elbows and pull your chin towards the wall, like a spring ready to be uncoiled. The action of pulling the chin closer to the poolside has the effect of lifting the upper body out of the water. Your chin is now about 10 cm from the starting block. On the start command, drive your head upwards and backwards by straightening your legs at the knees and pressing with your toes and feet on the pool wall.

Simultaneously, push down and inwards with your arms. The shoulders – which until now have been curled – arch as the head and shoulders rotate backwards. Then release your arms, which swing rapidly forwards in front of the head (having been swung in a lateral manner along the same plane as the shoulders). Too much arching of the back is prevented by the use of the external and oblique muscles in the abdomen.

The arms conclude their swing forwards by coming together in front of the head, and the toes point in order to stretch the legs. Your aim is to cut through the surface by way of a parabolic curve, in order to get your body in the right position for a long glide and the added advantage of those dolphin leg kicks.

Tips on diving

- Avoid throwing the arms too high in the air by following through and forwards too strongly.
- Keep the head down throughout.
- Keep the arm-swing strong and controlled in order to achieve a good transfer of momentum.
- Try to cut through the surface of the water with the hands, and avoid surface friction by allowing the torso to land on the surface.

Reviewing the turns

Freestyle (tumble) turn

Gradually the tumble turn has superseded all other forms of freestyle turn (*see* fig. 14.5). The extra speed and superior body position it offers after it has been executed have led to other turns becoming more or less extinct. How then do you learn the turn? The best way is in the shallow end of the pool, on your own with very few other people around you.

Start with your body horizontal in line with the water surface. Tuck your chin on to your chest and, at the same time as your face begins to go under the water, pull hard with your hands in a 180-degree movement in line with your shoulders. Your

Figure 14.5 Freestyle (tumble) turn

hands effectively start by facing down towards the bottom of the pool, stretched out in front of your shoulders, and finish with the backs of the hands facing up towards the ceiling. In addition to the movements of the chin and the hands, the knees bend to the stomach to aid the rotational movement.

After a little practice, you will find that you can rotate your body along its central and vertical axis until it returns to its starting position. You may find that until you are used to the movement, the water goes up your nose. To counteract this, you need to cup your lower lip and literally blow up your nose in order to create an air pocket.

Once you are getting the hang of it, incorporate it into your swimming. Swim very slowly with breaststroke arms and freestyle legs towards the pool wall. When you are one stroke away from the wall, carry out the movement. After a little trial and error, you will find that once your body has rotated, your heels land up on the wall. As soon as they make contact, push off on your back with your hands above your head.

The next refinement is to carry out the turn in the same way, but twisting your feet through 180 degrees on the wall. In this way your whole body will be facing the bottom of the pool during the glide.

When you are confident with this, you can carry out the whole movement approaching the wall on freestyle rather than breaststroke arms. When your lead arm reaches the wall, the palm of the hand is turned towards the wall so that the forearm rests on the wall and diagonally down towards the bottom of the pool. At this initial stage, the forearm can then be fixed on the wall and used to assist in the initial rotation when the chin drops down to the chest.

Breaststroke and butterfly turns

The breaststroke and butterfly turns are similar in competition (*see* fig. 14.6). In both cases, the hands have to touch the wall simultaneously to comply with the rules.

Both turns can be learned quite simply and applied immediately without any staged build-up. Let us imagine that you are turning around your left shoulder. You approach the swimming pool wall. On reaching out with both arms outstretched, quickly bend your elbows so that the shoulders are drawn towards the wall. Keep your head down to facilitate the movement.

As the top part of your head almost reaches the wall and your knees bend in towards your hips, place your left hand in the water to steady yourself. The right arm is bent at the elbow and thrown in a circular manner over the water until it joins the left to start the push-off. The head stays down until the left hand moves away from the wall.

What, then, is the difference between a butterfly and breaststroke turn? There are a number. The first difference is that in butterfly, you are approaching the wall at greater speed and therefore need to bend the elbows more quickly when your hands first touch the wall. There is also more momentum throughout the turn on butterfly as a result of this initial speed. On breaststroke, the push-off needs to be made a little deeper in order to allow for the underwater pull. Also on breaststroke, the swimmer is allowed one complete pull and recovery underwater before the head breaks the surface. The deeper glide can be achieved by allowing the feet to drop lower on the wall in order to let the centre of gravity also drop. The fingers of both hands need to be pointed diagonally towards the bottom of the wall at the other end of the pool.

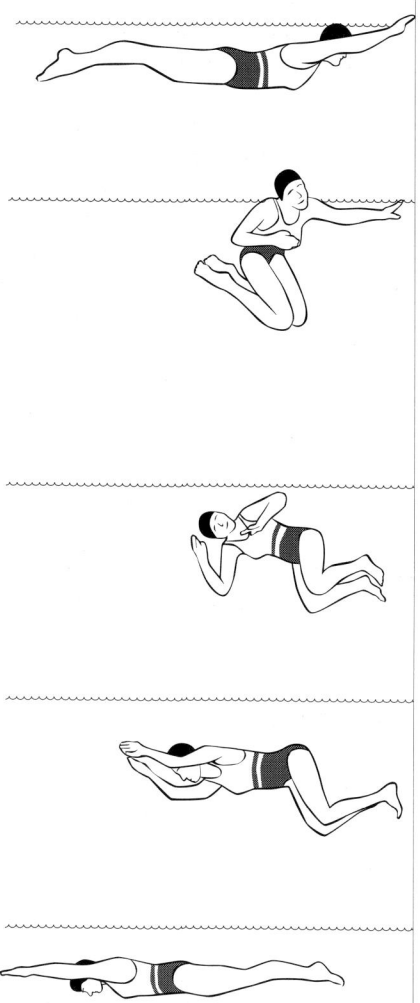

Figure 14.6 *Breaststroke and butterfly turn*

The underwater breaststroke pull

The breaststroke underwater pull (*see* fig. 14.7) is executed at the end of the push-off from the turn. As the glide slows down to swimming speed, make a long and wide breaststroke pull. When your hands become level with your shoulders, push them down to the thighs. Effectively, the hands 'fix' when they are in line with the shoulders and the body is pushed past the hands.

In the meantime, bend your legs and lift your heels ready for the recovery. When your hands have reached the outside part of the thighs, recover your arms under the water by bending the elbows and bringing the hands forwards together under the body. The hands should face down towards the bottom of the pool throughout this

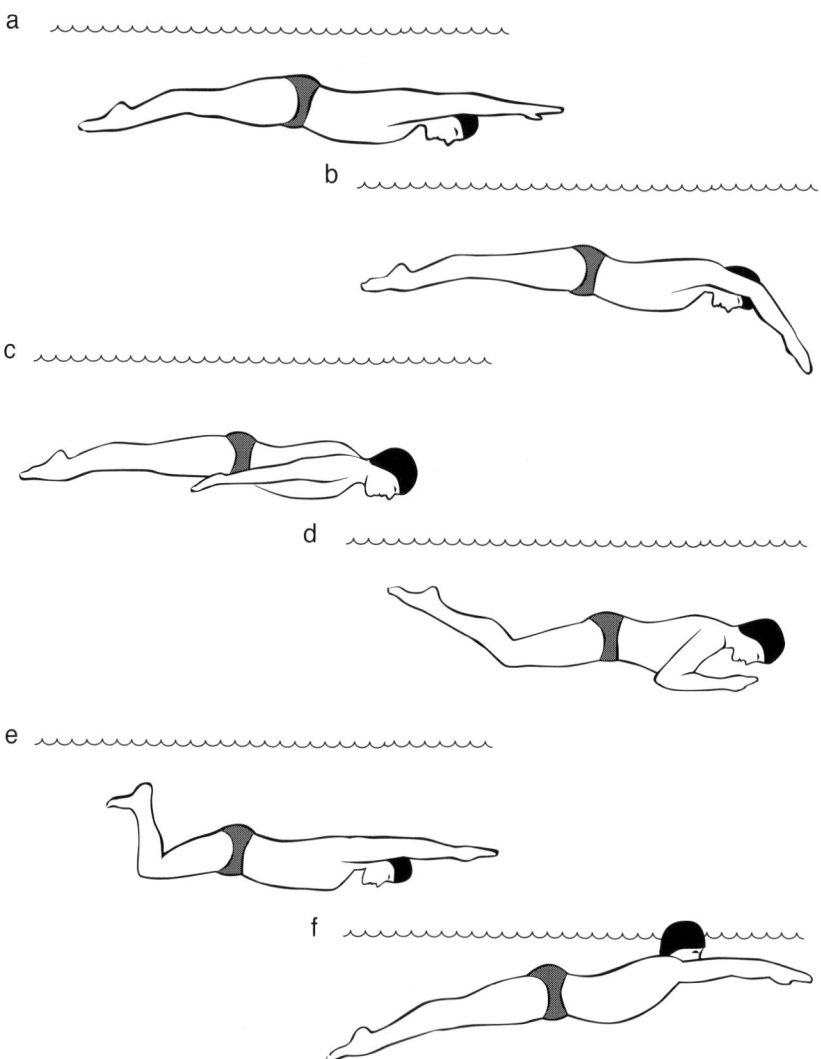

Figure 14.7 Underwater pull breaststroke

recovery phase. As this arm recovery takes place, the legs make a normal breaststroke kick in order to drive the body back to the surface. Your head should now break the surface and – with your body in a straight line and arms stretched out ahead – you are now ready for your next stroke on the surface.

Backstroke turn

Like freestyle, backstroke has undergone a number of experimental and different turns in the last 20 years as swimmers have searched for ever-increasing speed (*see* fig. 14.8). Changes to FINA Laws mean that in race situations, backstrokers no longer need to touch the wall with their hands when turning. The result has been a gradual movement towards the flip or backstroke tumble turn.

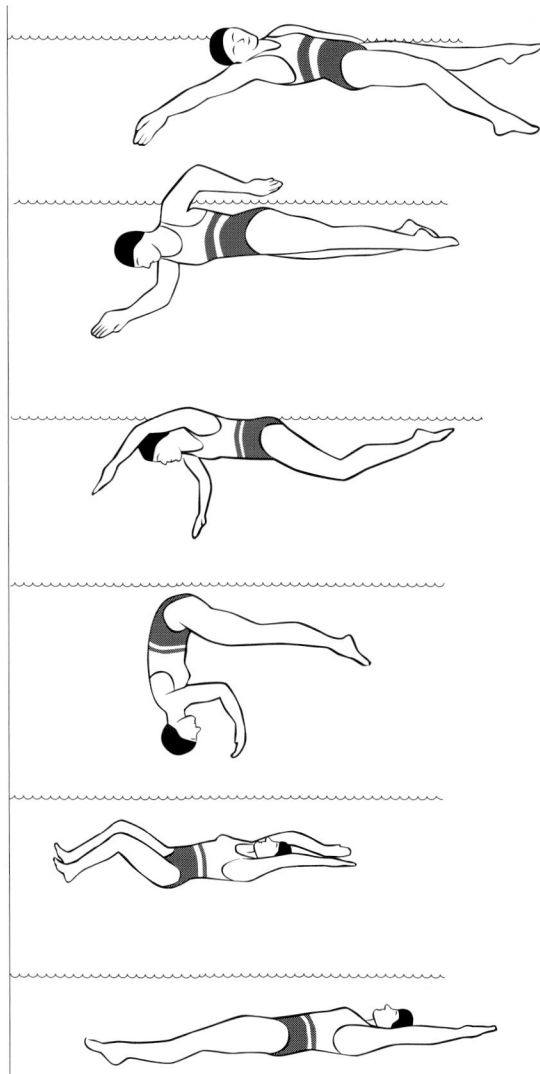

Figure 14.8 Backstroke turn

If you can already tumble turn proficiently on freestyle then the backstroke turn will be easier for you. The practices for the tumble turn in backstroke are exactly the same as those previously described for the freestyle turn.

As you approach the wall on your back and one arm is halfway through its recovery, turn your hand so that the palm is facing down toward the bottom of the pool. Sweep this arm laterally across your chest so as to place it beyond the opposite shoulder. Your other hand stabilises the body by remaining beside your hips and then joins the hand of the lateral sweeping arm in front of the original shoulder position. Now roll your body on to its front and before reaching the wall tuck your chin and knees in so that you emulate the freestyle tumble turn.

Plant your feet on the wall in order to push off and bring your hands together to effectively make a hole for your head to push through. Straighten your arms at the elbows and the legs at the knees and 'squeeze' the wall in the push off.

When the speed of your glide starts to slow down, you can make a number of dolphin leg movements to extend the push off before your fingers bring you back to the surface where normal swimming stroke recommences.

Further information

This chapter is intended to help you to find more information to support your training programme.

Swimming associations

Amateur Swimming Association, Harold Fern House, Derby Square, Loughborough, Leics, LE11 5AL. Tel 01509 618700

Federation Internationale De Natation Amateur, Avenue de Beaumont 9, 1012 Lausanne, Switzerland. Tel (00 41) 21 312 6602, Fax (00 41) 21 312 6610

Ulster Region Swim Ireland, House of Sport, Upper Malone Road, Belfast, N Ireland, BT9 5LA. Tel 028 903 83807

Scottish Sports Council, Caledonia House, South Gyle, Edinburgh, EH12 9DQ. Tel 0131 317 7200, Fax 0131 317 7202

Scottish Swimming, Holmhills Farm, Cambuslang, Glasgow, G72 8DT. Tel 0141 646 0490, Fax 0141 646 0491, email scotswim@aol.com

Sport England, 16 Upper Woburn Place, London, WC1 0QP. Tel 020 8778 8600

Sports Council For Wales, National Sports Centre For Wales, Sophia Gardens, Cardiff, CF1 9SW. Tel 029 20 300500, Fax 01222 300600

Welsh Amateur Swimming Association, Roath Park House, Ninian Road, Cardiff, CF2 5ER. Tel 02920 488820

Information on where to swim

Institute of Sports and Recreation Management, Giffard House, 36–38 Sherrard Street, Melton Mowbray, Leics.,LE13 1XJ. Tel 01664 565531

Institute of Leisure and Amenity Management, ILAM House, Lower Basildon, Reading, Berks, RG8 9NE. Tel 01491 874222, Fax 01491 874059

Swimming injuries

Association of Chartered Physiotherapists in Sports Medicine, 81 Heol West Place, Cotty, Bridgend, Mid Glamorgan, CF35 6BA. Tel 01656 665310

British Association of Sport and Medicine, Birch Lea, 67 Springfield Lane, Eccleston, St Helens, Merseyside, WA10 5HB. Tel 01744 28198, Fax 01744 28198

Society of Sports Therapists, 45c Carrick Street, Glasgow, G2 8PJ. Tel 0141 221 3660, Fax 0141 221 1525

Visually impaired swimming

British Blind Sport, 67 Alert Street, Rugby, Warwks., CV21 2SN. Tel 01788 536142, Fax 01788 536676

Deaf swimming

British Deaf Sports Council, 7A Bridge Street, Otley, West Yorkshire, LS21 1BQ. Tel 01943 850214, Fax 01943 850828

Diet

British Nutrition Foundation, High Holborn House, 52–54 High Holborn, London, WC1V 6RQ. Tel 0207 404 6504, Fax 0207 404 6747

Disabled swimming

British Paralympic Association, Norwich Union Building, 69 Park Lane, Croydon, Surrey, CR9 1BE. Tel 020 7662 8882, Fax 020 7662 8310

Disability Sport England, N17 Studio 5, Unit 4G, 784–788 High Road, Tottenham, N17 0DA. Tel/fax 020 8801 4466

Open water swimming

Amateur Swimming Association, contact David Fytche, National Development Officer. Tel 023 92570865, email dfytche@asagb.org

British Long Distance Swimming Association, 16 Elmwood Road, Barnton, Norwich, Cheshire, CW8 4NB. Tel 01606 75298

Channel Swimming Association, The Hermitage, 12 Vale Square, Ramsgate, Kent, CT11 95X. Tel/fax 01843 852772

Magazines and publications

Aquazone, c/o Swimming Times

Peak Performance, 67–71 Gosditch Rd, London, EV1V 7EP. Tel 020 7251 9037

Swim News, 356 Sumach Street, Toronto, Ontario, Canada, M4X 1V4. Tel (001) 416 963 5599

Swimming Times, 41 Granby Street, Loughborough, Leics, LE11 3DU. Tel 01509 632206, email swimtime@asag.org.uk

Swimming World and Swimming Technique, via Swimshop, 228 Nevada Street, El Segunda, California 90245. Tel (001) 800 352 7948

UK Swimmer, PO Box 26, Ledbury, Herefordshire, HR8 2YB. email: ukswimming@moose.co.uk

Watermarks, Plantagent Buildings, 100 Spencer Street, Birmingham, B18 6DB. Tel 0121 523 7961, email Water-marks@freeuk.com

Wavelength, ASA Newsletter, c/o Amateur Swimming Association. Tel 01509 618756, e.mail Helen@asag.org.uk

What About Masters? Newsletter, c/o Amateur Swimming Association

Videos and where to purchase them

Don Gambril's classic series:

Art of Swimming

Alexander Popov – What's the Limit

Excellence in Stroke Technique

Fast Lane Series – Basic Training

Gold Medal Series (covers all strokes)

21st Century Swimming

All available from SwimShop, 228 Nevada Street, El Segundo, California 90245, USA. Tel (001) 800 35 7946

Master Class Video, 25 Hartlington Road, High Lane, Stockport, Cheshire, SK6 8BZ

Training World Class Swimming, c/o Scottish Swimming (address above)

Also, if you have a computer, you can view videoclips of the top swimmers by going to the following web site:
www.geocities.com/colosseum/court/5811/agevideo/realvids.htm

Adult Swim Fit Award Scheme

ASA Awards Centre, Unit 1, Kingfisher Enterprise Park, 50 Arthur Street, Redditch, Worcs., B98 8LG. Tel 0800 220292, email, sales@asa-awards.co.uk

Books

The Complete Guide to Exercise in Water by Debbie Lawrence (A & C Black, 1998)

The Complete Guide to Sports Nutrition by Anita Bean (A & C Black, 2000)

The Fit Swimmer, 120 Workouts and Tips by Marianne Brems (Contemporary Books, 1984)

The Handbook of Swimming by David Wilkie and Kelvin Juba (Pelham Books, 1986)

Know The Game Swimming (A & C Black, 2000)

The Science of Winning by J Olbrect, 2000 (through Swimshop, 3 Dencora Way, Luton, LU3 3HP, Tel 01582 562111, email swimshopuk@aol.com

Strength Training by Anita Bean (A & C Black, 1998)

Swimming Coaching by Joseph Dixon (Crowood Press, 1996)

Swimming Drills For Every Stroke by Ruben Guzman (Human Kinetics, 1998)

Swimming Dynamics: Winning Techniques and Strategies by Cecil Colwin (Masters Press, 1998)

Swimming Even Faster by Ernest W Maglischo (Mayfield Publishing, 1982)

Swimming For Fitness by George Austin and Jim Noble (ASA Publications, 1990)

Swimming Into The 21st Century by Cecil M Colwin (Human Kinetics, 1992)

Useful web sites

Amateur Swimming Association
www.britishswimming.org.uk

Association of British swimmers with Physical Disabilities
www.lut.ac.uk/research/paad/wheelpower/swim.htm

Department for Culture Media and Sport
www.culture.gov.uk

Institute of Leisure and Amenity Management
www.ilam.co.uk

Institute of Sport and Recreation Management
www.isrm.co.uk

Institute of Swimming Teachers and Coaches
www.swimming.org.uk

List of masters swimming clubs through the world
www.swimsearch.com

Long distance swimming event details
Ali38crossings@aol.com
Maurice.Ferguson@virgin.net

Masters Aquatic Coaches Association
www.macacoach.org/

National Coaching Foundation
www.ncf.org.uk

National Sports Medicine Institute of the UK
www.nsmi.org.uk

Sport England
www.english.sports.gov.uk

United States Masters Swimming
www.usms.org

Professional bodies

British Swimming Coaches and Teachers Association, 82 St Michael's Road, Aldershot, Hants, GU12 4JW. Tel 01452 409251, email, admin@bscta.com

Institute of Swimming Teachers and Coaches, Dawson House, 63 Forest Road, Loughborough, Leics, LE11 3NW. Tel 01509 264357

Software

Workout Manager, Hytek Ltd, 01494 510938, email, www.hy-tekltd.com

Aquapacer™, SwimTec (Heartrate UK) Ltd., 2 Church View, York Road, York, YO24 4NW. Tel/fax 01904 788427

Swimming records

Masters swimming records, like any other records, continue to tumble. Both the ASA and FINA update records on their web sites on a fairly regular basis (*see* Further information for addresses). The following list is by no means exhaustive but gives some of the most important World, European and British records.

Short Course Records
Event : 50 m Freestyle

	25–29	30–34	35–39	40–44	45–49	50–54	55–59	60–64
British men	Craig Eddlestone & Roland Lee 23.75	Roland Lee 24.11	Nicholas Vaughan 24.00	Tom Greenwood 25.07	Peter Projdekker 25.76	Tony Cherrington 26.85	Tony Cherrington 27.20	Hugh Cumberford 29.15
British women	Helen Sadler 27.09	Maxine McKinnell 27.28	Alyson Jones 28.19	Judy Hattle 28.88	Susan Shrimpton 29.73	Carol Fellows 30.29	Judy Wilson 30.56	Jan Asher 33.54
European men	Handler Reiko 23.50	Lars Johansson 23.151	Janne Virtamen 23.64	Vladimir Galavtine 24.62	Vladimir Galavtine 24.14	Bernd Scroeder 26.81	Stanley Clarke 27.06	Peter Berengren 27.42
European women	Manuela Schubert 26.62	Maxine McKinnell 27.28	Karin Seick 27.52	Guylaine Berger 27.97	Conny Boer Buys 29.14	Carol Fellows 30.29	Susana Barkley 31.18	Jane Asher 33.54
World men	Robert Peel 22.48	Rowdy Gaines 22.82	John Miranda 22.44	Bret Barnes 24.09	V Galavtine 24.14	Roger Hawkins 25.49	Donald Hill 26.60	Katsuki Ishihara 27.06
World women	Hageman/Schubert 26.63	Anna Pettis-Scott 26.46	Sandy Neilson-Bell 26.13	Beth Knight 26.95	Laura Val 28.11	Carol Fellows 30.29	Ardeth Mueller 30.37	Jayne Bruner 33.07

	65–69	70–74	75–79	80–84	85–89	90–94	95–99	100–104
British men	Joseph Phillips 29.65	Jack Hale 29.65	Jack Hale 32.48	Gordon Newman 40.12	John Harrison 51.60			
British women	Jane Asher 34.34	Doreen Cope 38.95	Betty Condon 44.83	Edith Newitt 51.50	Willy Van Rysel 1:00.11			
European men	Bernhard Schlurike 29.50	Jack Hale 31.01	Jack Hale 32.48	Rein Stadler 37.79	Rein Stadler 38.82	Hans Paul 56.38		
European women	Jane Asher 34.34	Kerstin Gjores 38.38	Margaret Pfannmuller 43.57	Ursula Oehmke 48.63	Nella Gamenara 56.37	Margarete Gottschalk 1:13.90		
World men	Cav Caanaugh 27.68	Takahiko Noma 30.21	Keijro Nakamura 32.09	Jim Eubank 36.90	Woodrow Bowersock 37.75	Gastao Figueiredo 46.94	Gus Langner 57.57	Tom Lane 2:06.66
World women	Gail Roper 34.17	Gail Roper 35.37	Olga Johnson 39.73	Hatsuho Sugaya 44.57	Julie Doice 51.99	Margot Bates 1:11.85	Marge Anderson 2:02.29	

Age range

157

Short Course Records
Event : 100 m Freestyle

	Age range							
	25–29	30–34	35–39	40–44	45–49	50–54	55–59	60–64
British men	Roland Lee 51.62	Mike Fibbens 50.37	Nocolus Vaughan 53.06	Paul Blackbeard 55.23	Peter Prijdekker 56.86	Ally McGregor 59.12	Duncan McCreadie 59.98	Geoff Stokes 1:05.04
British women	Helen Sadler 59.78	Maxine McKinnell 59.00	Alyson Jones 1:00.71	Margaret Smith 1:02.86	Susan Shrimpton 1:05.20	Carol Fellows 1:06.25	Judy Wilson 1:11.08	Jane Asher 1:13.68
European men	Roland Lee 51.62	Jochen Bruha 51.50	Edwin van Norden 52.23	Laci Perenyi 54.78	Galavtine 55.82	Hans Ljungberg 58.98	Duncan McCreadie 59.98	Peter Berengren 1:01.51
European women	Manuela Stellmach 58.63	Manuela Stellmach 58.78	Karin Seick 57.75	Guylaine Berger 1:00.47	Conny Buys Boer 1:03.75	Carol Fellows 1:06.25	Susana Barkley 1:09.41	Jane Asher 1:13.68
World men	Bjorn Zikarsky 49.91	Mike Fisher 50.37	John Miranda 49.53	Rick Abbott 53.25	Terry Downes 54.64	Keefe Lodwig 56.63	Jack Geoghegan 59.49	Peter Bergenren 1:01.51
World women	Sheila Taormina 56.30	Sandy Neilson 57.35	Sandy Neilson-Bell 57.71	Berger-Talachino 1:00.47	Laura Val 1:01.76	Ardeth Mueller 1:06.41	Susan Barkley 1:09.41	Yoshiko Osaki 1:12.22

	65–69	70–74	75–79	80–84	85–89	90–94	95–99	100–104
British men	Joseph Phillips 1:08.92	Jack Hale 1:10.56	Jack Hale 1:13.35	H.P. Dodd 1:35.02	John Harrison 1:56.57			
British women	Jane Asher 1:17.08	Doreen Cope 1:33.51	Vivienne Cherriman 1:45.53	Vivienne Cherriman 1:53.70	Willy Van Rysel 2:16.87			
European men	Roberto Albeiche 1:02.77	Jack Hale 1:10.56	Jack Hale 1:13.35	Otto Claus 1:20.96	Rein Stadtler 1:36.18	Fritz Mouke 2:11.91		
European women	Jane Asher 1:17.08	Brit Grilli 1:30.85	Virgine Keteleer 1:42.00	Britt Nordin Maj 1:53.21	Nella Gamenara 2:15.70			
World men	Cav Caanaugh 1:02.41	Frank Piemme 1:09.00	Jack Hale 1:13.35	Hikoji Ueki 1:18.80	Jim Eubank 1:23.20	Gastaa Figueiredo 1:56.88	Gus Langner 2:19.51	Tom Lane 4:32.29
World women	Gail Roper 1:16.26	Gail Roper 1:18.67	Margery Meyer 1:33.87	Rita Simonton 1:42.38	Julie Doice 2:05.74	Margot Bates 2:58.33	Marge Anderson 4:35.98	

Short Course Records

Event : 200 m Freestyle

Age range	25–29	30–34	35–39	40–44	45–49	50–54	55–59	60–64
British men	Steven Mellor 1:51.34	Juan Vallejo 1:54.75	Edwin van Norden 1:53.66	Tom Greenwood 2:05.55	Ivan Myall 2:07.16	Ally McGregor 2:08.87	Duncan McCreadie 2:11.21	Geoff Stokes 2:23.18
British women	Alyson Jones 2:09.36	Sarah Garrett 2:11.12	Nuala Muir-Cochrane 2:12.25	Margaret Smith 2:17.34	Jayne Ball 2:25.21	Carol Fellows 2:33.27	Flora Connolly 2:44.69	Jane Asher 2:49.55
European men	Steven Mellor 1:51.34	Juan Vallejo 1:54.75	Edwin van Norden 1:53.66	Thomas Greenwood 2:02.55	Ivan Myall 2:07.16	Alistar MacGregor 2:08.87	Duncan McCreadie 2:11.21	Geoff Stokes 2:23.18
European women	Barbara Kehbein 2:06.08	Barbara Kehbein 2:07.07	Barbara Seick 2:08.12	Margaret Smith 2:17.34	Conny Buys Boer 2:24.31	Brigitte Berten 2:31.95	Susana Barkley 2:37.70	Jane Asher 2:49.55
World men	John Keppeler 1:48.81	Rowdy Gaines 1:50.91	Edwin van Norden 1:53.66	Hess Yntema 1:57.83	Tim Broderick 2:00.13	R Tod Spieker 2:06.51	Duncan McCreadie 2:11.21	Graham Johnston 2:21.31
World women	Sheila Taormina 1:59.78	K. Pipes-Neilsen 2:04.64	K. Pipes-Nielsen 2:03.56	Beth Knight 2:09.53	Laura Val 2:16.07	Diane Foster 2:24.43	Ardeth Mueller 2:28.30	Yoshiko Osaki 2:38.32

Age range	65–69	70–74	75–79	80–84	85–89	90–94	95–99	100–104
British men	Arthur Lowe 2:39.51	Jack Hale 2:47.16	Forbes Gentleman 3:14.16	H.P. Dodd 3:33.0	John Harrison 4:27.88			
British women	Jane Asher 2:50.40	Doreen Cope 3:40.75	Vivienne Cherriman 3:52.86	Edith Hewitt 4:07.83	Willy van Rysel 4:51.48			
European men	Roberto Alberiche 2:22.13	Jesus Dominguez 2:40.15	Karl Hauter 2:54.54	Otto Claus 3:24.58	Rein Stadtler 3:44.09			
European women	Jane Asher 2:50.40	Grethe Beodtsen 3:25.23	Virgine Keteleer 3:41.78	Gertrud Meerwald 4:02.27	Nella Gamenara 5:28.97			
World men	Graham Johnston 2:22.07	William Phillips 2:34.64	Ray Taft 2:48.67	Ray Taft 3:00.63	Jim Eubank 3:13.45	Gasteo Figueredo 4:20.43	Gus Langner 5:13.46	
World women	Jane Asher 2:50.40	Gail Roper 2:25.06	Margery Meyer 3:27.92	Rita Simonton 3:37.21	Maria Lenk 4:36.42	Jewell Cooke 5:45.22		

Short Course Records
Event : 400 m Freestyle

Age range	25–29	30–34	35–39	40–44	45–49	50–54	55–59	60–64
British men	Steven Mellor 3:57.24	Roland Lee 4:05.17	Martyn Price 4:13.48	Ian Proud 4:21.44	Eddie Riach 4:27.42	Sandy Galletly 4:38.22	Duncan McCreadie 4:41.19	Geoff Stokes 5:07.50
British women	Lynne Marshall 4:30.49	Sally Dearden 4:36.31	Nuala Muir-Cochrane 4:33.34	Margaret Smith 4:50.83	Jayne Ball 5:08.10	Sandra O'Neill 5:24.35	Judy Wilson 5:40.90	Jane Asher 5:56.20
European men	Steven Mellor 3:57.24	Roland Lee 4:05.17	Edwin van Norden 4:07.22	Ian Proud 4:21.44	Eddie Riach 4:27.42	Sandy Galletly 4:38.22	Duncan McCreadie 4:41.19	Geoff Stokes 5:07.50
European women	Chantal Duck 4:26.56	Karin Seick 4:33.51	Nuala Muir-Cochrane 4:33.45	Margaret Smith 4:50.83	Karin Milger 5:02.44	Sandra O'Neill 5:24.35	Susana Barkley 5:29.06	Jane Asher 5:56.20
World men	Alex Kostich 3:58.23	Bruce Hayes 3:59.83	Edwin van Norden 4:07.22	William Specht 4:09.10	Jim McConica 4:14.73	R Tod Spieker 4:28.84	Duncan McGesdie 4:43.10	Graham Johnston 4:56.69
World women	Sheila Taormina 4:24.18	K. Pipes-Neilsen 4:22.70	K. Pipes-Nielsen 4:22.56	S. Heim-Bowen 4:34.83	Laura Val 4:49.52	Barbara Dunbar 4:59.56	Ardeth Mueller 5:15.91	Yoshiko Osaki 5:30.24

Age range	65–69	70–74	75–79	80–84	85–89	90–94	95–99	100–104
British men	Arthur Lowe 5:40.29	Ken McKay 6:10.48	Ray Brookouse 7:07.90	H.P Dodd 7:32.46	John Harrison 9:28.06			
British women	Jane Asher 6:00.99	Jane Asher 6:10.10	Vivienne Cherriman 7:56.05	Vivienne Cherriman 8:51.10	Willy van Rysel 9:58.35			
European men	Don Bland 5:40.29	Jesus Dominguez 5:53.77	Karl Hauter 6:04.20	Otto Kutz 7:16.62	Rein Stadtler 8:25.47			
European women	Jane Asher 6:00.99	Brit Grill 7:02.30	Virgine Keteleer 7:43.40	Gertrud Meerwald 8:10.68				
World men	Graham Johnston 5:09.09	Frank Piemme 5:35.49	Ray Taft 6:02.95	Ray Taft 6:27.60	Jim Eubank 7:22.31	Gus Langner 8:50.65	Gus Langner 10:51.93	
World women	Jane Asher 6:00.99	Gail Roper 6:27.21	Margery Meyer 7:01.36	Rita Simonton 7:33.69	Maria Lenk 9:27.25	Anna Bauscher 14:16.35		

Short Course Records

Event : 800 m Freestyle

Age range	25–29	30–34	35–39	40–44	45–49	50–54	55–59	60–64	100–104
British men	Neil Sloan 8:45.00	Colin Ovington 8:45.41	Ian Proud 9:13.06	Willaim Hempel 9:17.35	Eddie Riach 9:27.49	Sandy Galletly 9:38.02	Sandy Galletly 9:47.45	Geoff Stokes 10:44.13	
British women	Carol MacIntyre 9:26.95	Susan Hill 9:37.42	Nuala Muir-Cochrane 9:23.86	Margaret Smith 10:04.87	Jayne Ball 10:36.68	Sandra O'Neill 11:24.29	Jane Asher 12:02.16	Jane Asher 12:29.23	
European men	Tony Lennartson 8:29.19	Tony Lennartson 8:35.17	Juan Vallejo 9:04.25	White 9:04.91	Eddie Riach 9:27.49	Uijtenbogart 9:35.73	Sandy Galletly 9:47.45	Fabrizo Momoni 10:43.50	
European women	Chantal Duck 9:15.02	Susan Hill 9:37.42	Nuala Muir-Cochrane 9:23.79	Margaret Smith 10:04.87	Jayne Ball 10:36.68	Margareta Rainer 11:19.71	Hannelore Rose 11:55.75	Jane Asher 12:29.23	
World men	Alex Kostich 8:14.75	Bruce Hayes 8:19.44	Bobby Patten 8:29.31	Hess Yntema 8:49.83	Tim Broderick 8:56.08	R Tod Spieker 9:12.81	Sandy Galletly 9:47.45	Graham Johnston 10:27.62	
World women	Sheila Taormina 8:51.18	K. Pipes-Neilsen 9:08.34	K. Pipes-Nielsen 9:15.40	S. Heim-Bowen 9:29.90	Laura Val 9:56.23	Diane Foster 10:23.48	Jen Thomasson 11:04.01	Yoshiko Osaki 11:18.60	

Age range	65–69	70–74	75–79	80–84	85–89	90–94	95–99	100–104
British men	Donald Bland 11:39.71	Jack Hale 13:01.75	Ray Brookouse 14:22.51	Jim Masterson 16:07.20	John Harrison 19:25.93			
British women	Jane Asher 12:26.75	Jane Asher 12:32.86	Willy van Rysel 17:02.67	Vivienne Cherriman 18:11.91	Willy van Rysel 20:13.49			
European men	Don Bland 11:39.71	Jesus Dominguez 12:05.80	Celio Brunelleschi 13:14.50	Nils Ferm 15:23.05	John Harrison 19:25.93			
European women	Jane Asher 12:26.85	Brit Grilli 14:15.96	Willy van Rysel 17:02.67	Vivienne Cherriman 18:11.91				
World men	Graham Johnston 10:35.13	Frank Piemme 11:38.41	Ray Taft 12:45.40	Ray Taft 13:29.27	Tokushi Komeda 16:19.95	Gus Langer 22:05.55	Gus Langer 22:05.55	
World women	Jane Asher 12:26.85	June Krauser 13:07.28	Margery Meyer 14:46.26	Rita Simonton 15:49.21	Maine Merlino 19:41.58	Anna Bauscher 28:45.45		

Short Course Records
Event: 1500 m Freestyle

Age range	25–29	30–34	35–39	40–44	45–49	50–54	55–59	60–64
British men	Tony Day 16:26.54	Colin Ovington 16:49.97	Robin Brew 16:57.90	Ian Proud 17:42.29	Eddie Rich 18:05.56	Sandy Galletly 18:32.56	Sandy Galletly 18:51.83	Michael Edwards 20:59.93
British women	Deborah Hamilton 18:18.84	Claire Sweeney 19:00.40	Nuala Muir-Cochrane 17:54.55	Margaret Smith 19:20.62	Jayne Ball 20:40.70	Sandra O'Neill 21:52.62	Elaine Blower 23:08.81	Jane Asher 24:21.16
European men	Tony Day 16:26.54	Edwin van Norden 16:47.64	Jimmy Furrer 16:47.64	Jimmy Furrer 17:40.77	Uijtenbogaart 18:23.21	Uijtenbogaart 18:18.49	Sandy Galletly 18:51.83	Michael Edwards 20:59.93
European women	Deborah Hamilton 18:18.84	Judith Heydens 18:44.91	Nuala Muir-Cochrane 17:54.55	Lorraine Betts 20:19.97	Karin Milger 20:35.48	Sandra O'Neill 21:52.62	Hannelore Rose 22:40.31	Jane Asher 24:21.16
World men	Alex Kostich 15:41.81	Bruce Hayes 16:21.25	Bobby Patten 15:58.20	Hess Yntema 16:51.71	Jim McConica 16:51.21	R Tod Spieker 17:36.51	Sandy Galletly 18:51.83	Graham Johnston 19:48.44
World women	Sheila Taormina 16:36.07	Karen Burton 17:23.16	K. Pipes-Nielsen 17:36.24	S. Heim-Bowen 18:02.62	Laura Val 18:55.82	Barbara Dunbar 19:59.03	Jen Thomasson 20:49.11	Yoshiko Osaki 21:59.83

Age range	65–69	70–74	75–79	80–84	85–89	90–94	95–99	100–104
British men	Donald Bland 21:56.09	Forbes Gentleman 24:50.67	Ray Brookhouse 28:02.03	Harold Dodd 31:20.10	John Harrison 36:57.22			
British women	Jane Asher 23:44.34	Daphne Gilbert 30:50.18	Willy Van Rysel 32:16.46	Vivienne Cherriman 35:44.26				
European men	Donald Bland 21:56.09	Valentin Weber 23:32.02	Kar Bayerlein 27:35.06	Otto Kutz 29:54.78	John Harrison 36:57.22			
European women	Jane Asher 23:44.34	Daphne Gilbert 30:50.18	Willy van Rysel 32:16.46	Vivienne Cherriman 35:44.26				
World men	Graham Johnston 19:53.18	William Phillips 22:30.87	Aldo Da Rosa 24:46.19	Ray Taft 25:35.01	Tokushi Komeda 30:31.85	Gus Lagner 44:48.99	Gus Langner 41:29.87	
World women	Clara Walker 23:38.44	June Krauser 24:57.85	Margery Meyer 27:47.25	Rita Simonton 29:48.75	Maxine Merlino 37:28.53			

Short Course Records
Event: 50 m Backstroke

Age range	25–29	30–34	35–39	40–44	45–49	50–54	55–59	60–64
British men	Martin Harris 25.43	Martin Harris 26.03	Paul Morris 29.10	Kevin Parfoot 29.61	Eddie Riach 30.05	Graham Sykes 31.60	Graham Sykes 32.40	Graham Sykes 33.89
British women	Kitty Edbrooke 31.14	Helen Jameson 30.94	Helen Jameson 31.03	Lesley Wilde 33.31	Sylvia Platt-Rogers 34.70	Carol Fellows 34.97	Margaret Wilding 36.99	Margaret Wilding 36.92
European men	Martin Harris 25.43	Martin Harris 26.03	Craig Norrey 27.77	Dariusz Wolny 28.57	Laci Perenyi 29.33	Graham Sykes 31.06	Joszef Csikany 31.92	Frans van Enst 33.84
European women	Cornelia Seithe 30.87	Therese Lundin 29.13	Helen Jameson 31.03	Lesley Wilde 33.31	Bendicte Duprez 33.95	Carol Fellows 34.97	Margaret Wilding 36.99	Margaret Wilding 36.92
World men	Martin Harris 25.43	Martin Harris 26.03	Clay Britt 26.84	William Specht 27.84	Claflin/Galavtin 28.81	Hugh Wilder 29.50	Robert Smith 30.35	Akihiko Yabe 33.62
World women	Gisele Pereira 30.32	D. Graner 30.14	K.Pipes-Nielsen 30.73	Laura Val 31.55	Laura Val 32.39	Carol Fellows 34.97	S Nabuco de Abreu 35.82	Margaret Wilding 37.75

Age range	65–69	70–74	75–79	80–84	85–89	90–94	95–99	100–104
British men	Cliff Ward 36.83	Jack Hale 36.97	Jack Hale 38.83	Graham Huxtable 51.64	John Harrison 54.49	George Onion 1:32.79		
British women	Jane Asher 42.67	Willy Van Rysel 45.08	Willy Van Rysel 48.75	Willy Van Rysel 55.58	Willy Van Rysel 1:01.63			
European men	Cliff Ward 36.83	Jack Hale 36.97	Jack Hale 38.83	Otto Claus 43.17	Reinstadtler 47.17			
European women	Grethe Bendtsen 142.00	Grethe Bendtsen 42.86	Willy Van Rysel 46.79	Willy Van Rysel 55.58	Dorothy Weston 1:10.95	Margarete Gottschalk 1:15.02		
World men	Yoshi Oyakawa 33.38	Paul Hutinger 35.71	Keiro Nakamura 37.47	Shoichi Sakamoto 42.16	Joshiji Sato 46.08	Gastao Figueiredo 1:01.03	Gus Langner 1:27.67	Tom Lane 2:02.52
World women	Doris Steadman 40.48	Doris Steadman 42.58	Doris Steadman 44.76	Willy Van Rysel 55.58	Masa Shigemitsu 58.58	M Gottschalk 1:15.02	Marge Anderson 2:05.36	

Short Course Records
Event: 100 m Backstroke

Age range	25–29	30–34	35–39	40–44	45–49	50–54	55–59	60–64
British men	Martin Harris 54.82	Martin Harris 55.78	Steve Burcham 1:02.19	Steve Burcham 1:02.35	Eddie Riach 1:04.11	Graham Harris 1:09.58	John Gordon 1:12.44	Graham Sykes 1:17.46
British women	Kitty Edbrooke 1:06.14	Jo Swatton 1:06.73	Helen Jameson 1:07.87	Lesley Wilde 1:10.99	Sylvia Platt-Rogers 1:15.46	Sandra O'Neill 1:19.16	Margaret Wilding 1:20.73	Margaret Wilding 1:21.88
European men	Martin Harris 54.82	Martin Harris 55.78	Edwin van Norden 59.11	Dariusz Wolny 1:01.11	Vladimir Galavtine 1:02.31	Ioszef Csikany 1:10.20	Ioszef Csikany 1:10.36	Graham Sykes 1:17.46
European women	Berit Puggaard 1:04.50	Therese Lundin 1:06.62	Karin Seick 1:05.93	Lesley Wilde 1:10.99	Sylvia Platt-Rogers 1:15.45	Sandra O'Neill 1:19.16	Margaret Wilding 1:20.73	Margaret Wilding 1:21.88
World men	Martin Harris 54.82	Martin Harris 55.78	Clay Britt 58.25	William Specht 59.26	V. Galavtin 1:02.31	Hugh Wilder 1:04.17	Richard Burns 1:08.34	Gary Chase 1:12.42
World women	Berit Puggaard 1:04.50	K.Pipes-Nielsen 1:03.96	K. Pipes-Nielsen 1:03.56	Laura Val 1:10.45	Laura Val 1:10.76	Sandra O'Neill 1:19.16	Satoko Takeuji 1:19.61	Margaret Wilding 1:22.31

Age range	65–69	70–74	75–79	80–84	85–89	90–94	95–99	100–104
British men	Roger Burrell 1:22.53	Jack Hale 1:25.01	Jack Hale 1:26.40	Graham Huxtable 1:55.29	John Harrison 2:04.07	George Onion 3:22.97		
British women	Jane Asher 1:32.80	Willy Van Rysel 1:44.02	Willy Van Rysel 1:48.13	Willy Van Rysel 2:03.47	Willy Van Rysel 2:14.54			
European men	Roger Burrell 1:22.53	Jack Hale 1:25.01	Jack Hale 1:26.40	Reinstadtler 1:43.79	Reinstadtler 1:50.96	George Onion 3:22.97		
European women	Grethe Bendtsen 1:31.33	Grethe Bendtsen 1:34.51	Willy Van Rysel 1:48.13	Willy Van Rysel 2:03.47	Dorothy Weston 2:23.91	Margarete Gottschalk 2:45.49		
World men	Yoshi Oyakawa 1:14.66	Paul Hutinger 1:21.74	Keijro Nakamura 1:24.21	Ray Taft 1:33.58	Toshiji Sato 1:40.25	Nori Yamanoto 2:29.06	Gus Langner 3:38.07	
World women	Doris Steadman 1:30.41	Doris Steadman 1:35.66	Doris Steadman 1:40.47	Edith Thein 1:57.69	Maria Lenk 2:11.54	M Gottschalk 2:45.496		

Short Course Records
Event : 200 m Backstroke

Age range	25–29	30–34	35–39	40–44	45–49	50–54	55–59	60–64
British men	Martin Harris 2:01.78	Paul Griffiths 2:10.35	Edwin van Norden 2:09.92	Eddie Riach 2:18.26	Eddie Riach 2:18.26	Ivan Mayall 2:31.43	Joszef Czikany 2:34.67	Tom Walker 2:49.19
British women	Michelle Bingham 2:24.51	Jo Swatton 2:19.66	Nuala Muir-Cochrane 2:28.24	Lesley Wilde 2:30.26	Anne Cork 2:41.91	Sandra O'Neill 2:52.16	Margaret Wilding 2:58.47	Margaret Wilding 2:57.92
European men	Martin Harris 2:01.78	Paul Griffiths 2:10.35	Edwin van Norden 2:09.92	Eddie Riach 2:18.26	Eddie Riach 2:18.98	Ivan Mayall 2:31.43	Joszef Czitany 2:34.67	Thomas Walker 2:49.19
European women	Jolande de Rover 2:17.86	Jo Swatton 2:19.66	Daphne Fuchs 2:22.81	Lesley Wilde 2:32.03	Bendicte Duprez 2:38.02	Sandra O'Neill 2:52.16	Margaret Wilding 2:58.47	Margaret Wilding 2:57.92
World men	Martin Harris 2:01.78	John Keppeler 2:02.91	Jerome Frentsos 2:07.12	Willian Specht 2:09.61	Eddie Riach 2:18.98	R. Tod Spieker 2:20.42	John Calvert 2:26.64	Jack Beattie 2:40.75
World women	Jolande de Rover 2:17.86	K. Pipes-Nielsen 2:16.62	K. Pipes-Nielsen 2:14.10	Lesley Wilde 2:32.88	Nancy Fisher 2:37.35	Ardeth Mueller 2:48.88	Margaret Wilding 2:58.47	Betsy Jordan 3:05.27

Age range	65–69	70–74	75–79	80–84	85–89	90–94	95–99	100–104
British men	Tom Walker 2:59.59	Jack Hale 3:13.43	John Davis 3:50.34	Bob Taylor 4:14.28	John Harrison 4:17.43	George Onion 7:12.87		
British women	Flora Connolly 3:18.42	Willy Van Rysel 3:53.86	Willy Van Rysel 3:59.85	Willy Van Rysel 4:35.63	Dorothy Weston 5:28.52			
European men	Thomas Walker 2:59.59	Jack Hale 3:13.43	Jack Hale 3:17.80	Carl Scherer 3:40.75	Carl Scherer 4:05.25	George Onion 7:12.87		
European women	Flora Connolly 3:18.42	Grethe Bendtsen 3:30.33	Willy Van Rysel 3:59.85	Willy Van Rysel 4:35.63	Rina Davoglia 5:23.00			
World men	S. Sekikawa 2:47.59	Roger Franks 2:55.73	Keijiro Nakamura 3:09.22	Ray Taft 3:23.73	Carl Sherrer 4:05.25	Gastao Figuerdo 4:56.91	Gus Langner 8:32.34	
World women	Doris Steadman 3:15.72	Doris Steadman 3:27.79	Doris Steadman 3:38.25	Edith Thein 4:03.55	Maria Lenk 4:41.34	Jewell Cooke 6:32.92		

Short Course Records
Event: 50 m Butterfly

Age range	25–29	30–34	35–39	40–44	45–49	50–54	55–59	60–64
British men	Martin Harris 25.41	Mike Fibbens 25.50	Nicolus Vaughan 26.13	Paul Morris 26.43	Tony Jarvis 28.44	Eric Henderson 29.20	Bod Lord 30.92	Jack Hale 32.48
British women	Sharron Davies 29.63	Suki Brownsdon 29.33	Marie Sadler 30.38	Marie Sadler 29.45	Liz Rutherford 32.65	Judy Wilson 33.09	Judy Wilson 31.92	Jane Asher 38.40
European men	Jiri Mikula 25.10	Mike Fibbens 25.50	Edwin van Norden 25.95	Paul Morris 26.43	Vladimir Galavtine 28.00	Bernd Schroeder 28.35	Josep Claret 28.92	Peter Berengren 30.25
European women	Monica Cuervo 28.95	Suki Brownsdon 29.33	Barbara Gellrich 29.81	Marie Sadler 29.45	Angela Zingler 31.52	Judy Wilson 33.09	Judy Wilson 31.92	Haike Holer 37.14
World men	Jonas Akesson 25.20	Brian Alderman 24.64	William Specht 25.89	Ramon Gamboa 25.80	Dan Thompson 27.08	Steve Borowski 27.55	Jim Dragon 28.57	Chitoshi Konishi 29.81
World women	Sheila Taormina 28.68	Wenke Hansen 28.84	Tracie Moll 29.29	Laura Val 30.17	Laura Val 30.50	Judy Wilson 33.09	Judy Wilson 33.23	Yoshiko Osaki 36.04

Age range	65–69	70–74	75–79	80–84	85–89	90–94	95–99	100–104
British men	John Jacey 34.25	Jack Hale 35.35	Jack Hale 38.00	Ernest Clemmett 1:06.65				
British women	Jane Asher 39.11	Jane Asher 41.79	Margaret Evans 59.56	Dorothy Weston 1:07.83	Dorothy Weston 1:24.60			
European men	Jack Hale 32.48	Jack Hale 35.35	Robert Pfersdorff 37.18	Gerhard Hein 48.81	Reinstadtler 57.89			
European women	Jane Asher 39.11	Edith Bohm 45.44	Agnes Plisson 55.56	Gertrud Meerwald 1:01.24				
World men	Ron Johnson 31.65	Frank Piemme 34.77	Robert Pferdorf 37.18	Andrew Holden 41.87	Walter Pfeiffer 52.74	Jim Penfold 1:16.38		
World women	Hisako Sato 38.09	Gail Roper 40.60	Lois Kivi Nochman 47.88	Gertrud Meerwald 1:01.24	Jean Durston 1:07.35	Jewel Cooke 1:49.08		

Short Course Records
Event: 100 m Butterfly

Age range	25–29	30–34	35–39	40–44	45–49	50–54	55–59	60–64
British men	John Bradley 57.17	Ian Beck 57.65	Paul Morris 58.16	Paul Morris 59.78	Eric Henderson 1:03.42	Peter Godfrey 1:05.89	Derek Parr 1:10.78	David Cumming 1:13.35
British women	Jackie Thompson 1:05.24	Kate Veale 1:04.51	Marie Sadler 1:08.55	Marie Sadler 1:06.45	Judy Wilson 1:14.85	Judy Wilson 1:17.39	Judy Wilson 1:15.03	Flora Connolly 1:29.99
European men	John Bradley 57.17	Ian Beck 57.65	Paul Morris 58.16	Paul Morris 59.78	Eric Henderson 1:03.42	Peter Godfrey 1:05.89	Bernd Schroder 1:06.29	David Cumming 1:13.35
European women	Monica Cuervo 1:04.96	Katherine Veale 1:04.51	Barbara Gellrich 1:06.53	Marie Sadler 1:06.45	Conny Boer Buijs 1:13.20	Susana Beakley 1:16.06	Judy Wilson 1:15.03	Christel Schulz 1:27.62
World men	Roberto Neto 55.85	Hiroshi Miura 54.82	William Specjt 57.02	William Specht 56.18	Tom Perrin 1:01.13	Boo Graner Gallas 1:02.54	Poiteman/Schroder 1:06.29	Chitoshi Konishi 1:09.68
World women	Sheila Taormina 1:01.33	K.Pipes-Nielsen 1:03.80	K. Pipes-Nielsen 1:03.29	Marie Sadler 1:06.61	Laura Val 1:07.80	Ardeth Mueller 1:12.66	Judy Wilson 1:16.17	Yoshiko Osaki 1:23.78

Age range	65–69	70–74	75–79	80–84	85–89	90–94	95–99	100–104
British men	Seymour Banning 1:25.21	Jack Hale 1:27.28	Donald Leader 1:55.33	Ernest Clemmett 2:36.15				
British women	Flora Connolly 1:36.95	Margaret Evans 1:57.43	n/a	Dorothy Weston 2:29.66				
European men	Werner Muller 1:20.01	Karl Heinz Knops 1:27.21	Robert Pfersdorff 1:32.07	Luigi Davoglio 1:50.97	Reinstadler 2:23.30			
European women	Flora Connolly 1:36.95	Silvia Neuhauser 1:46.23	Anne Pottier 2:18.68	Gertrud Meerwald 2:22.05				
World men	Ron Johnson 1:16.70	Joe Kurtzman 1:26.98	Paul Krup 1:36.80	Paul Krup 1:47.20	Walter Pfeiffer 2:04.50			
World women	Gail Roper 1:33.10	Gail Roper 1:37.56	Lois Kivi Nochman 1:56.42	Gertrud Meerwald 2:22.05	Jean Durston 2:36.50	Jewell Cooke 4:06.32		

Short Course Records
Event : 200 m Butterfly

Age range	25–29	30–34	35–39	40–44	45–49	50–54	55–59	60–64
British men	Steven Mellor 2:05.26	Ian Beck 2:05.73	Ian Beck 2:11.74	Allan Gentleman 2:19.94	Eric Henderson 2:27.64	Sandy Galletly 2:36.26	Derek Parr 2:42.36	David Cumming 2:54.48
British women	Jackie Thompson 2:23.30	Kate Veale 2:24.17	Lesley Norton 2:36.03	Judy Hattle 2:34.41	Jayne Ball 2:57.91	Bernice Wilkins 3:04.03	Judy Wilson 3:02.63	Flora Connolly 3:17.00
European men	Steven Mellor 2:05.26	Ian Beck 2:05.73	Ian Beck 2:11.74	Hugo Bregman 2:16.22	Lorenzo Marugo 2:26.38	Jacek Krawczyk 2:26.45	Bernd Schroder 2:41.73	Gunter Schopke 2:46.18
European women	Barbara Kehbein 2:20.82	Katherine Veale 2:24.17	Barbara Gellrich 2:29.56	Judy Hattle 2:34.41	Bloch Morche 2:55.10	Susana Backley 3:02.43	Judy Wilson 3:02.63	Flora Connolly 3:17.00
World men	Gavin Lilley 2:05.97	Hiroshi Miura 2:00.21	Bobby Patten 2:04.50	William Specht 2:02.97	David Vandam 2:18.31	Boo Graner Gallas 2:21.58	Robert Poiletman 2:31.16	Gunter Schopke 2:46.18
World women	S. Palmer White 2:17.13	K. Pipes Neilsen 2:19.64	K. Pipes Neilsen 2:18.41	Laura Val 2:29.19	Laura Val 2:32.52	Barbara Dunbar 2:44.84	Ardeth Mueller 2:55.05	Yoshiko Osaki 3:05.20

Age range	65–69	70–74	75–79	80–84	85–89	90–94	95–99	100–104
British men	Seymour Banning 3:17.13	Donald Leader 3:54.53	Donald Leader 4:15.30	Ernest Clemmett 5:47.33				
British women	Flora Connolly 3:31.57	Margaret Evans 4:17.53	n/a	Dorothy Weston 5:39.29				
European men	Jesus Dominguez 3:13.57	Robert Pfersdorff 3:26.72	Ernest Clemett 5:47.33					
European women	Flora Connolly 3:31.57	Silvia Neuhauser 3:53.51	Anne Pottier 7:07.32	Dorothy Weston 5:39.29				
World men	Werner Muller 3:06.32	Jesus Dominguez 3:13.57	Robert Pferdorf 3:26.72	Anton Cerer 4:00.64	Walter Pfeiffer 4:45.09			
World women	Flora Connolly 3:31.57	June Krauser 3:38.39	Lois Kivi Nochman 4:08.39	Maxine Merlino 5:22.65	Jean Durston 5:42.80			

Short Course Records
Event: 50 m Breaststroke

Age range	25–29	30–34	35–39	40–44	45–49	50–54	55–59	60–64
British men	Nick Polkinghorne 29.12	Paul Shackley 30.24	Jim Hobsley 31.23	Simon Garside 31.45	Neville Barton 32.53	John Liron 33.32	Chris Jones 36.20	Tom Walker 36.60
British women	Charlotte Mustard 34.12	Suki Brownsdon 33.08	Verity Dobble 36.29	Marggie Kelly 33.83	Elaine Bromwich 38.67	Elaine Bromwich 39.24	Elain Bromwich 40.28	Flora Connolly 42.96
European men	Peter Lang 28.90	Willy Penet 29.58	Gerald Morken 28.87	Gerhard Ammer 29.50	Kees Uijtenhout 31.87	John Liron 33.32	Gunter Schmah 34.25	Eron Henninger 34.88
European women	Ria Willemse 33.60	Suki Brownsdon 33.13	Dagma Hilbig 33.89	Maggie Kelly 33.83	Bea Pool 37.45	Erna Vahrmijer 38.82	Minka Senftleben 38.98	Edith Bohm 42.02
World men	Hideaki Togo 28.69	Dean Putterman 29.21	Wally Dicks 28.82	Gerhard Ammer 29.50	Robert Strand 31.83	Don McKenzie 31.24	Hiroshi Kotegawa 33.17	Yoshiko Osaki 33.64
World women	Ria Willemse 33.60	Suki Brownsdon 33.13	Caroline Krattli 34.38	Eva M. Hakansson 35.22	Naomi Heimbach 36.69	Ian MacLeod 38.48	Monika Senftleben 38.98	Jaoann Leilich 41.35

Age range	65–69	70–74	75–79	80–84	85–89	90–94	95–99	100–104
British men	Tom Walker 39.05	Roy Romain 42.74	Roy Romain 43.19	Ken Stillwell 55.52	Derrick Davey 59.95	George Onion 1:38.97		
British women	Flora Connolly 44.87	Maud Povey 49.15	Maud Povey 54.77	Dorothy Weston 1:10.27	Dorothy Weston 1:10.47			
European men	Jack Anderson 38.01	Karl Heinz Knops 38.99	Robert Pfersdorff 40.22	Karl Wittenberg 45.52	Karl Wittenberg 51.17	Hans Paul 1:05.73		
European women	Elaine Pellis 43.27	Edith Bohm 45.08	Ingeborg Fritze 53.28	Gertrud Meerwald 59.26	Pauli Emmi 1:09.28	Margarete Gottschalk 1:25.24		
World men	Hiroshi Katewawa 35.96	Toshio Tajima 38.60	Toshio Tajima 39.97	Y Miyamoto 44.56	Hiromu Yoshimoto 48.82	Hans Paul 1:05.70	Gus Langner 1:31.60	
World women	Elaine Pellis 43.27	Edith Boehm 45.08	Satoko Suzuki 49.57	Gertrud Meerwald 59.29	Maria Lenk 1:08.39	Margarete Gottschalk 1:25.24		

Short Course Records
Event : 100 m Breaststroke

Age range	25–29	30–34	35–39	40–44	45–49	50–54	55–59	60–64
British men	Nick Polkinghorne 1:03.29	Nick Gillingham 1:04.59	Dave Milburn 1:08.20	Anthony O'Driscoll 1:08.48	Neville Barton 1:13.23	Denis Thys 1:18.49	Tom Walker 1:19.42	Tom Walker 1:20.29
British women	Helen Douthwaite 1:13.99	Suki Brownsdon 1:11.81	Verity Dobble 1:20.14	Maggie Kelly 1:14.29	Elaine Bromwich 1:25.20	Elaine Bromwich 1:28.34	Flora Connolly 1:28.13	Flora Connolly 1:32.12
European men	Nick Polkinghorne 1:03.29	Glen Christiansen 1:04.10	Gerald Morken 1:04.02	Glen Christiansen 1:06.72	Lorenzo Marugo 1:11.50	Gianni Gross 1:14.70	Gunter Schmah 1:17.06	Tom Walker 1:20.29
European women	Manueka Nackel 1:10.71	Suki Brownsdon 1:11.81	Dagma Hilbig 1:16.40	Maggie Kelly 1:14.29	Ulrike Urbaniak 1:21.29	Christane Heeren 1:24.45	Flora Connolly 1:28.13	Flora Connolly 1:32.12
World men	Hideaki Togo 1:02.87	Roque Santos 1:03.64	Wally Dicks 1:03.18	Ron Schafer 1:06.50	Robert Strand 1:09.44	Robert Strand 1:09.96	Manuel Sangully 1:16.32	Jack Kelso 1:17.85
World women	Manueka Naechel 1:10.71	Wenke Hansen 1:11.13	Caroline Krattli 1:15.00	Eva Hakannson 1:18.59	Ulrike Urbaniak 1:21.38	Christane Heeren 1:24.45	Bonnie Pronk 1:25.92	Joann Leilich 1:30.58

Age range	65–69	70–74	75–79	80–84	85–89	90–94	95–99	100–104
British men	Tom Walker 1:24.82	Jim Motion 1:42.10	Ray Brookhouse 1:52.48	Phil Merryweather 2:14.10	Derrick Davey 2:14.35			
British women	Flora Connolly 1:34.93	Margaret Evans 1:53.73	Audrey Gathercole 2:03.82	Dorothy Weston 2:14.40	Dorothy Weston 2:38.91			
European men	Tom Walker 1:24.94	Robert Pfersdorff 1:28.61	Augusto Romano 1:46.59	Rolf Abel 2:10.09				
European women	Flora Connolly 1:34.93	Edith Bohm 1:42.62	Hildegard Messing 1:59.41	Gertrud Meerwald 2:08.23	Dorothy Weston 2:38.75	Margarete Gottschalk 3:25.74		
World men	Nick Templeman 1:21.34	Barton Greenberg 1:29.48	Robert Pfersdorf 1:28.61	Y Miyamoto 1:43.91	Hiromu Yoshimoto 1:50.32	Jim Penfield 2:45.20	Gus Langner 3:35.33	
World women	Masayo Azuma 1:34.50	Edith Boehm 1:42.62	Satoko Suzuki 1:49.77	Gertrud Meerwald 2:08.23	Maria Lenk 2:329.90	Margarete Gottschalk 3:25.74		

Short Course Records
Event : 200 m Breaststroke

Age range	25–29	30–34	35–39	40–44	45–49	50–54	55–59	60–64
British men	Martin Douglas 2:23.66	Nick Gillingham 2:25.43	Dave Milburn 2:30.29	Anthony O'Driscoll 2:29.86	Bill Price 2:48.61	Charles Doxat 2:52.28	Tom Walker 2:54.70	Tom Walker 2:57.08
British women	Helen Gorman 2:37.35	Suki Brownsdon 2:40.08	Verity Dobble 2:53.58	Amanda Heath 2:49.01	Jennifer Merritt 3:02.78	Diane Ford 3:06.63	Elaine Bromwich 3:11.28	Flora Connolly 3:19.67
European men	Martin Douglas 2:23.66	Glen Christiansen 2:22.80	Edwin van Norden 2:26.33	Glen Christiansen 2:27.86	Gerd Kruger 2:40.98	Peter Hofft 2:48.77	Tom Walker 2:54.70	Tom Walker 2:57.08
European women	Nathalie Elorrietta 2:37.16	Sylvia Gerasch 2:39.65	Dagma Hilbig 2:44.81	Dagmar Hilbig 2:47.54	Ulrike Urbaniak 2:54.97	Christiane Heeren 3:00.98	Hannelore Rose 3:10.93	Flora Connolly 3:19.67
World men	Abraham Solano 2:20.43	Roque Santos 2:17.56	Serge Score 2:22.64	Ron Schafer 2:25.58	Rick Colella 2:34.24	Robert Strand 2:34.71	Tegze Haraszti 2:49.21	Michael Molony 2:56.18
World women	N Elorrieta 2:37.16	Wenke Hansen 2:34.09	Caroline Krattli 2:43.61	Dagmar Hilbig 2:47.54	Ulrike Urbaniak 2:54.97	Christiane Heeren 3:00.98	Bonnie Pronk 3:08.87	Joann Leilich 3:18.34

Age range	65–69	70–74	75–79	80–84	85–89	90–94	95–99	100–104
British men	Tom Walker 3:03.31	Roy Romain 3:43.09	John Davis 4:05.51	Ken Stillwell 4:41.47	Chester Kozlowski 5:40.93			
British women	Flora Connolly 3:25.67	Margaret Evans 3:55.30	Dorothy Williams 4:25.13	Dorothy Weston 4:45.97				
European men	Tom Walker 3:03.31	Karl Hauter 3:16.44	Karl Hauter 3:21.50	Johann Morscher 4:07.75	Chester Kozlowski 5:40.93			
European women	Flora Connolly 3:25.67	Sylvia Neuhauser 3:45.96	Agnes Plisson 4:20.48	Dorothy Weston 4:45.97				
World men	Peter Bell 3:05.24	Karl Hauter 3:16.44	Robert Pfersdorf 3:24.84	Aldo Da Rosa 3:56.61	Hiromu Yoshimoto 4:20.67	Gus Langner 6:41.56	Gus Langner 7:29.31	
World women	Flora Connolly 3:25.67	Sylvia Neuhauser 3:45.96	Agnes Plisson 4:20.48	Rita Simonton 4:49.62	Marti Gogniat 5:59.36	Jewel Cook 9:03.85		

Short Course Records

Event: 100 m individual medley

Age range	25–29	30–34	35–39	40–44	45–49	50–54	55–59	60–64	100–104
British men	Martin Harris 56.90	Martin Harris 58.09	Robin Brew 1:100.17	Paul Morris 1:04.22	Trevor Clark 1:06.20	Alistair MacGregor 1:07.66	Duncan McCreadie 1:10.29	Keith Ingram 1:17.18	
British women	Sarah Garrett 1:07.48	Suki Brownsdon 1:06.40	Alyson Jones 1:11.40	Maggie Kelly 1:08.48	Sandra O'Neill 1:15.52	Carol Fellows 1:17.98	Judy Wilson 1:24.25	Margaret Wilding 1:24.97	
European men	Martin Harris 56.90	Martin Harris 58.09	Edwin Van Norden 59.29	Dariusz Wolny 1:01.95	Vladimir Galavtine 1:03.22	Alistair MacGregor 1:07.66	Bernd Schroder 1:09.59	Peter Bergengren 1:13.81	
European women	Manueka Nackel 1:06.60	Sylvia Gerasch 1:05.10	Ineke Hond 1:09.96	Maggie Kelly 1:08.48	Angela Zingler 1:14.23	Carol Fellows 1:17.98	Susana Barkley 1:20.81	Christel Schultz 1:24.53	
World men	Martin Harris 56.90	Hiroshi Miura 57.84	Jerome Frentsos 59.11	Dariusz Wolny 1:01.95	Tom Reudy 1:02.99	Robert Strand 1:04.97	Robert Smith 1:09.02	Jack Kelso 1:09.93	
World women	Wenke Hansen 1:05.67	Wenke Hansen 1:04.96	K. Pipes-Neilsen 1:05.74	Jenny Whiteley 1:11.13	Laura Val 1:11.82	Carol Fellows 1:17.98	Susana Barkley 1:20.81	Yoshiko Osaki 1:23.16	

Age range	65–69	70–74	75–79	80–84	85–89	90–94	95–99
British men	Tom Walker 1:21.83	Forbes Gentleman 1:30.41	Roy Romain 1:41.20	Ray Brookhouse 1:58.34	John Harrison 2:29.18		
British women	Jane Asher 1:30.70	Margaret Evans 1:52.06	Audrey Gathercole 2:00.14	Dorothy Weston 2:07.57	Dorothy Weston 2:32.74		
European men	Roberto Alberiche 1:16.79	Karl Hauter 1:26.25	Karl Hauter 1:25.36	Herhard Hein 1:48.40	Rein Stadtler 1:56.26		
European women	Jane Asher 1:30.70	Grethe Bendsten 1:39.14	Agnes Plisson 1:51.58	Gertrud Meerwald 2:03.87	Dorothy Weston 2:32.74		
World men	Ron Johnson 1:15.61	Frank Piemme 1:20.99	Ray Taft 1:27.43	Ray Taft 1:35.31	Walter Pfeiffer 1:51.87	Nori Yamauoto 2:32.79	Gus Langner 3:33.98
World women	Gail Roper 1:28.95	Gail Roper 1:32.23	Doris McEwan 1:47.56	Gertrud Meerwald 2:03.87	Maria Lenk 2:22.10	Jewel Cook 3:13.87	

Short Course Records
Event : 200 m individual medley

Age range	25–29	30–34	35–39	40–44	45–49	50–54	55–59	60–64
British men	Martin Harris 2:10.48	Paul Brew 2:06.69	Robin Brew 2:10.84	Eddie Riach 2:21.13	Eddie Riach 2:22.11	Ally MacGregor 2:28.22	Duncan McCreadle 2:32.71	Tom Walker 2:50.79
British women	Helen Gorman 2:25.04	Kate Veale 2:24.30	Angela Wilson 2:35.78	Lesley Wilde 2:36.14	Anne Cork 2:46.69	Sandra O'Neil 2:53.94	Flora Connolly 3:05.23	Margaret Wilding 3:11.04
European men	Patric Robertsson 2:09.06	Edwin Van Norden 2:08.41	Edwin Van Norden 2:08.21	Eddie Riach 2:21.13	Eddie riach 2:22.11	Allyy MacGregor 2:28.22	Duncan McGesdie 2:32.71	Adu Hewicke 2:47.21
European women	Birgit Deurnig 2:23.47	Kate Veale 2:24.30	Karin Seick 2:25.26	Lesley Wilde 2:36.24	Brigitte Merten 2:44.20	Brigitte Merten 2:48.78	Susana Barkley 2:58.20	Margaret Wilding 3:11.04
World men	John Keppeler 2:05.93	Hiroshi Miura 2:05.59	Edwin Van Norden 2:08.21	Jim Sorensen 2:12.25	Tom Reudy 2:16.97	Robert Strand 2:25.01	John Calvert 2:27.19	Jack Kelso 2:35.04
World women	Wenke Hansen 2:21.79	K. Pipes-Neilsen 2:20.90	K Pipes-Neilsen 2:20.79	Laura Val 2:33.89	Laura Vale 2:37.59	Brigitte Merten 2:48.78	Ardeth Mueller 2:52.43	Yoshiko Osaki 2:59.95

Age range	65–69	70–74	75–79	80–84	85–89	90–94	95–99	100–104
British men	Tom Walker 3:05.60	Forbes Gentleman 3:27.39	Don Leader 3:45.85	Ernest Clemett 4:56.38				
British women	Flora Connolly 3:15.59	Margaret Evans 3:58.74	Margaret Evans 4:35.80	n/a				
European men	Roberto Alberiche 2:49.10	Jesus Dominguez 3:00.88	Karl Hauter 3:10.06	Hans Larsson 4:36.05				
European women	Flora Connolly 3:17.55	Sylvia Neuhauser 3:47.88	Agnes Plisson 4:07.53					
World men	Roberto Alberiche 2:49.10	Jesus Dominguez 3:00.88	Karl Hauter 3:12.01	Aldo Da Rosa 3:35.06	Walter Pfeiffer 4:21.90			
World women	Flora Connolly 3:17.55	Gail Roper 3:30.92	Lois Kivi Nochman 4:08.84	Maria Lenk 4:40.77	Maria Lenk 5:09.92	Jewel Cooke 6:56.70		

Short Course Records
Event: 400 m individual medley

Age range	25–29	30–34	35–39	40–44	45–49	50–54	55–59	60–64
British men	Matthew Driscoll 4:38.48	Roland Lee 4:43.72	Robin Brew 4:40.84	Eddie Riach 4:56.49	Eddie Riach 5:04.83	Sandy Galletly 5:18.03	Sandy Galletly 5.29.09	Tom Walker 6:09.77
British women	Helen Slatter 5:01.26	Suki Brownsdon 5:06.05	Angela Wilson 5:34.70	Lesley Wilde 5:37.23	Jayne Ball 5:56.92	Julie Crayford 6:26.65	Flora Connolly 6:36.03	Flora Connolly 6:58.16
European men	Mathias Haak 4:37.03	Edwin Van Norden 4:42.23	Edwin Van Norden 4:39.42	Dariusz Wolny 4:47.71	Lorenzo Marugo 4:57.94	Sandy Galletly 5:18.03	Sandy Galletly 5:29.09	Tom Walker 6:09.77
European women	Helen Slatter 5:01.26	Suki Brownsdon 5:06.05	Barbara Gellrich 5:28.67	Lesley Wilde 5:38.68	Ulrike Urbaniak 5:53.97	Brigitte Merten 6:03.68	Hannelore Rose 6:34.91	Helga Reich 7:09.37
World men	John Keppeler 4:26.79	Roque Santos 4:26.74	Jerome Frentsos 4:34.06	Hess Yatsma 4:43.28	Tom Reudy 4:57.34	R Tod Spieker 5:12.31	Sandy Galletly 5:29.09	Drury Galopher 5:39.12
World women	Wenke Hansen 5:02.54	K. Pipes-Neilsen 4:53.85	K Pipes-Neilsen 4:52.85	Robynn Masters 5:22.59	Laura Vale 5:33.37	Ardeth Mueller 5:56.24	Jen Thomason 6:11.73	Yoshiko Osaki 6:28.22

Age range	65–69	70–74	75–79	80–84	85–89	90–94	95–99	100–104
British men	Tom Walker 6:34.82	Donald Leader 7:39.23	Donald Leader 7:56.54	Ernest Clemett 10.42.14				
British women	Flora Connolly 6:57.58	Margaret Evans 8:06.71						
European men	Roberto Alberiche 6:07.00	Jesus Dominguez 6:47.09	Karl Hauter 7:02.03	Reinstadtler 10.36.295				
European women	Flora Connolly 6:58.31	Sylvia Neuhauser 7:52.30	Gertrud Meerwald 9:23.96					
World men	Graham Johnston 6:04.40	Frank Piemme 6:38.98	Karl Hauter 7:02.03	Ray Taft 7:37.58	Walter Pfeiffer 9:31.75			
World women	Flora Connolly 6:58.31	June Krauser 7:24.32	Lois Kivi Nochman 8:30.82	Maine Merlino 9:50.43	Jean Durston 10:55.73	Jewel Cooke 14.55.37		

Long Course Records
Event: 50 m Freestyle

Age range	25–29	30–34	35–39	40–44	45–49	50–54	55–59	60–64
British men	Roland Lee 24.29	Mike Fibbens 23.73	David Lowe 24.30	Tom Greenwood 26.08	Alexander Mills 26.62	Tony Jarvis 26.86	Duncan McCredie 28.30	Hugh Cumberford 29.66
British women	Alison Sheppard 26.20	Maxine McKinnell/ Sarah Eames 27.97	Linzi Gaywood 28.97	Margaret Smith 29.62	Carol Fellows 30.31	Carol Fellows 30.10	Judy Wilson 30.33	Jane Asher 33.60
World men	Kevin DeForrest 22.59	Rowdy Gaines 23.21	Rowdy Gaines 23.20	Brent Barnes 24.25	Gary Schats 24.75	Richard Abrahams 24.60	Steve Clark 26.33	Jeff Farrell 26.70
World women	Alison Sheppard 26.20	Angel Martino 26.25	Tracie Moll 26.66	S. Neilson-Bell 27.39	Jackie Hirsty 28.30	Ardeth Mueller 29.33	Judy Wilson 30.33	Olga Krejci 32.92

Age range	65–69	70–74	75–79	80–84	85–89	90–94	95–99	100–104
British men	Joseph Phillips 30.52	Allen Miles 31.85	Jack Hale 32.92	Fred Bramhall 39.73	John Harrison 53.11			
British women	Jane Asher 34.61	M Cunningham 36.39	Betty Condon 44.09	Edith Hewitt 50.18	Dorothy Weston 58.21			
World men	Ronald Johnson 28.04	Kelley Lemmon 29.35	Frank Piemne 31.19	Woodrow Bowersock 33.88	Woodrow Bowersock 35.77	Gastao Figuiredo 46.24	Gus Lagner 55.88	Tom Lane 2:05.49
World women	Jayne Bruner 33.55	Gail Roper 35.28	J. Drake-Brockman 38.22	J. Drake-Brockman 40.89	Ume Wada 49.84	Aileen Soule 55.76	Mary M Anderson 1:55.57	Mary Maina 5:10.84

Long Course Records
Event: 100 m Freestyle

Age range	25–29	30–34	35–39	40–44	45–49	50–54	55–59	60–64
British men	Mike Fibbens 52.18	Mike Fibbens 52.05	David Lowe 54.41	Paul Blackbeard 57.65	Alexander Mills 58.45	Alistair MacGregor 59.24	Duncan McCreadie 1:01.77	Balazs Gyorffy 1:06.92
British women	Alison Sheppard 58.22	Sarah Garrett 1:00.46	Alyson Jones 1:02.70	Margaret Smith 1:04.72	Carol Fellows 1:07.32	Carol Fellows 1:07.34	Judy Wilson 1:09.00	Jane Asher 1:14.25
World men	Jim Montgomery 51.23	Rowdy Gaines 51.50	Rowdy Gaines 51.49	Jack Groselle 53.78	Jack Groselle 53.90	Terry Downes 56.69	Timothy Garton 58.41	Jeff Farrell 1:00.11
World women	Alison Sheppard 58.22	Angel Martino 57.09	Tracie Moll 58.38	S. Neilson-Bell 1:00.63	Laura Val 1:02.42	Carol Fellows 1:07.34	Judy Wilson 1:09.00	Yoshiko Osaki 1:12.87

Age range	65–69	70–74	75–79	80–84	85–89	90–94	95–99	100–104
British men	Arthur Lowe 1:09.48	Jack Hale 1:10.96	Alexander Laylee 1:27.87	Ray Brookhouse 1:36.90	John Harrison 2:02.85			
British women	Jane Asher 1:17.73	M Cunningham 1:25.23	Audrey Gathercole 1:45.41	Edith Hewitt 1:58.71				
World men	Roberto Alberiche 1:03.39	Chuck Baldwin 1:08.27	Ray Taft 1:13.84	Hikoji Ueki 1:19.28	Hikoji Ueki 1:26.71	Gastao Figuiredo 1:56.60	Gus Lagner 2:29.32	Tom Lane 4:25.98
World women	Jane Asher 1:15.29	Gail Roper 1:19.94	J. Drake-Brockman 1:30.42	Ume Wada 1:39.30	Ume Wada 2:00.66	Aileen Soule 2:19.62	Mary M Anderson 4:06.70	

Long Course Records
Event: 200 m Freestyle

Age range	25–29	30–34	35–39	40–44	45–49	50–54	55–59	60–64
British men	Neil Tait 1:54.87	Roland Lee 1:59.32	David Dunne 2:03.61	Thomas Greenwood 2:07.89	Alexander Mills 2:07.54	Alistair MacGregor 2:08.98	Duncan McCreadie 2:16.10	Geoff Stokes 2:28.71
British women	Sharron Davies 2:07.14	Susan Hill 2:14.25	Nuala Muir-Cochrane 2:16.49	Margaret Smith 2:21.67	Jayne Bell 2:27.76	Sandra O'Neil 2:37.27	Jane Asher 2:46.28	Jane Asher 2:51.82
World men	John Keppeler 1:52.17	Rowdy Gaines 1:54.04	Rowdy Gaines 1:55.36	Joseph Rhyne 2:01.07	Jack Groselle 2:01.54	Jim McConica 2:02.50	Tim Burnie 2:15.00	Jeff Farrell 2:20.54
World women	Sara Shand 2:07.11	Beth Knight 2:07.84	K. Pipes-Neilsen 2:06.94	Jill Hermamdez 2:13.10	Laura Val 2:17.12	Barbara Dunbar 2:28.11	Ardeth Mueller 2:34.88	Yoshiko Osaki 2:40.63

Age range	65–69	70–74	75–79	80–84	85–89	90–94	95–99	100–104
British men	Jack Hale 2:35.38	Jack Hale 2:45.92	Ray Brookhouse 3:18.16	Ray Brookhouse 3:42.21	John Harrison 4:22.14			
British women	Jane Asher 2:53.14	M Cunningham 3:12.54	Vivienne Cherriman 3:52.90	Vivienne Cherriman 4:16.48				
World men	Roberto Alberiche 2:21.74	William Phillips 2:37.00	Frank Piemme 2:50.01	Hikoji Ueki 3:03.45	Hikoji Veki 3:13.78	Gus Lagner 4:28.34	Tom Lagner 5:30.23	
World women	Clara Walker 2:48.51	Gail Roper 3:01.28	Margery Meyer 3:19.07	Ume Wada 3:44.00	Ume Wada 4:26.52	Julia Dolce 5:19.36		

Long Course Records
Event: 400 m Freestyle

Age range	25–29	30–34	35–39	40–44	45–49	50–54	55–59	60–64
British men	Roland Lee 4:07.72	Roland Lee 4:14.62	Ian Beck 4:27.10	Simon Veale 4:37.30	Eddie Riach 4:40.95	Sandy Galletly 4:46.50	Sandy Galletly 4:53.35	Geoff Stokes 5:25.16
British women	Lynn Marshall 4:36.79	Deborah Hamilton 4:45.69	Nuala Muir-Cochrane 4:40.68	Margaret Smith 4:59.29	Jayne Bell 5:09.73	Sandra O'Neil 5:32.05	Judy Wilsonr 5:51.61	Jane Asher 6:11.09
World men	Alex Kositch 4:03.63	Rowdy Gaines 4:07.04	Rowdy Gaines 4:07.64	Joseph Rhyne 4:15.86	Jim McConica 4:21.16	Jim McConica 4:19.47	Tim Burnie 4:46.92	Drury Gallagher 5:04.45
World women	Sara Shand 4:27.53	K. Pipes-Neilsen 4:28.76	K. Pipes-Neilsen 4:26.17	Jill Hernandez 4:38.89	Laura Val 4:52.03	Barbara Dunbar 5:11.22	Ardeth Mueller 5:25.59	Yoshiko Osaki 5:46.79

Age range	65–69	70–74	75–79	80–84	85–89	90–94	95–99	100–104
British men	Don Bland 5:46.48	Jack Hale 6:01.57	Ray Brookhouse 7:08.51	Ray Brookhouse 7:58.20	John Harrison 9:06.01			
British women	Jane Asher 6:09.73	Daphne Gilbert 7:55.56	Vivienne Cherriman 8:09.29	Vivienne Cherriman 9:44.26				
World men	Graham Johnston 5:03.36	William Phillips 5:40.41	Domel Suzaki 6:17.36	Hikoji Ueki 6:40.63	Hikoji Veki 7:05.53	Alfredo Cherchi 9:40.04	Gus Lagner 11:30.53	
World women	Lavelle Stoinoff 5:54.90	Clara Walker 6:33.15	Margery Meyer 7:16.82	Rita Simonton 7:53.37	Ume Wada 9:31.21	Julia Dolce 11:44.11		

Long Course Records
Event: 800 m Freestyle

Age range	25–29	30–34	35–39	40–44	45–49	50–54	55–59	60–64
British men	Neil Tait 8:32.92	Ian Beck 8:47.93	Ian Beck 9:27.77	Eddie Riach 9:31.86	Eddie Riach 9:39.25	Sandy Galletly 9:49.89	Sandy Galletly 10:03.22	Geoff Stokes 11:24.04
British women	Karen Clifton 9:28.85	Deborah Hamilton 9:52.29	Nuala Muir-Cochrane 9:36.96	Margaret Smith 10:22.52	Jayne Bell 10:56.22	Sandra O'Neill 11:36.23	Penny Webster 12:21.88	Jane Asher 12:41.37
World men	Graham Johnson 10:29.26	Rowdy Gaines 8:40.19	Rowdy Gaines 8:38.73	Joseph Rhyne 8:48.69	Jim McConica 8:58.84	Jim McConica 9:05.69	Sandy Galletly 10:03.22	Drury Gallagher 10:29.40
World women	Eva Mortensen 9:17.09	Lynn Marshall 9:16.82	K. Pipes-Neilsen 9:16.20	Jill Hernandez 9:31.64	Laura Val 10:08.23	Dianne Foster 10:36.52	Ardeth Mueller 11:15.07	Yoshiko Osaki 11:44.16

Age range	65–69	70–74	75–79	80–84	85–89	90–94	95–99	100–104
British men	Jack Hale 11:36.97	Ken McKay 13:41.97	Ray Brookhouse 14:47.77	Ray Brookhouse 17:11.82	John Harrison 19:06.39			
British women	Jane Asher 12:41.94	Daphne Gilbert 16:46.13	Willy Van Rysel 17:50.00	Vivienne Cherriman 20:14.29				
World men	Graham Johnston 10:29.26	Frank Piemme 12:03.73	Frank Piemme 12:52.31	Norbert Artus 13:50.05	Takushi Komeda 15:59.86	Gus Langner 20:13.74	Gus Langner 22:28.28	
World women	Lavelle Stoinoff 12:23.32	June Krauser 13:15.45	Margery Meyer 14:32.25	Rita Simonton 16:05.85	Jean Durston 19:12.10	Anna Bauscher 30:55.09		

Long Course Records
Event: 1500 m Freestyle

Age range	25–29	30–34	35–39	40–44	45–49	50–54	55–59	60–64
British men	Matthew Driscoll 16:46.97	Ian Beck 17:11.09	Andrew Gristwood 18:18.15	Eddie Riach 18:28.59	Eddie Riach 18:30.13	Sandy Galletly 18:49.43	Sandy Galletly 19:09.48	Mike Edwards 21:39.89
British women	Deborah Hamilton 18:58.28	Deborah Hamilton 18:52.01	Nuala Muir-Cochrane 18:25.65	Helen Kula-Prezwanski 20:35.75	Jayne Bell 21:20.48	Sandra O'Neil 22:17.09	Jane Asher 23:51.95	Barbara Fentiman 25:07.30
World men	Alex Kostich 16:13.89	Bobby Patten 16:36.06	Rowdy Gaines 16:37.34	Hess Yntema 16:58.52	Todd Bryan 17:31.23	Jim McConica 17:08.33	Sandy Galletly 19:09.48	Graham Johnston 20:04.73
World women	Amy Pope 17:38.78	Karen Burton 17:38.70	Penny Bond 17:55.34	S. Heim-Bowen 18:14.34	Laura Val 19:26.97	Barbara Dunbar 20:22.69	Ardeth Mueller 21:09.91	Lavelle Stoinoff 22:50.81

Age range	65–69	70–74	75–79	80–84	85–89	90–94	95–99	100–104
British men	Don Bland 22:16.14	Jack Hale 24:13.81	Don Leader 29:01.22	Ernest Ckemett 34:17.13	John Harrison 36:15.45			
British women	Jane Asher 24:43.09	Willy Van Rysel 33:34.89	Yvonne Hodges 38:46.75	Willy Van Rysel 39:49.97				
World men	Graham Johnston 20:16.54	Roger Franks 22:59.14	Domei Suzuki 24:51.78	Ray Taft 26:52.93	Takushi Komeda 30:14.52	Gus Langner 36:47.02	Gus Lagner 47:30.40	
World women	Lavelle Stoinoff 23:42.01	June Krauser 25:11.23	Margery Meyer 28:38.34	Rita Simonton 30:41.01	Jean Durston 36:42.65	Julia Dolce 50:26.55		

Long Course Records
Event: 50 m Backstroke

Age range	25–29	30–34	35–39	40–44	45–49	50–54	55–59	60–64
British men	Martin Harris 26.66	Martin Harris 26.66	Craig Norrey 29.02	Simon Garside 30.79	Eddie Riach 31.08	Graham Sykes 31.85	Graham Sykes 33.04	Graham Sykes 34.49
British women	Helen Slatter 31.14	Helen Jameson 31.72	Lesley Webb 34.25	Lesley Wilde 34.46	Sylvia Platt-Rogers 35.31	Carol Fellows 35.85	Margaret Wilding 36.77	Margaret Wilding 37.39
World men	Martin Harris 26.68	Martin Harris 26.66	J Clay Britt 27.60	Peter Rocca 28.69	Tom Wolf 29.85	Hugh Wilder 30.63	Robert Smith 31.52	Yoshi Oyanawa 33.13
World women	Kaoru ono 30.73	D. Graner-Gallas 30.94	K. Pipes-Neilsen 31.43	Laua Val 32.25	Laura Val 32.93	Satoko Takeuji 34.87	Satoko Takeuji 36.08	Margaret Wilding 37.39

Age range	65–69	70–74	75–79	80–84	85–89	90–94	95–99	100–104
British men	Jack Hale 32.61	Jack Hale 39.52	Alexander Laylee 43.59	Fred Bramhall 46.97	John Harrison 53.21			
British women	Jane Asher 42.98	Willy Van Rysel 46.81	Willy Van Rysel 46.64	Willy Van Rysel 55.92	Dorothy Weston 1:05.05			
World men	Yoshi Oyanawa 33.54	Paul Huntinger 37.10	Keijiro Nakamura 37.51	Shochi Sakomoto 40.71	Toshikija Sato 45.16	Nori Yamamoto 1:02.91		Tom Lane 2:05.54
World women	Clara Walker 39.85	Doris Steadman 42.49	Doris Steadman 44.43	Betty Stern 51.41	Aileen Soule 58.42	Aileen Soule 1:03.49	Mary M Anderson 1:57.79	

Long Course Records
Event: 100 m Backstroke

Age range	25–29	30–34	35–39	40–44	45–49	50–54	55–59	60–64
British men	Martin Harris 57.93	Martin Harris 57.24	Craig Norrey 1:04.03	Eddie Riach 1:05.94	Eddie Riach 1:04.69	John Gordon 1:12.47	John Gordon 1:14.37	Alan Jackson 1:20.25
British women	Alison Sheppard 1:05.02	Jo Swatton 1:08.24	Nuala Muir-Cochrane 1:14.41	Lesley Wilde 1:12.00	Sylvia Platt-Rogers 1:16.35	Margaret Wilding 1:21.01	Margaret Wilding 1:24.41	Margaret Wilding 1:22.07
World men	Jon Winter 57.45	Martin Harris 57.24	J Clay Britt 1:00.13	William Specht 1:02.48	Tom Wolf 1:03.68	Hugh Wilder 1:07.16	Tim Burnie 1:09.27	Barry Young 1:14.53
World women	Alison Sheppard 1:05.02	D. Graner-Gallas 1:05.42	K. Pipes-Neilsen 1:06.29	Laura Val 1:11.03	Laura Val 1:12.70	Satoko Takeuji 1:18.86	Satoko Takeuji 1:19.65	Margaret Wilding 1:24.24

Age range	65–69	70–74	75–79	80–84	85–89	90–94	95–99	100–104
British men	Jack Hale/Roger Burrell 1:24.88	Jack Hale 1:26.53	Alexander Laylee 1:41.24	Fred Bramhall 1:53.40	John Harrison 2:04.44			
British women	Flora Connolly 1:36.52	Willy Van Rysel 1:47.39	Willy Van Rysel 1:48.78	Willy Van Rysel 2:07.93				
World men	Yoshi Oyanawa 1:16.78	Paul Huntinger 1:24.14	Keijiro Nakamura 1:26.00	Ray Taft 1:35.36	Toshikija Sato 1:41.25	Nori Yamamoto 2:18.51		Tom Lane 4:57.01
World women	Doris Steadman 1:31.58	Doris Steadman 1:35.11	Doris Steadman 1:39.06	J. Drake-Brockman 1:58.08	Aileen Soule 2:13.13	Aileen Soule 2:23.23	Mary M Anderson 4:16.79	

Long Course Records
Event : 200 m Backstroke

Age range	25–29	30–34	35–39	40–44	45–49	50–54	55–59	60–64
British men	Martin Harris 2:05.86	Martin Harris 2:06.30	Eddie Riach 2:21.67	Eddie Riach 2:23.74	Eddie Riach 2:22.45	Ivan Myall 2:38.75	John Gordon 2:44.11	Tom Walker 2:54.19
British women	Alison Sheppard 2:20.88	Jo Swatton 2:24.25	Nuala Muir- 2:34.92	Lesley Wilde 2:34.37	Anne Cork 2:47.09	Sandra O'Neil 2:57.59	Margaret Wilding 3:08.24	Margaret Wilding 3:08.57
World men	Martin Harris 2:05.86	Sean Murphy 2:05.62	Daniel Veatch 2:09.26	William Specht 2:15.49	Tom Wolf 2:21.66	Jim McConica 2:25.70	Tim Burnie 2:30.84	Barry Young 2:40.83
World women	Diane Graner 2:19.97	K. Pipes-Neilsen 2:18.98	K. Pipes-Neilsen 2:18.20	Zena Courtney 2:34.18	Cecilla McCloskey 2:42.60	Satoko Takeuji 2:51.11	Satoko Takeuji 2:56.13	Betsy Jordan 3:06.23

Age range	65–69	70–74	75–79	80–84	85–89	90–94	95–99	100–104
British men	Jack Hale 2:59.42	Jack Hale 3:12.55	John Davis 3:43.83	Roy Hodges 4:47.34	John Harrison 4:32.32			
British women	Flora Connolly 3:24.65	Margaret Evans 3:58.55	Willy Van Rysel 4:07.04	Dorothy Weston 4:43.51				
World men	S. Sekikawa 2:51.19	Roger Franks 3:04.42	Keijiro Nakamura 3:10.64	Ray Taft 3:31.36	Toshikija Sato 3:48.38	Gastao Figueredo 5:06.10		
World women	Lavekke Stoinoff 3:16.02	Doris Steadman 3:28.69	Doris Steadman 3:39.41	Edith Thein 4:11.83	Aileen Soule 4:47.82	Aileen Soule 5:29.07		

Long Course Records
Event : 50 m Butterfly

Age range	25–29	30–34	35–39	40–44	45–49	50–54	55–59	60–64
British men	Mike Fibbens 25.37	Mike Fibbens 25.93	David Lowe 26.44	Tony Jarvis 27.95	Eric Henderson 28.69	Tony Jarvis 28.72	Bob Lord 30.81	John Cardwell 32.77
British women	Sharron Davies 28.87	Maxine McKinnell 29.68	Marie Sadler 30.56	Marie Sadler 30.40	Sylvia Platt-Rogers 32.43	Carol Fellows 32.80	Judy Wilson 32.24	Jane Asher 38.54
World men	Jon Winter 24.88	Brian Alderman 25.16	J. Tyler 25.77	William Specht 26.33	Rick Abbott 26.97	Richard Abrahams 27.13	Richard Abrahams 27.76	Chitoshi Konishi 29.89
World women	Marja Parssinen 28.09	Tracie Moll 29.07	Tracie Moll 28.32	Laura Val 29.89	Ardeth Mueller 30.74	Ardeth Mueller 31.69	Judy Wilson 32.24	Yoshiko Osaki 36.87

Age range	65–69	70–74	75–79	80–84	85–89	90–94	95–99	100–104
British men	Jack Hale 33.34	Jack Hale 35.13	Roy Romain 39.37	Roy Romain 52.17				
British women	Jane Asher 40.29	M Cunningham 49.00	Margaret Evans 59.48	Dorothy Weston 1:05.05				
World men	Ronald Johnson 30.81	Frank Piemme 33.79	Frank Piemme 35.66	Andrew Holden 41.89	Jesse Coom 57.93	Jesse Coom 1:23.87		
World women	Gail Roper 39.18	Gail Roper 41.26	Lois Kivi Nochman 47.86	Gertrud Meerwald 1:00.50	Jean Durston 1:11.58	Anna Bauscher 4:57.25		

Long Course Records
Event: 100 m Butterfly

Age range	25–29	30–34	35–39	40–44	45–49	50–54	55–59	60–64
British men	Steven Mellor 58.23	Mike Fibbens 56.68	Nicolus Vaughan 1:00.32	Trevor Clark 1:02.82	Eric Henderson 1:03.73	Tony Jarvis 1:05.82	Roger Lloyd-Mostyn 1:10.74	David Cumming 1:15.75
British women	Jackie Thompson 1:05.29	Nikki Gordon 1:07.79	Marie Sadler 1:08.73	Marie Sadler 1:08.11	Judy Wilson 1:16.67	Judy Wilson 1:17.63	Judy Wilson 1:13.71	Christine Parfect 1:34.98
World men	Mike Bottom 56.49	Roberto Neto 56.49	J. Tyler 56.39	William Specht 57.79	Bradley Homer 1:00.42	Richard Abrahams 1:02.25	Richard Abrahams 1:03.90	Chitoshi Konishi 1:11.56
World women	Rosemarie Seaman 1:03.91	Angel Martino 1:00.03	Tracie Moll 1:03.79	Laura val 1:06.27	Laura Val 1:08.02	Ardeth Mueller 1:13.86	Judy Wilson 1:13.71	Yoshiko Osaki 1:27.05

Age range	65–69	70–74	75–79	80–84	85–89	90–94	95–99	100–104
British men	Seymour Banning 1:26.31	Roy Romain 1:46.72	Roy romain 1:44.82	Ernest Clemett 2:48.66	Dorothy Weston 2:45.28			
British women	Flora Connolly 1:40.35	Margaret Evans 2:00.57	n/a	Dorothy Weston 2:29.87				
World men	Ronald Johnson 1:15.69	Joseph Kurtzman 1:24.84	Frank Piemme 1:35.81	Andrew Holden 1:47.88	Walter Pfeiffer 2:10.28	Jesse Coon 3:29.53		
World women	Gail Roper 1:36.68	June Krauser 1:40.85	Lois Kivi Nochman 1:56.92	Gertrud Meerwald 2:21.88	Jean Durston 2:40.11			

Long Course Records
Event: 200 m Butterfly

Age range	25–29	30–34	35–39	40–44	45–49	50–54	55–59	60–64
British men	Richard Stent 2:11.00	Ian Beck 2:06.84	Ian Beck 2:12.86	Steve Nash 2:21.12	Eric Henderson 2:30.57	Alex Galletly 2:40.14	Derek Parr 2:49.59	David Cumming 2:57.43
British women	Helen Slatter 2:20.72	Diane Brades 2:28.06	Lesley Norton 2:41.23	Judy Hattle 2:42.96	Bernice Watkins 3:02.64	Julie Crayford 3:16.15	Judy Wilson 3:05.21	Flora Connolly 3:26.76
World men	M. Lukasek 2:05.25	Bobby Patten 2:03.85	Jeff Stuart 2:06.74	William Specht 2:09.47	James Densmuir 2:17.71	Dave Tanner 2:26.11	Robert Poiletman 2:33.48	Gunter Schopke 2:52.73
World women	S. Palmer White 2:18.69	Eugeniya Ojoguina 2:20.07	K. Pipes-Neilsen 2:20.21	S. Heim-Bowen 2:32.14	Laura Val 2:31.37	Barbara Dunbar 2:44.93	Hannelore Roese 3:14.39	Flora Connolly 3:26.76

Age range	65–69	70–74	75–79	80–84	85–89	90–94	95–99	100–104
British men	Seymour Banning 3:20.21	Forbes Gentleman 3:29.28	Don Leader 4:24.84	Ernest Clemett 5:53.76				
British women	Flora Connolly 3:33.04	Margaret Evans 4:32.32						
World men	Joseph Kurtzman 3:08.79	Valentin Weber 3:22.01	Anton Cerer 3:43.56	Anton Cerer 4:11.09	Walter Pfeiffer 5:06.00	Jesse Coon 8:22.48		
World women	Flora Connolly 3:33.04	June Krauser 3:39.81	Lois Kivi Nochman 4:19.81	Jean Durston 5:24.52	Jean Durston 5:49.75			

Long Course Records
Event: 50 m Breaststroke

Age range	25–29	30–34	35–39	40–44	45–49	50–54	55–59	60–64
British men	James Parrack 28.68	Nick Gillingham 29.98	Anthony O'Driscoll 31.96	Simon Garside 31.98	Neville Barton 33.29	John Liron 34.07	Tom Walker 35.80	Tom Walker 37.04
British women	Charlotte Mustard 34.59	Margaret Hohmann 34.56	A. Glynne-Jones 36.66	Margaret Hohmann 36.56	Elaine Bromwich 39.43	Elaine Bromwich 39.29	Elaine Bromwich 40.81	Christine Parfect 43.40
World men	James Parrack 28.68	David Guthrie 29.42	Wally Dicks 29.09	Gerhard Ammer 30.51	C. Miltenberger 31.54	Robert Strand 32.16	Hiroshi Kotegawa 33.03	Akio Sugiyama 34.59
World women	S. Seminatore 32.01	Wenke Hansen 33.84	L. Wetzel-Osborne 34.41	Dagmar Hilbig 34.97	Susan Roy 36.97	Jan Macleod 38.04	Monika Senftleben 39.43	Jayne Bruner 41.43

Age range	65–69	70–74	75–79	80–84	85–89	90–94	95–99	100–104
British men	Tom Walker 39.36	Roy Romain 41.20	Roy Romain 44.22	Roy Romain 50.50	Derrick Davey 1:01.01			
British women	Flora Connolly 45.98	M. Cunningham 50.78	Maud Povey 54.78	Dorothy Weston 59.60				
World men	Hiroshi Kotegwa 36.38	Chuch Baldwin 37.96	Toshio Tajima 40.51	Y. Miyamoto 43.62	Hiromu Yoshimoto 49.46	Hans Paul 1:08.90	Gus Langner 1:26.61	
World women	Edith Boehm 43.42	Edith Boehm 43.98	Satoko Suzuki 50.65	Dorothy Weston 59.60	Maria Lenk 1:07.88	Margarete Gottschalk 1:26.57		

Long Course Records
Event: 100 m Breaststroke

Age range	25–29	30–34	35–39	40–44	45–49	50–54	55–59	60–64
British men	James Parrack 1:04.11	Nick Gillingham 1:05.02	Anthony O'Driscoll 1:12.41	Anthony O'Driscoll 1:09.31	Neville Barton 1:15.30	Denis Thys 1:20.93	Tom Walker 1:20.20	Tom Walker 1:20.56
British women	Charlotte Mustard 1:15.31	Margaret Hohmann 1:14.52	A. Glynne-Jones 1:21.47	Alison Nye 1:22.28	Elaine Bromwich 1:27.15	Elaine Bromwich 1:28.05	Elaine Bromwich 1:30.30	Flora Connolly 1:35.86
World men	James Parrack 1:04.11	Nick Gillingham 1:05.02	Wally Dicks 1:05.03	David Guthrie 1:08.01	Jack Groselle 1:12.29	Robert Strand 1:11.90	Albert Kostitsyu 1:17.18	Drury Gallagher 1:19.82
World women	Manuela Naeckel 1:13.15	M. Hohmann 1:14.52	Caroline Krattli 1:16.36	Dagmar Hilbig 1:16.81	Susan Roy 1:22.27	Shirley Turner 1:28.05	Bonnie Pronk 1:29.11	Joann Leilich 1:32.37

Age range	65–69	70–74	75–79	80–84	85–89	90–94	95–99	100–104
British men	Tom Walker 1:26.54	Roy Romain 1:39.19	Roy Romain 1:47.76	Roy Romain 2:04.47	Derrick Davey 2:23.17			
British women	Flora Connolly 1:38.37	Margaret Evans 1:55.17	Audrey Gathercole 2:07.40	Dorothy Weston 2:16.91	Dorothy Weston 2:34.97			
World men	Manuel Sanguily 1:24.16	Robert Pfersdorff 1:31.05	Robert Pfersdorff 1:35.70	W. Miyamoto 1:45.24	Hiromu Yoshimoto 1:53.70	Hans Paul 2:39.02	Gus Langner 3:38.45	
World women	Masayo Azuma 1:37.48	Edith Boehm 1:43.86	Satoko Suzuki 1:52.54	Gertrud Meerwald 2:10.47	Dorothy Weston 2:34.97	Margarete Gottschalk 3:21.95		

Long Course Records
Event: 200 m Breaststroke

Age range	25–29	30–34	35–39	40–44	45–49	50–54	55–59	60–64
British men	Murray Buswell 2:29.38	Nick Gillingham 2:20.43	Barry O'Brien 2:40.59	Anthony O'Driscoll 2:34.96	Bill Price 2:49.58	Mike Wake 2:58.99	Tom Walker 2:56.20	Tom Walker 2:58.37
British women	Sharron Davies 2:42.02	Verity Dobbie 2:54.99	Antonia Jones 2:58.39	Amanda Heath 2:57.68	Jennifer Merritt 3:09.97	Elaine Bromwich 3:11.56	Elaine Bromwich 3:15.32	Flora Connolly 3:24.83
World men	Abraham Solano 2:24.57	Nick Gillingham 2:20.43	David Guthrie 2:24.37	David Guthrie 2:28.54	Gerhard Preiner 2:41.02	Robert Strand 2:40.57	William Gonzalez 2:50.44	Thomas Walker 2:58.37
World women	Sharron Davies 2:42.02	Wenke Hansen 2:41.51	Caroline Krattli 2:46.38	Dagmar Hilbig 2:49.95	Ulrike Urbaniak 2:57.38	Christiane Heeren 3:08.74	Hannelore Roese 3:14.40	Joann Leilich 3:23.62

Age range	65–69	70–74	75–79	80–84	85–89	90–94	95–99	100–104
British men	Tom Walker 3:08.19	Roy Romain 3:42.25	Roy Romain 4:02.71	Roy Romain 4:33.85	Chester Kozlowski 5:42.96			
British women	Flora Connolly 3:30.95	Margaret Evans 4:03.16	Dorothy Williams 4:35.26	Dorothy Weston 5:01.36				
World men	Tom Walker 3:08.19	Karl-Heinz Knops 3:26.27	Karl Hauter 3:33.27	Ray Taft 3:42.04	Hiromu Yoshimoto 4:22.99	Gus Langner 6:24.54	Gus Langner 7:37.70	
World women	Flora Connolly 3:30.95	Silvia Neuhauser 3:51.31	Olga Kokorina 4:08.40	Gertrud Meerwald 4:42.75	Emmi Pauli 5:36.62	Del Rowley 10:39.50		

Long Course Records
Event: 200 m individual medley

Age range	25–29	30–34	35–39	40–44	45–49	50–54	55–59	60–64
British men	Roland Lee 2:10.70	Roland Lee 2:15.75	Calvin Harris 2:20.73	Eddie Riach 2:24.02	Eddie Riach 2:25.19	Sandy Galletly 2:33.73	Duncan McCreadie 2:37.89	Tom Walker 2:53.72
British women	Sharron Davies 2:22.00	Sarah Garrett 2:28.27	Julia Robinson 2:37.63	Lesley Wilde 2:39.08	Patricia Legge 2:48.90	Sandra O'Neil 2:56.61	Flora Connolly 3:10.88	Flora Connolly 3:15.30
World men	Nicolas Granger 2:07.00	Nicolas Granger 2:08.89	Jerome Frentsos 2:13.02	James Sorenson 2:15.53	Tim Broderick 2:22.06	Jim McConica 2:25.77	John Calvert 2:30.33	Drury Gallagher 2:41.71
World women	Sharron Davies 2:22.00	Karlyn Pipes 2:25.68	K. Pipes-Neilsen 2:25.31	Jill Hermantez 2:30.96	Danielle Ogier 2:40.28	Brigitte Merten 2:52.11	Yoshiko Osaki 2:59.15	Yoshiko Osaki 3:05.90

Age range	65–69	70–74	75–79	80–84	85–89	90–94	95–99	100–104
British men	Vincent Miller 3:10.47	Forbes Gentleman 3:29.28	Roy Romain 3:46.62	Ernest Clemett 4:57.27				
British women	Flora Connolly 3:24.08	Margaret Evans 4:05.44	Margaret Evanss 4:45.35	Dorothy Weston 4:54.26				
World men	Roberto Alberiche 2:49.71	Jesus Dominguez 3:06.43	Frank Piemme 3:18.35	Ray Taft 3:43.19	Takushi Komeda 4:30.49	Jesse Coon 6:25.78		
World women	Jane Asher 3:20.26	Gail Roper 3:32.94	Agnes Plisson 4:07.53	Gertrud Meerwald 4:39.22	Jean Durston 5:16.68	Anna Bauscher 12:10.93		

Long Course Records
Event : 400 m individual medley

Age range	25–29	30–34	35–39	40–44	45–49	50–54	55–59	60–64
British men	Peter O'Sullivan 4:44.58	Ian Beck 4:53.73	Calvin Harris 5:00.87	Eddie Riach 5:07.04	Eddie Riach 5:09.11	Sandy Galletly 5:25.57	Sandy Galletly 5:43.50	Tom Walker 6:21.48
British women	Sharron Davies 5:05.29	Kate Veale 5:17.34	Julia Robinson 5:36.78	Lesley Wilde 5:41.83	Anne Cork 6:09.70	Julie Crayford 6:36.53	Flora Connolly 6:42.85	Flora Connolly 6:57.33
World men	Nicolas Granger 4:31.47	Nicolas Granger 4:39.92	Jerome Frentsos 4:43.17	Danusz Wolney 4:49.62	Eddie Riach 5:09.11	John Calvert 5:20.78	John Calvert 5:26.63	Barry Young 5:51.70
World women	Sharron Davies 5:05.29	Hideka Koshimizu 5:05.05	K. Pipes-Neilsen 5:07.21	Jill Hernandez 5:21.32	Danielle Ogier 5:45.85	Barbara Dunbar 6:03.12	Yoshiko Osaki 6:18.94	Yoshiko Osaki 6:50.29

Age range	65–69	70–74	75–79	80–84	85–89	90–94	95–99	100–104
British men	Roger Burrell 7:11.05	Donald Leader 7:55.54	Donald Leader 8:12.25	Ernest Clemett 11:37.87				
British women	Flora Connolly 7:06.75	Margaret Evans 8:29.65						
World men	Roberto Alberiche 6:05.15	Frank Piemme 6:52.07	Karl Hauter 7:19.76	Ray Taft 8:05.14	Walter Pfeiffer 9:42.77	Jesse Coon 13:52.72		
World women	Flora Connolly 7:06.75	June Krauser 7:30.91	Lois Kivi Nochman 8:59.25	Gertrud Meerwald 9:45.48	Jean Durston 11:10.37			

Index

Page numbers in italics refer to illustrations